GENERAL CUSTER AND THE BATTLE OF THE LITTLE BIG HORN: The Federal View

GENERAL CUSTER AND THE BATTLE OF THE LITTLE BIG HORN:
The Federal View

Edited by John M. Carroll

J. M. CARROLL & COMPANY
Bryan and Mattituck

International Standard Book Number 0-8488-0017-6 (hardcover)
International Standard Book Number 0-8488-0018-4 (softcover)

To order contact
J. M. Carroll & Company
PO Box 1200
Mattituck, New York 11952

Frontispiece: *Death of Custer*

FOR MY FRIENDS
JIM AND MARY ELLEN BOREN

Manufactured in the United States of America by The Mad Printers of Mattituck

TABLE OF CONTENTS

LIST OF ILLUSTRATIONS

PREFACE

Much of the Custer story has been told and retold. Here for the first time, however, Mr. Carroll's diligent efforts have brought together a large portion of that work previously inaccessible to the curious and scholarly alike. It seems entirely appropriate that with the publication of this series of documents, we examine the directions and approaches writers and researchers interested in Custer and Custeriana might now take.

Controversy had raged as hotly over Custer and the Battle of the Little Big Horn as over any other officer and engagement in our military history. News of the disaster was headlined around the country and, predictably, accusations and insinuations followed hard on its heels. President and pleb alike directed the fault variously at Custer, Reno, Benteen and others. Charges and counter-charges flowed freely and have continued almost unabated to this day. Custer has been charged with rashness, outright disobedience and even drunkenness. In turn, his defenders have attacked both Reno and Benteen—Reno for his failure to hold the ground in the valley and both for their failure to march to the sound of Custer's guns. The controversy has raged on and on, with the partisans unable—or unwilling—to defend one without attacking the other.

Though I am not wholly disposed to a Macaulàyian disregard for *where* or *how* events unfolded on the Little Big Horn, it seems obvious that the time has come to weigh the value added (or lost) by continuing to focus our efforts on the *truth* about Custer's Last Stand. In the last one hundred years a mass of evidence and a number of interpretations have been put forward. Now, most all of the "official" testimony has been gathered by Mr. Carroll into a single publication. It is time to turn and build on this strong foundation, not new accounts of the limited subjects with which we have so commonly worked, but rather interpretation with wider vision. Armed now with rather precise, if always controversial information, we should attempt to apply it to the broader aspects of America's history. When we consider that disastrous day at the Little Big Horn, let us not turn inward to the battle, but rather outward. How did the country react, a single day after its centennial anniversary, when the terrible news reached it? What was the effect of those horrifying headlines? Why did this tragedy become a political football? How correct was Charles F. Bates when, fifty years later, he wrote, "Custer lost his fight against the Indians, but he did not lose the fight he had made against corruption in the administration of Indian affairs." How did news of the event affect the pattern of that seemingly irresistible westward flow of Americans? These, I believe, are some of the questions which will turn our investigations in both rewarding and more profitable new directions. These are the kinds of questions that would demonstrate the true significance of those events in American history.

Certain other tasks also offer a rewarding challenge. One—which incidentally would complement this series of Custeriana handsomely—is the collection and publication of the Custer correspondence. There are a large number of unpublished Custer letters scattered among manuscript collections across the country. These should be gathered together and made available to researchers everywhere. Sadly, it appears the largest single collection of letters —those collected by Marguerite Merington in *The Custer Story* —has been destroyed. This is truly a loss, for despite its valuable contribution, her editing of the letters to fit the confines and direction of her story has surely eliminated much valuable material. In addition, there is a question as to the accuracy of her dating of the Kentucky period (1871-1873)—four of six originally undated letters are dated incorrectly. Because errors of this nature can lead to false conclusions and because almost every Custer scholar since 1950 has relied heavily on this source, it seems obvious that a reexamination is in order.

To those *aficionados* who insist on retaining a focus narrower than I am calling for, let me suggest that there remain unexplored gaps that need to be filled. My own research has dealt extensively with Custer's two years in Elizabethtown, Kentucky; yet much in this period remains to be done. Little, for example, is known of Custer's horse racing interests (which, incidentally, I believe are much more limited than has been commonly held). In addition, there is the myth that Custer aided General Phil Sheridan in Chicago after the great fire. Evidence is massing to allay this fable, but the *coup de grace* is yet to be administered. In some ways the more that is done, the more that remains to be done. Mr. Carroll's recent *Custer In Texas* is an excellent example. It admirably fills many of the gaps in our knowledge of that period in the General's life, but like any worthwhile work it raises as many questions as it answers. No doubt there will continue to be any number of areas that both invite examination and offer a measure of profit in return for the effort expended.

The scope of Mr. Carroll's *Custeriana* series is a measure of the great work already done. At the same time, it alerts us to the tasks, large and small, that remain and should warn us against the fruitless, partisan bickering that has so frequently dominated the field. The task of each new effort should be the relationship of the value added to the effort required. Wisely directed, our efforts will not only enhance our knowledge of the colorful George A. Custer but will also increase our understanding of America's rich heritage. In this effort, Mr. Carroll's *Custeriana* series will be an invaluable and indispensable tool, and this volume should become the basic reference on a subject that continues to intrigue and confound us today.

THEODORE J. CRACKEL
Major, U.S.A.
Command and General Staff School
Fort Leavenworth, Kansas

FOREWORD

The Custer story began the day George Armstrong Custer first picked up a toy sword. Since then he has been the subject of countless books, articles and newspaper columns. Some say more has been written about him than any other American military figure. Others say there has been more literature produced about Custer's last battle than on any other incident in American history.

The graphic arts have not been an exception. Several years ago an attempt was made to catalogue the renditions offered in the various media. What first was to be a checklist of the Custer battle illustrations was enlarged to include every known illustration pertaining to the Little Big Horn incident. The compilers arrived at a total of 967! It is reasonable to assume the checklist would now go well over 1,000.

One artistic effort alone has been the means of introducing the story of Custer to more people than any other. Near the turn of the century the Anheuser-Busch Brewing Association produced a lithograph called "Custer's Last Fight." With 150,000 copies distributed to taverns throughout the country for over half a century, there seems to be little doubt more people have gazed at this work of art than any other painting in the world.

Though school texts and most histories say little or nothing at all about Custer and his last stand, artists, authors, television, motion pictures and newsmen keep the story alive. Rare is the week in which some mention of Custer is not made. Each year sees an ascending number of books and articles published pertaining to the Custer story.

Mounting interest is also evident by the annual increase in attendance at the Custer Battlefield National Monument and several other Custer exhibits around the country.

One organization—The Little Big Horn Associates—with a membership of well over 200 serious students, historians, artists, authors and collectors of Custeriana, directs its efforts "to seek the truth about the Battle of the Little Big Horn and all of Custeriana."

Its *Research Review* contains valuable research material and articles. By uncovering facts, debunking myths and fiction, much of worth has been added to the Custer literature.

In 1939, Fred Dustin made the first attempt to provide a comprehensive bibliography of Custeriana. Unfortunately, he introduced statements indicating his personal bias. There were inaccuracies, and the list was incomplete, but it was of considerable assistance to the beginning student of this intriguing personage and the events and characters influencing and surrounding his life.

In 1953, Colonel William Graham reprinted the Dustin bibliography and augmented it with items that subsequently had been published. Others have endeavored to develop a more comprehensive and complete list. Even though a complete one eventually may be published, the agonizing fact remains that the majority of the materials are unavailable at any one place. The only possible sources for anything resembling a complete bibliography are the Custer Battlefield National Monument and a very few private collections.

To the writer, the researcher, the artist, the historian or the Custer buff, having all of the known literature on the subject readily available is of inestimable value. To have this type of collection bound and readily available to students of both Custeriana and Indianania would fill a huge gap the average library fails to supply, so it is especially gratifying to know that such a collection as Federal documents is being made available. It will join those other volumes relating to the subject as an important resource area.

John Carroll, the editor, has collected and evaluated Custer writings for many years. The Federal documents he is making available here—many for the first time—are extremely difficult to obtain and have been known to most Custerphiles only in footnotes. He is to be complimented for this incredible undertaking.

LAWRENCE A. FROST
Custer Curator
Monroe Historical Museum
Monroe, Michigan

INTRODUCTION

About the Documents

The federal reports concerning the Battle of the Little Big Horn and the death of General Custer and members of the Seventh U.S. Cavalry at the hands of the Sioux, Northern Cheyenne and Arapaho fiat have long been available to the general public; most have lain—practically hidden and almost inaccessible to most persons —within the covers of official publications. These publications have now become even more rare, and those libraries which have them are few and far between. Some are War Department reports; others are reports of Engineers or they are reports of the Commissioner of Indian Affairs. Still others are Senate and House of Representative documents. All relate to the subject of the Sioux War of 1876, and each will be discussed in turn to enable the Federal view of the Custer battle to be more easily understood.

The Sioux Campaign of 1876 did not end with the death of General Custer and the near annihilation of the Seventh U.S. Cavalry; indeed, this was but one moment in the total story. How the campaign was to end was obvious from the start. Everything pointed to success for the Federal forces in their eventual "conquest" of the Native Americans who populated the Northern Plains. What was not predicted, of course, was that dramatic confrontation on the Little Big Horn on June 25, 1876, and *its* results and consequences.

From the very start there were conflicting reports of this event. It is doubtful if the whole and true story can ever be told. Even today recent discoveries have verified the rumor that Major Reno proposed to Captain Benteen the abandonment of the wounded after their first day of fighting at what is now called Reno Hill. There are always new documents being uncovered as well as new interpretations being presented, all of which tend to alter many of the original interpretations of what happened that day. With this in mind—and considering what else that still may be hidden—it is no wonder the complete story will never be told. The military brotherhood banded together—as so many of us have believed they should have done —at the Reno Court of Inquiry, and there, too, the whole story was not revealed. Even Captain Benteen wrote Colonel (State National Guard rank) Goldin many years later that the prosecution did not know how to bring out the whole truth from him even though they believed he was not telling all. And so this historic battle still rages, never to be resolved—at least in the light of what is now presently known.

Most of what has been written about this famous conflict between the Indian and the military was based on official reports as well as eye witness accounts, letters, narratives, journals and diaries. Some were based on the accounts by "survivors" who managed to pop up now and then with an alarming degree of regularity. However, it is the mass of Federal documents—the Federal view—which must be considered the most important source, and, surprisingly, they have never been published as a group in a single reference before now. None here will have seen complete reprint since their first appearance. But that is not so unusual when one considers the restricted availability of complete runs of the Federal Serials.

Where to begin was at first a difficult problem but it was decided that *Senate Executive Document No. 52,* 44th Congress, 1st Session, April 26, 1876, qualified for the distinction of being first. It is a "Letter From The Secretary Of The Interior" transmitting a "copy of the report of the Commissioner of Indian Affairs in relation to the present situation of Indian disturbances in the Sioux reservation." It includes reports from agents and representatives of the Commissioner of Indian Affairs written between November 9, 1875, and April 3, 1876. In effect, these reports—which predated the Custer massacre and which were presented to our Federal assembly exactly two months prior to the Little Big Horn confrontation— must be considered the first *major* indications of the approaching "show-down" even though there were isolated, individual reports prior to this which seem to have gotten lost in all the publishing efforts and needs of the Federal Government. This consolidated report also sets the stage for the Custer disaster as well as the subsequent events.

Next in chronological importance are the two appendices to the "Annual Report of the Chief of Engineers for the Fiscal Year Ending June 30, 1876." The first is Appendix MM (Luther #41) written by Major G. L. Gillespie on the explorations and surveys, Military Division of the Missouri, which "briefly summarizes the overall army operations in the Sioux war." The other is Appendix 00 (Luther #44) written by Lieutenant Edward Maguire on the explorations and surveys in the Department of Dakota. Of it Luther says, "Maguire was with the column under Terry and Gibbon that arrived at the battlefield on June 27. His report contains an important map of the battlefield." That map is faithfully reproduced in this publication.

Luther (his #42) says of the next in this compilation that "Of major significance . . . is Lt. E. J. McClernand's daily journal of the Montana forces under Gibbon during 1876 and Lt. Geo. D. Wallace's journal of the Custer column from June 22 to June 25, 1876. These were printed in the 1877 report as they were received too late for inclusion with that for 1876. Also noteworthy is Sgt. James E. Wilson's journal of the activities of the steamer *Far West* from June 24 through June 29." He is writing, of course, of Appendix PP in Part II, "Annual Report of the Chief of Engineers for the Fiscal Year Ending June 30, 1877"; Lieutenant Edward Maguire's report is of explorations and surveys in the Department of Dakota. This report is found in *House of Representatives Executive Document #1, Part 2, Volume II,* 45th Congress, 2nd Session, June 30, 1877. Significantly, Dustin has several references to this document in his bibliography; they are his #'s 175, 177, 181 and 268.

House of Representatives Executive Document No. 1, Part 2, 44th Congress, 2nd Session, November 25, 1876, can be found in Volume I of the "Report of the Secretary of War . . . 1876." This is the "Report of Lieutenant General P. H. Sheridan" which contains the various reports including those of Major Reno, Captain Benteen, General Terry, Colonel Gibbon and many others. It is listed by Luther as his High Spot #40, and are Dustin's #'s 14, 118, 137, 207, 229, 248, 249, 257 and 258. In Dustin's #258 citation he states that "all but the stolen 'confidential' report will be found [in this] report." Dustin and his "lost, stolen, hidden and secret" documents have befogged the real Custer story for too many years, and it is hoped this presentation will expose his kind of history by insinuation.

The situation and disposition of the Sioux and their allies, the Northern Cheyenne and Arapaho, before and after the Little Big Horn and the Sioux Campaign of 1876 is the subject of the next two documents, both of which are extractions from the *Annual Report of the Secretary of the Interior, Commissioner of Indian Affairs Report for 1877,* and one treats of the Sitting Bull Commission especially. It is illustrative of the international consequences and concerns generated by the military/Indian actions of the previous three years. It is also illustrative of the genuine respect and appreciation existing between the Federal forces of this country and their counterparts in Canada, and how both were working to resolve a difficult problem created by the presence of the Sioux and some of their allies and friends in Canada—a refuge, they believed, for themselves.

"Message From The President Of The United States," *Senate Executive Document No. 81,* 44th Congress, 1st Session, July 13, 1876, has to be considered the next document of importance in this progression. Although this document was not included in either of the two major bibliographic checklists by Dustin and Luther, it was deemed invaluable since it does officially open the door to the flood of Federal publications involving this single incident in our history. This publication raised points which enabled the other reports to be written and published; in fact, there seemed to be a lot of doubt generated by Secretary George C. Gorham when transmitting various reports, one of which was to resolve "whether the recent reports of an alleged disaster to our forces under General Custer in that region are true." These reports ended with the following statement by General Alfred Terry: "I have as yet received no official reports in regard to the battle, but what is stated herein is gathered from the officers who were on the ground there, and from those who have been over it since." Then came the flood!

As previously mentioned, the Battle of the Little Big Horn and Custer's defeat on June 25, 1876, did not constitute the termination of the Sioux campaign; it was not officially declared ended until 1877, and then only after many other engagements. What was not over after that date was the tally sheet, the computations for the expenses of the campaign. On February 21, 1878, Part I of *Senate Executive Document No. 33,* 45th Congress, 2nd Session was released. Part II was released almost one month later, on March 26,

1878. Both addressed themselves to the cost of the "late war with the Sioux Nation." Although both parts had financial considerations and charts and equipment breakdowns, Part I also addressed itself to the casualties experienced by the army commencing in February, 1876. Of all the units in the field on this campaign—2nd, 3rd, 4th, 5th and 7th Cavalries; 4th, 5th, 6th, 17th and 22nd Infantries; the Medical Department and the Indian scouts—the 7th U.S. Cavalry led the statistics in all categories except in Commissioned Officers Wounded. The 3rd Cavalry was second highest in total reported killed. These statistics, however, as accurate as they were thought to have been at the time, were incorrect. In fact, the total number was debated for many years. This chart does not list civilians who were killed on the campaign.

The Sioux Campaign of 1876 was one conducted by the Federal Government as an outgrowth of our westward expansion which was an inevitable fact that would have to have been faced sooner or later; its manner of solution was the only thing in doubt. The Indian waged a war of survival—survival for life as well as for a way of life. The tactics used by either forces were often questionable. History has proven the expansion to have been in the best interest of this nation, but it has also proven to be a long period of disgrace and of conquest at any price. One's interpretations and conclusions can come only from that body of literature relating to the subject, and one as a result must read all of them in order to reach anything remotely reflective of a complete answer. It is fervently hoped this compilation of related documents will further the students' research and make it more possible to arrive at a conclusion which we can all accept.

About The Contributors

This publication could not have been realized had it not been for the generosity and artistry and scholarship of all the contributors. In alphabetical order, they are:

Bjorklund, Lorence—(P.O. Box 265, Croton Falls, New York, 10519)—Larry has illustrated over three hundred books, several of which have been mine. Born in Minnesota, he began his illustrating career in the New York area where he began to build his reputation as an illustrator of the western scene by supplying drawings for the popular western pulp magazines of the 1930's and 1940's. He is also the author of two highly successful books, *Faces of the Frontier* and *The Bison: The Great American Buffalo.*

Crackel, Major Theodore J.—I have counted Ted as a friend for several years now. We first met as a result of his paper on Custer at Elizabethtown. Having seen a copy, I was interested in writing to the gentleman to express my admiration for the amount of excellent research and writing which I recognized as being evident in his paper. To my surprise I learned he lived just three or four miles from me and was attending Rutgers University where he was working on his Ph.D. Ted was subsequently assigned on a tour of duty in Viet Nam, and in fact wrote the first draft of his Preface while on duty there. He was then returned to the United States and assigned as an instructor of American History at the United States Military Academy at West Point where we again picked up our friendship which had been interrupted by his tour of duty overseas. His reassignment in the same capacity to the Command and General Staff School at Fort Leavenworth was the result of recognition of him as an outstanding scholar and teacher. His study of Custer—though limited to Elizabethtown—was a first on the subject and set the standard.

Crandall, Jerry—(P.O. Box 6783, Torrance, California, 90504)—Jerry (The Little General) has been a friend for only a year. I had been aware of his great work on canvas and was pleasantly surprised when I had the opportunity to meet him at the 2nd Annual Conference of the Little Big Horn Associates in Billings, Montana, in 1975. His work can be seen throughout the Southwest including Petersen Galleries in Beverly Hills, California; Overland Trail Galleries in Jackson Hole, Wyoming; Saddleback Galleries in Santa Ana, California; Gallery '85 in Billings, Montana and the Fenn Galleries in Santa Fe, New Mexico. His contributions to this book are handsome, indeed, and I hope they will not be the last of his to appear in any of my books in the future.

Frost, Dr. Lawrence—Larry, a long-time friend, and an internationally recognized authority of the Custer story, resides in Monroe, Michigan, the home of the Custers and the Bacons. His involvement in Custer history is well known and resulted in *The Custer Album, The Custer Court-Martial* and the soon-to-be-released biography of Elizabeth Custer. He also co-edited a book with me, *The Private Theodore Ewert Diary of the Black Hills Expedition of 1874*. As curator of the Custer Museum at Monroe, Larry has had the unique opportunity of knowing many of the Custer family. His contributions to Custeriana are always welcome.

Lorimer, Thomas—(652 Temple Avenue, Long Beach, California, 90814)—I have known Tom but a short time, but during that period I have had the opportunity to view and judge his work. I am most impressed, as so should the reader be. His childhood love of cowboy and Indian lore and his strong desire to paint all came together at a time when America's nostalgia for things past and curiosity about her own history have brought renewed status to western artists. Two years of training in Chicago and his subsequent work as an illustrator helped him define his goals, and led him to California where he graduated from Art Center College of Design in 1970. Since that time his works, done mostly in watercolor and egg tempera, have grown in scope and historical import.

Powell, Dave—(Route #3, Kalispell, Montana, 59901)—Dave is an acquaintance of long standing. He and his father, the well-known Ace Powell, have always been particular favorites of mine, and when I first met Dave, his artifact drawings impressed me greatly. He was a young teenager then, but since that time many summers ago he has grown as an artist and has demonstrated a capability far larger than his age would normally dictate.

Reedstrom, Lisle—(9907 West 109th Avenue, Cedar Lake, Indiana 46303)—Lisle, a long-time friend and a companion in the Little Big Horn Associates, has contributed two very major drawings to this book. Nationally known for his authentic portrayals and book and story illustrations dealing with the Civil War period, the early western frontier movement and Indian and Military tactics, he is considered by many to be an expert in his field. Early training in the Art Institute of Chicago instilled in him all the qualities necessary for an art historian. Additional training at Arizona School of Art enabled him to establish his reputation as one of our best art illustrators.

Steffen, Randy—(Route #4, Dublin, Texas, 76446)—Randy is one of my closest friends, and a visit with him and his wife, Dorothy, at their Walking S Ranch is always a pleasure. He is a native of Texas. His art is widely celebrated for its beauty, accuracy and fidelity; he works in ink, oil, watercolor and bronze. I have never held the fact that he graduated from the United States Naval Academy against him. This book will be the first of two of mine which will contain this fine gentleman's work; the second will be the dust jacket picture for my *Custer in the Civil War*, due for release in the fall of this year. Randy has illustrated literally hundreds of articles and books of military and western history, and has recently seen the release of one of his very own, *United States Military Saddles: 1812-1943;* it was established as a classic in its field almost immediately upon publication.

Terry, Jack—(415 West 15th Street, Austin, Texas, 78701)—Jack is one of my newest friends in the western art field. Born in Sweetwater, Texas, he is only twenty-four years old and already imbued with the traditions of the American West. He began to paint at age 9, and won a blue ribbon in his first art exhibit. Since that time he has amassed more than 150 awards for his work. In the early 1970's he studied art with Dalhart Windberg, then entered the University of Texas where he earned a degree in Journalism in 1973. He has held over six one-man shows, and this year will be exhibited in the rotunda of the Texas State Capitol. Though he does not consider himself to be strictly a western artist, it is this theme which has won for him most of his recognition.

    The collaboration of all this talent has enabled me to complete this project which has been "on the boards" for over three years. I thank each and every one of them for their generosity.

JOHN M. CARROLL
New Brunswick, New Jersey

LETTER

FROM THE

SECRETARY OF THE INTERIOR,

TRANSMITTING,

In answer to a Senate resolution of April 19, 1876, a copy of the report of the Commissioner of Indian Affairs in relation to the present situation of Indian disturbances in the Sioux reservation.

APRIL 26, 1876.—Referred to the Committee on Indian Affairs and ordered to be printed.

DEPARTMENT OF THE INTERIOR,
Washington, April 25, 1876.

SIR: I have the honor to acknowledge the receipt of the following resolution passed by the Senate April 19, 1876:

"*Resolved,* That the Secretary of the Interior be directed to communicate to the Senate any information in his possession in relation to the present situation of Indian disturbances in the Sioux reservation, or unceded Indian territory of said Sioux, and whether military force has been interposed therein ; and, if so, whether at the instance of the Interior Department, and the reasons for such interposition."

In answer to said resolution, I transmit, herewith, copy of report, dated the 22d instant, from the Commissioner of Indian Affairs, together with accompanying copies of papers therein referred to.

I have the honor to be, very respectfully, your obedient servant,

Z. CHANDLER,
Secretary.

The PRESIDENT OF THE SENATE.

DEPARTMENT OF THE INTERIOR,
OFFICE OF INDIAN AFFAIRS,
Washington, D. C., April 22, 1876.

SIR: I have the honor to acknowledge the receipt, by reference from the Department, of United States Senate resolution of April 19, 1876, which directs the Secretary of the Interior " to communicate to the Senate any information in his possession in relation to the present situation of Indian disturbances in the Sioux reservation, or unceded territory of said Sioux, and whether military force has been interposed therein, and, if so, whether at the instance of the Interior Department, and the reasons for such interposition."

3

Assuming that the disturbances alluded to are those arising out of the course pursued for a long time past by lawless Indians under the leadership of the notorious Sioux chief Sitting Bull, in Western Dakota and Eastern Montana, I beg leave to say that this Office has but meager information in regard to the present situation of the troubles with these Indians.

Herewith I transmit a copy of the correspondence on file here, showing the measures adopted by mutual understanding between the War and Interior Departments for inducing, as well as compelling, if need be, Sitting Bull and his followers to go upon their reservation in Dakota and remain there. It will be seen that the insolent and destructive attitude of these Indians rendered the use of military force a necessity. For the maintenance of good order and the protection of the whites, an order had been issued by this Department in December, 1875, that these troublesome and defiant Indians should go upon their reservation by the 31st of January last, or they would be regarded as hostile, and so treated by the military. As this order, which had been communicated to them by couriers from several of the Indian agencies, seemed to be utterly disregarded, this Office, taking into consideration the opinion of the General and Lieutenant-General of the Army, that a movement against them would be entirely practicable, and inferring that the force at command would be sufficient to restrain the Sioux Indians now at the several agencies from an outbreak, as a diversion in favor of the hostiles, on the 21st of January, ultimo, in a report to the Department, expressed the conviction that enough had been done to fully commit the Department to the policy of force should the hostile bands further refuse to comply with its order. Acting upon that report, the Department, under date of the 1st of February, ultimo, communicated with the Secretary of War, and turned over these Indians to his Department for appropriate action by the Army; and, on the 3d of said month, the Secretary of War replied that the Adjutant-General had directed the General of the Army to take immediate measures to compel the Indians to return to, and remain upon, their reservation.

As to the result of the military expedition against these Indians, this Office has no other information than that furnished in reports from Agents Hastings and Howard, respectively in charge of the Red Cloud and Spotted Tail agencies in Nebraska, and Agent Clapp, of the Crow agency in Montana, all having some bearing upon the subject, and of which copies are herewith submitted.

The resolution of the Senate is herewith returned.

Very respectfully, your obedient servant,

J. Q. SMITH,
Commissioner.

The Hon. SECRETARY OF THE INTERIOR.

SENATE EXECUTIVE DOCUMENT NO. 52
44th CONGRESS, 1st SESSION

A Northern Cheyenne Warrior

WASHINGTON, D. C., *November* 9, 1875.

SIR: I have the honor to address you in relation to the attitude and condition of certain wild and hostile bands of Sioux Indians in Dakota and Montana, that came under my observation during my recent tour through their country, and what I think should be the policy of the Government toward them.

I refer to Sitting Bull's band and other bands of the Sioux Nation, under chiefs or "head-men" of less note, but no less untamable and hostile. These Indians occupy the center, so to speak, and roam over Western Dakota and Eastern Montana, including the rich valleys of the Yellowstone and Powder Rivers, and make war on the Aricka-rees, Mandans, Gros Ventres, Assinaboines, Blackfeet, Piegans, Crows, and other friendly tribes on the circumference.

Their country is probably the best hunting-ground in the United States, "a paradise" for Indians, affording game in such variety and abundance that the need of Government supplies is not felt. Perhaps for this reason, they have never accepted aid or been brought under control. They openly set at defiance all law and authority, and boast that the United States authorities are not strong enough to conquer them. The United States troops are held in contempt, and, surrounded by their native mountains, relying on their knowledge of the country and powers of endurance, they laugh at the futile efforts that have thus far been made to subjugate them, and scorn the idea of white civilization.

They are lofty and independent in their attitude and language to Government officials, as well as the whites generally, and claim to be the sovereign rulers of the land. They say they own the wood, the water, the ground, and the air, and that white men live in or pass through their country but by their sufferance.

They are rich in horses and robes, and are thoroughly armed. Nearly every warrior carries a breech-loading gun, a pistol, a bow and quiver of arrows. From their central position they strike to the east, north, and west, steal horses, and plunder from all the surrounding tribes, as well as frontier settlers, and luckless white hunters, or emi-grants who are not in sufficient force to resist them, and fortunate, indeed, is the man who thus meets them, if, after losing all his worldly possessions, he escapes with his scalp.

And yet these Indians number, all told, but a few hundred warriors, and these are never all together, or under the control of one chief.

In my judgment, one thousand men, under the command of an experienced officer, sent into their country in the winter, when the Indians are nearly always in camp, and at which season of the year they are the most helpless, would be amply sufficient for their capture or punishment.

The Government has done everything that can be done, peacefully to get control of these Indians, or to induce them to respect its authority. Every effort has been made, but all to no purpose. They are still as wild and untamable, as uncivilized and savage, as when Lewis and Clark first passed through their country.

The injurious effects of the repeated attacks made by these bands on the peaceful, friendly tribes heretofore mentioned cannot be over-estimated. No people can reasonably be expected to make progress in the arts of peace, if they must be constantly armed, and prepared to defend their houses and property. No Indians can be expected to "civilize," to learn to cultivate the soil, or the machanic acts, if, while they have the implements of labor in one hand, they must carry the gun in the other for self-defense. Their natural instincts come to the surface at once, and the Indian agent or missionary who is zealously laboring for the advancement of the people under his care, and to carry out the humane policy of our Government, the only policy worthy an enlightened Christian nation, finds his labors vastly increased and discouragements multiplied by this state of affairs.

These wild bands are but as a drop in the bucket in number compared to the great body of Indians who have accepted the peaceful policy, made treaties with the Government, and are keeping them, or have been supplied with provisions, goods, and farming-implements, without treaty stipulations, and are under the care of agents, friendly, and making fair progress in the way of civilization. In interviews with the Indians along the Missouri River and through Montana, during my recent tour of inspection, they invariably spoke of this subject, and complained bitterly that the Government was not protecting them as it had promised, and frequently closed the case by saying "they might just as well go out and kill white men, as to try to be good Indians, for they get no protection or extra reward for being good." When I told them the Sioux would be punished, they said, "We have heard that before; we'll wait and see." While I am not disposed to be needlessly alarmed, and do not agree with the writers of articles published in numerous territorial papers of a sensational character on this subject, yet I think there is danger of some of the young warriors from friendly tribes falling off and joining with these hostile bands, until, with these accessions, they would be somewhat formidable, and might make a simultaneous attack on the white settlers in some localities, if they are thus allowed to gather head.

The true policy, in my judgment, is to send troops against them in the winter—the sooner the better—and whip them into subjection. They richly merit the punishment for their incessant warfare on friendly tribes, their continuous thieving, and their numerous murders of white settlers and their families, or white men wherever found unarmed.

The Government owes it, too, to these friendly tribes, in fulfillment of treaty stipulations. It owes it to the agents and employés, whom it has sent to labor among the Indians at remote and almost inaccessible

6

places, beyond the reach of aid, in time to save. It owes it to the frontier settlers, who have, with their families, braved the dangers and hardships incident to pioneer life. It owes it to civilization and the common cause of humanity.

Very respectfully, your obedient servant,

E. C. WATKINS,
United States Indian Inspector.

Hon. E. P. SMITH,
Commissioner of Indian Affairs, Washington, D. C.

2.

DEPARTMENT OF THE INTERIOR,
OFFICE INDIAN AFFAIRS,
November 27, 1875.

SIR: I have the honor to transmit herewith, inclosed, a special report from E. C. Watkins, United States Indian inspector, dated the 9th instant, in relation to the status and condition of certain wild and lawless bands of Sioux Indians, giving an expression of his views in reference to the future action of the Government toward them.

Inspector Watkins refers to Sitting Bull's band, and others, who roam over Western Dakota and Eastern Montana, including the rich valley of the Yellowstone and Powder Rivers, and make war on the Arickarees, Mandans, Gros Ventres, Assinaboines, Blackfeet, Piegans, Crows, and other friendly tribes; and he suggests, for reasons stated by him, that one thousand men, under the command of an experienced officer, be sent into the country of these hostile Indians (numbering but a few hundred) during the winter season, and compel them to submit to the authority of the Government.

I respectfully recommend that this communication be referred to the War Department for consideration and such action as may be deemed best by Lieutenant-General Sheridan, who is personally conversant with the situation on the Upper Missouri, and with the relations of Sitting Bull's band to the other Sioux tribes.

Very respectfully, your obedient servant,

EDW. P. SMITH,
Commissioner.

The Hon. SECRETARY OF THE INTERIOR.

3.

DEPARTMENT OF THE INTERIOR,
Washington, December 3, 1875.

SIR: Referring to your communication of the 27th ultimo, relative to the status of certain Sioux Indians residing without the bounds of their reservation, and their continued hostile attitude toward the whites, I have to request that you direct the Indian agents at all the Sioux agencies in Dakota, and at Fort Peck, Montana, to notify said Indians that unless they shall remove within the bounds of their reservation (and remain there) before the 31st of January next, they shall be deemed hostile, and treated accordingly by the military force.

Please instruct said agents to acknowledge the receipt of your order, and notify you of the execution of it.

Very respectfully, your obedient servant,

Z. CHANDLER,
Secretary.

The COMMISSIONER OF INDIAN AFFAIRS.

4.

DEPARTMENT OF THE INTERIOR,
OFFICE INDIAN AFFAIRS,
December 6, 1875.

SIR: I am instructed by the honorable Secretary of the Interior, under date of the 3d instant, to direct you to notify Sitting Bull's band, and other wild and lawless bands of Sioux Indians residing without the bounds of their reservation, who roam over Western Dakota, and Eastern Montana, including the rich valley of the Yellowstone and Powder Rivers, and make war on the Arickarees, Mandans, Gros Ventres, Assinaboines, Blackfeet, Piegans, Crows, and other friendly tribes, that unless they shall remove within the bounds of their reservation (and remain there) before the 31st of January next, they shall be deemed hostile, and treated accordingly by the military force.

You will acknowledge the receipt of this order, and notify this Office of the execution of it.

Very respectfully, your obedient servant,

EDW. P. SMITH,
Commissioner.

J. S. HASTINGS, Esq.,
United States Indian Agent, Red Cloud Agency, Nebraska.

Letter to the same effect addressed the same day to Agents Howard, Bingham, Burke, Livingstone, Beckwith, Reily, and Alderson.

5.

WAR DEPARTMENT,
Washington City, January 12, 1876.

SIR: Referring to a previous correspondence with your Department on the subject of the appearance of hostile bands of Sioux outside their reservation, I have now the honor to transmit copy of a report of the commanding general, Division of the Missouri, concerning these Indians, and to invite your attention to the request of General Sheridan, concurred in by the General of the Army, that should operations against them be determined upon, he may be so advised as speedily as possible.

Very respectfully, your obedient servant,

H. T. CROSBY, *Chief Clerk.*
(For the Secretary of War, in his absence.)

The Hon. the SECRETARY OF THE INTERIOR.

Indorsements on copy of correspondence concerning status of certain wild bands of Sioux, covering report of Indian Inspector Watkins.

WAR DEPARTMENT, ADJUTANT-GENERAL'S OFFICE,
Washington, December 11, 1875.

Official copies, respectfully referred through headquarters of the Army to commanding general Military Division of the Missouri.

By order of the Secretary of War:

E. D. TOWNSEND,
Adjutant-General.

HEADQUARTERS OF THE ARMY,
Saint Louis, December 13, 1875.

Respectfully referred to Lieutenant-General P. H. Sheridan, commanding Division of the Missouri, for report as to the plausibility of military operations against Sitting Bull and his tribe, this winter.

By command of General Sherman:

A. McD. McCOOK,
Colonel and A. D. C.

HEADQUARTERS OF THE ARMY,
Saint Louis, Mo., January 7, 1876.

Respectfully returned to the Secretary of War, inviting attention to General Sheridan's letter, herewith inclosed. Midwinter is the best time to strike hostile Indians in the latitude of the Yellowstone, but we should have timely notice of the object to be accomplished and the means for its attainment.

W. T. SHERMAN, *General.*

[Inclosure to preceding indorsement.]

HEADQUARTERS MILITARY DIVISION OF THE MISSOURI,
Chicago, Illinois, January 4, 1876.

GENERAL: I have the honor to reply to your request as indorsed on certain papers, forwarded from the Secretary of the Interior, requesting military operations against Sioux Indians, in case they refuse to occupy the reservation assigned them by the Indian Bureau, on or before the 31st day of January, 1876.   *   *   *

As Generals Terry and Crook command the departments in which these hostile Indians are located, I respectfully forward their opinions on the subject.

General Terry is of the opinion that Sitting Bull's band of hostile Indians is encamped at or near the mouth of Little Missouri, and that it can be reached by a quick movement, which may be decisive at this season of the year, and that he has sufficient troops and means to make such a movement.

General Crook is of the opinion that operations can be undertaken in his department against bands of hostile Sioux Indians whenever, in the opinion of the Indian Bureau, such action becomes necessary.

As the commands of these two officers embrace all the Indians against whom military action was contemplated, it will be seen that the movement is considered practicable, and I earnestly request, should operations be determined upon, that directions to that effect be communicated to me as speedily as possible, so that the enemy may be taken at the greatest disadvantage.

Very respectfully, your obedient servant,

P. H. SHERIDAN,
Lieutenant-General.

General W. T. SHERMAN,
Headquarters of the Army, Saint Louis, Mo.

6.

DEPARTMENT OF THE INTERIOR,
OFFICE INDIAN AFFAIRS,
January 21, 1876.

SIR: By Department reference of the 13th instant, I am in receipt of communication from the honorable the Secretary of War, inviting attention to the indorsement of Lieutenant-General Sheridan (therewith inclosed) that, should operations against the hostile bands of Sioux outside their reservation be determined on, the military may be so advised as speedily as possible.

From this indorsement, it appears to be the opinion of the accomplished officers under whose immediate supervision any movement against these Indians would be conducted—an opinion in which the General and Lieutenant-General of the Army concur—that such a movement at this season of the year is entirely practicable.

I am disposed to believe, also, although the question is not specifically raised by these papers, that the officers whose opinions are thus given have no doubt as to this ability to restrain, with the troops at their command, any possible outbreak (by way of a diversion in favor of Sitting Bull and the Indians who will be the direct objects of the attack) of the bands of Sioux now at the several agencies.

In compliance with your directions, I have the honor to report that the indorsement of Lieutenant-General Sheridan, above mentioned, was called out by a communication from this Office of November 27th last, in which the then Commissioner invited attention to the trouble which Sitting Bull and other lawless Sioux ranging over certain parts of Dakota and Montana were giving to friendly Indians and white settlers within their reach, this communication having been referred by you, in compliance with his recommendation, to the War Department.

Since the date of this communication, viz, on the 6th ultimo, my predecessor, acting under your instructions, directed the agents at the Red Cloud, Spotted Tail, Lower Brulé, Crow Creek, Cheyenne River, Standing Rock, Devil's Lake, and Fort Peck agencies to communicate, if practicable, to Sitting Bull and the other hostile Indians the requirements of the Government that they return within the bounds of their reservation on or before the 31st instant. Agent Howard, of the Spotted Tail agency, reported, under date of the 3d instant, his belief that their demands had by that time reached the northern camps, and that Sitting Bull is fully advised of the intentions of the Government.

Some of the agents named have not been heard from in regard to this matter, while no one has, as yet, clearly expressed a belief concurrent with that of Agent Howard. In my opinion, however, enough has been done to fully commit the Department to the policy of restraining, by force of arms, any further outbreak or insubordination on the part of these defiant and hostile bands, should they refuse to comply before the 31st instant with the demands thus made upon them. Certainly I can conceive of nothing more damaging to the authority of the Government, not yet fully recognized by other bands of Sioux, than a failure to execute threats of military operations so clearly made.

In further execution of the policy thus determined upon, and with a desire to afford the fullest information to all officers interested, I directed, on the 19th instant, the agents at the Red Cloud, Spotted Tail, Standing Rock, and Cheyenne River agencies, who would in my view be most likely to obtain reliable and early news of Sitting Bull's intentions and movements, to keep me fully advised by letter and telegraph of his acceptance or rejection of the conditions imposed upon him, or of any other intelligence concerning him.

Any information which I may receive in compliance with these instructions will be forwarded without delay to you, for transmission to the honorable the Secretary of War.

The communication of the honorable the Secretary of War is herewith returned.

I have the honor to be, very respectfully, your obedient servant,

J. Q. SMITH,
Commissioner.

The Hon. SECRETARY OF THE INTERIOR.

———

7.

DEPARTMENT OF THE INTERIOR,
Washington, D. C., February 1, 1876.

SIR: On the 3d December last I had the honor to address a communication to you relative to the hostile Sioux roaming in the Powder River country, under the leadership of Sitting Bull, informing you that I had directed couriers to be sent from each of the Sioux agencies, informing that chief that he must come in with his followers to one of the Sioux agencies, before the 31st ultimo, prepared to remain in peace near the agency, or he would be turned over to the War Department, and the Army be directed to compel him to comply with the orders of this Department.

The time given him in which to return to an agency having expired, and the advices received at the Indian Office being to the effect that Sitting Bull still refuses to comply with the directions of the Commissioner, the said Indians are hereby turned over to the War Department for such action on the part of the Army as you may deem proper under the circumstances.

I inclose copy of communication from the Commissioner of Indian Affairs, dated the 21st ultimo, recommending that hostilities be commenced.

Very respectfully, your obedient servant,

Z. CHANDLER,
Secretary.

The Hon. SECRETARY OF WAR.

———

8.

WAR DEPARTMENT,
Washington City, February 3, 1876.

SIR: Acknowledging the receipt of your letter of the 1st instant stating that the time given Sitting Bull and his followers to repair to an

S. Ex. 52——2

agency having expired, and this chief still refuses to comply with the directions of the Commissioner, and turning over the case to the War Department, in accordance with the recommendation of the Indian Bureau that hostilities be commenced against these Indians, I have the honor to inform you that the Adjutant-General has directed the General of the Army to take immediate measures to compel these Indians to return to and remain upon their reservation, as requested by your Department.

Very respectfully, your obedient servant,
W. W. BELKNAP,
Secretary of War.

The Hon. SECRETARY OF THE INTERIOR.

———

9.

CROW AGENCY, MONTANA,
March 10, 1876.

SIR: I have the honor to inclose herewith a report of murders and outrages committed by Sioux Indians in the valley of the Yellowstone since the first of last July.

It shows seventeen attacks made by them on parties of whites; nine white men killed and ten wounded, besides a large amount of property stolen or destroyed.

I estimate that they interfered with the building of this agency last summer to the amount of four to six thousand dollars. This is not a new condition of things. For several years, the eastern settlements of Montana have been harassed regularly every summer in the same manner. In fact, a regular predatory warfare has been carried on by the Sioux, and by Sioux that are receiving Government supplies.

The party that stole the agency horses and mules last summer left in the corral a blanket with the United States Indian Department brand. The party that attacked the agency train on July 2 and killed José Trojio, left flour-sacks bearing the brand of the United States inspector of Indian Department flour, (Clarkson.)

There is another very important consideration. The Crows have always been fast friends of the whites, and have largely assisted in protecting the eastern settlements of Montana.

The Sioux are now occupying the eastern and best portion of their reservation, and by their constant warfare paralyzing all efforts to induce the Crows to undertake agriculture or other means of self-support.

I respectfully ask attention to the importance of establishing a military post, or at least a summer camp, on the Yellowstone, near the mouth of the Big Horn.

There are fourteen companies stationed in Montana, in the district of which Fort Shaw is the headquarters, most of them at points where no hostile Indians have appeared for a long time. I think it will be evident to every person who is acquainted with the character and topography of the country that if several of these companies were stationed at the mouth of the Big Horn, and the others at Ellis and the forks of the Musselshell, complete protection could be afforded to the settlements, and the notorious Sitting Bull band of Sioux held in check. As it is, not only are men murdered and property destroyed every year, and the permanent good intended to the friendly Crows prevented, but large tracts of the best agricultural and pasture lands of Montana are made uninhabitable.

Very respectfully, your obedient servant,

DEXTER E. CLAPP, *Agent.*

Hon. J. Q. SMITH,
Commissioner of Indian Affairs.

P. S.—I open this to add that four Crows who accompanied General Brisbin's expedition to the mouth of the Big Horn, and remained behind, have just come in, and report that a very large force of Sioux are moving up the north bank of the Yellowstone. Nearly all the Crows have come in much earlier than usual, and report that they expect the Sioux to attack this agency and themselves in large force. They say they have received word from Fort Peck to that effect.

10.

SPOTTED TAIL AGENCY, NEBRASKA,
April 1, 1876.

SIR: I have the honor to submit this my monthly report of affairs at this agency for March, 1876:

* * * * * * *

During the month there was considerable drunkenness among the white and half-breed men, caused by liquor from Camp Sheridan, and I am very apprehensive that serious consequences will follow unless the sale of liquor be stopped.

I am informed that the internal-revenue officer at Cheyenne has issued license to sell liquor in Custer City, Dakota.

I have just read in a Cheyenne paper, "telegram of General George Crook, Fort Reno, March 22, 1876, stating that the village of Crazy Horse was attacked by the troops and destroyed on the 17th, finding it a perfect magazine of ammunition, war-material, and general supplies, and every evidence was found to prove that these Indians are in copartnership with those at the Red Cloud and Spotted Tail agencies, and that the proceeds of their raids upon the settlements had been taken to these agencies and supplies brought out in return." And further: "In this connection I would again urgently recommend the immediate transfer of these agencies to the Missouri."

Now, many unkind remarks find their way into the newspapers, and very few encouraging words for the successful efforts we have made for the civilization of these Indians. They are to-day, and have been for months, one of the best-behaved communities in the country, and that their improvement is not due to military influence is shown in the annual reports and in the reports of the Board of Indian Commissioners of 1875.

I here desire officially to state that very few Northern Indians have been here since the grand council of September last. No proceeds of raids upon settlements have been brought here; no supplies taken north in return. No arms have been sold by the agency trader to Indians for more than two years past, and but little ammunition; and, for two months, none of either.

Very few, if any, of these Indians have been north this season, and I have heard of none who were in copartnership with those of the north.

I respectfully suggest that General Crook be requested to produce some of the abundant evidence which he found.

*　　*　　*　　*　　*　　*　　*

I am, very respectfully, your obedient servant,

E. A. HOWARD,
United States Indian Agent.

Hon. COMMISSIONER INDIAN AFFAIRS,
Washington, D. C.

11.

RED CLOUD AGENCY, NEBRASKA,
April 3, 1876.

SIR: I have the honor to report that I have been on duty here during the month of March, 1876.

The Indians belonging here, who had been north to the buffalo, continued to arrive up to the last of the month. I am of the opinion that there are but few yet to come in; had there been food to issue them on their arrival, it would have been some satisfaction, but to find a comparatively empty warehouse and a limited supply of beef, the outlook was certainly discouraging, though they have showed no signs of ugliness. I have succeeded in keeping them in good spirits, and under control, by telling them that every effort was being made by the Department to procure for them more food. The last beef, consisting of about two-thirds of a regular ten days' allowance, was issued March 31.

I learn from one of the half-breed scouts, who was with Crook's expedition against the hostile camp, that it was a complete failure, with the exception of the killing of an old squaw and two children, and the destruction of about forty lodges, with a loss to the troops of four killed and six wounded. Seven hundred Indian ponies were captured, but were recaptured on the following day, with the exception of about seventy head. A dozen or more officers have been placed in arrest for cowardice, and the command have returned to the railroad.

Sensational newspaper reports from an Army officer correspondent with the expedition, to the effect that the Indians whom they encountered had "mines of ammunition and abundance of supplies, with evidences of having been procured from this and Spotted Tail agency," are very much exaggerated, and, I think, in the most part untrue. Five pounds of powder, twenty of lead, and six boxes of percussion-caps comprised all the ammunition that was found in the abandoned camp. It is generally known throughout this country that the "hostiles" do the principal part of their trading at points on the Missouri River. The agency Indians appear to take but little interest in what has transpired north; but the disastrous result may have a tendency to awaken the old feeling of superiority.

I have experienced no difficulty whatever in taking the census, but have been somewhat delayed on account of the weather. I expect to have it completed in about a week.

Very respectfully, your obedient servant,

JAS. S. HASTINGS,
United States Indian Agent.

Hon. J. Q. SMITH,
Commissioner of Indian Affairs, Washington, D. C.

ANNUAL REPORT OF THE CHIEF OF ENGINEERS FOR THE FISCAL YEAR ENDING JUNE 30, 1876 APPENDIX MM

Comanche (Capt. Keogh's Horse)

APPENDIX M M.

ANNUAL REPORT OF MAJOR G. L. GILLESPIE, CORPS OF ENGINEERS, FOR THE FISCAL YEAR ENDING JUNE 30, 1876.

EXPLORATIONS AND SURVEYS, MILITARY DIVISION OF THE MISSOURI.

HEADQUARTERS MILITARY DIVISION OF THE MISSOURI,
OFFICE OF THE CHIEF ENGINEER,
Chicago, Ill., July 11, 1876.

GENERAL: I have the honor to submit my annual report of operations as engineer officer at headquarters Military Division of the Missouri, for the fiscal year ending June 30, 1876.

The limited number of reliable itineraries of scouts received during the year at this office from the department engineers has not permitted any great or specially important changes to be made in existing maps of the Western Territories. Those that have reached me direct, as well as those accompanying reports to the adjutant-general of the division, and referred to me, have been carefully reduced, and when deemed reliable the information and changes contained therein have been added to the progress map of the division. Sheets Nos. 2 and 3 of map of Western Territories, under preparation in this office, have been completed. The latter was photo-lithographed in the office of the Chief of Engineers, January, 1876, and issued to the troops in the field in view of expected Indian operations in the Black Hills, and in the country adjacent, to the north and northwest, along the Yellowstone River and its principal tributaries, the Powder, Tongue, and the Big Horn. The former, which includes Texas, has been engraved on copper-plate in this office by Morton Collins, private Company B, Twenty-third Infantry, and is now ready to be printed. A proof-copy will accompany this report.

The engravings upon copper-plates, also executed by Private Collins, of the military reservations and plans of the military posts in the Military Division of the Missouri, mentioned in last annual report, have all been completed and one hundred copies of each printed. These reservations and plans of posts, together with a small map of the division, have been bound in the second edition of the book of "Outline Description of the Military Posts in the Military Division of the Missouri," which has been revised and corrected to date in this office, and to which some important information relative to Indian treaties and armaments of the posts has been added.

But little progress has been made in the preparation of sheet No. 4 of the Western Territories, as the manifold duties of the office have engrossed all the time of the one draughtsman allowed me.

A great deal of time is taken up in making tracings of sketches and maps accompanying reports passing through these headquarters, which tracings are required to perfect the files of reports kept in the office of the Adjutant-General.

The various duties of the year may be enumerated under the following heads:

1. Finished sheets 2 and 3 of map of Western Territories, scale 1-2,000,000. Sheet No. 4 of the same map in course of preparation, for which reductions have been made from Lieutenant Wheeler's sheets 50,

59, and 67; from Lieutenant Ruffner's map of New Mexico; from the Land-Office surveys in Colorado, and from various special surveys.

2. Revised and corrected Captain Raynolds's map 1859–'60 of the Yellowstone and Missouri Rivers.

3. Made additions and corrections on the map of Kansas, Texas, and Indian Territory, including operations of Colonel Mackenzie and Lieutenant-Colonel Shafter. Copy accompanies this report.

4. Revised and corrected "Outline Description of the Posts in the Military Division of the Missouri," and prepared maps for the same.

5. Made duplicate tracings of the following reservations and plans of posts : Camp Robinson, Nebraska ; Camp Sheridan, Nebraska ; Sidney Barracks, Nebraska ; Fort Hartsuff, Nebraska ; Cheyenne Agency, Dakota ; San Antonio, Tex. ; Camp Douglas, Utah ; Cantonment on the Sweetwater, Texas, and Fort Union, New Mexico.

6. Made duplicate tracings for the adjutant-general of the division of all sketches and maps accompanying reports referring to Indian operations.

7. Completed the engraving of sheet No. 2 of map of Western Territories, and that of the residue of the plans of posts and military reservations required to complete the book of "Outline Description," &c., mentioned under heading No. 4.

8. Compiled and arranged for the office files of this office every information that could be obtained relative to the date of declaration, the extent and establishment of the several military posts and reservations in the Military Division of the Missouri.

I accompany this report with a map showing to date the lines of march of the several columns of troops in the field operating against the hostile Sioux Indians, under command of Brig. Gen. A. H. Terry, U. S. A., Brig. Gen. George Crook, U. S. A., Col. John Gibbon, Seventh United States Infantry, and Col. Wesley Merritt, Fifth United States Cavalry.*

The first campaign, led by Brigadier-General Crook, and which had for its object the destruction of that band of the Sioux under a chief named Crazy Horse, left Fort Fetterman March 1, 1876. The column followed the old Phil. Kearney road to the Powder River at Fort Reno, thence moved direct to the headwaters of Tongue River, thence down the valley of the Tongue River to Red Clay, and thence by the valley of Otter Creek across to the Powder River, a short distance west of the forks, where a battle was fought March 17, resulting in the destruction of the village of Crazy Horse. Returning, the command reached Fort Fetterman March 26, 1876.

March 17, 1876, Colonel Gibbon left Fort Shaw for the Yellowstone River to take part in a general campaign against the Sioux, in connection with the column under General Crook from Fort Fetterman and with the column from Fort Lincoln under General Terry. The initial points of starting of these columns being so widely separated, no detailed plan of operation not subject to change could be adopted, but the movements of each were so ordered as to prevent primarily the Indians passing north of the Yellowstone, and it was designed and expected to confine the campaign to the country immediately adjacent to the Big Horn Mountains, or along the valleys of the rivers which have their sources in these mountains. Each column was to be strong enough to attack or defend itself against any force of Indians it might meet, and from the convergence of their lines of march and the proximity of the commands after the Sioux country had been reached, it was expected that any band of Indians driven by one column would inevitably be thrown upon the advance of the other columns.

---

* Map not printed.

In this way it was expected the Indians would be deprived of the means of escape otherwise afforded by the broken character of the country in which they operated, and be forced to fight until subdued or annihilated, or to return peaceably to their reservations under the terms dictated by the troops.

Colonel Gibbon's command was comprised of six companies of the Seventh Infantry and four of the Second Cavalry, aggregating 27 officers and 409 men. It moved down the Yellowstone River on the north side and reached Fort Pease, at the mouth of the Big Horn, May 9, 1876. A scout was sent from the mouth of the Big Horn to Fort C. F. Smith, thence across to Tullock's Fork, and thence down that valley to Fort Pease, returning May 14. No Indians were discovered. The command continued down the river to the mouth of the Rosebud, where it encamped May 20. May 17 General Terry left Fort Lincoln with twelve companies of the Seventh Cavalry, Lieut. Col. George A. Custer commanding, one company of the Sixth Infantry, two companies of the Seventeenth Infantry, a detatchment of the Twentieth Infantry serving Gatling guns, and thirty Indian scouts, aggregating 45 officers and 905 men. Lieut. Edward Maguire, United States Engineers, accompanied the column.

The column marched almost due west to the headwaters of the Heart River, and reached the Powder River 24 miles from its mouth, June 7, 1873.

On the 19th, a supply camp was formed on the Yellowstone, at the mouth of the Powder River, and General Terry from this point communicated with Colonel Gibbon at the mouth of the Rosebud.

General Crook opened his second campaign on the 29th of May. His command was composed of five companies of the Second Cavalry, ten companies of the Third Cavalry, and three companies of the Ninth Infantry, and three companies of the Fourth Infantry, aggregating 33 officers and 959 men, and was accompanied by Capt. W. S. Stanton, Corps of Engineers. The column moved north from Fort Fetterman, along the Fort Phil Kearney route, to the headwaters of the south fork of Tongue River, called Goose Creek, where a temporary camp was established on the 15th of June, 1876. On the 16th of June, General Crook moved down the valley of Goose Creek, thence over the Tongue River divide, and struck the Indians at the cañon at the head of Rosebud, on the 17th of June.

He returned to Cloud Peak Camp on Goose Creek June 19. No report has been received of subsequent field operations from that camp.

Immediately after reaching the Powder River, June 7, General Terry sent Major Reno of the Seventh Cavalry, with six companies, to scout up the Powder River to the Little Powder, thence down Mizpah Creek, thence over the divide to Pumpkin Creek, and thence to rejoin the command at the mouth of the Tongue River. After reaching the Little Powder River, Major Reno departed somewhat from his instructions, and moved directly across the country to the Rosebud, which he reached 25 miles from its mouth. Here he discovered an Indian trail leading up the creek. After following this for 20 miles, Major Reno returned on his trail and rejoined his command at the mouth of the Tongue River on June 19. June 21, (just four days after Crook's fight at the Rosebud Cañon,) General Terry and Colonel Gibbon united their commands at the mouth of the Rosebud.

In accordance with a plan then determined upon, Colonel Custer moved up the Rosebud with his regiment on the 22d. After striking the Indian trail discovered by Major Reno, he rapidly followed it till the morning of the 25th of June, when he suddenly came upon a large Indian village located on the left bank of the Little Horn, about 11 miles above its mouth. Major Reno was directed to cross the ford above the village, and make an attack on that side, while Custer led in person five companies in an attack on the north side, 3 miles below. Captain Benteen, with four companies, was held in reserve. Major Reno crossed the river, moved down 1 mile toward the village, and after encountering several attacks from Indians in large numbers, returned to the east bank, where he was joined by Captain Benteen and their position intrenched. But little is known positively of Colonel Custer's attack. This column reached the ford below, but could not effect a crossing, and on attempting to return it was surrounded by Indians and the whole command massacred after a bitter hand-to-hand fight. General Terry reached the mouth of Big Horn on the 24th of June. Colonel Gibbon's command was ferried across the Yellowstone in the afternoon and the advance toward the Little Horn commenced at once. Colonel Custer's battle-field was reached on the morning of the 27th, and Major Reno's command, which had been surrounded and several times attacked since the massacre, was rescued. After collecting the wounded and burying the dead, the united commands returned to the mouth of the Big Horn, where it is now refitting preparatory to a new campaign.

There are now *en route* to re-enforce this column four companies of the Twenty-second Infanty, 12 officers and 140 men, and six companies of the Fifth Infantry, 17 officers and 216 men.

To prevent Indians withdrawing from the Red Cloud and Spotted Tail agencies to assist Sitting Bull, and also to intercept war parties returning from Sitting Bull's command, eight companies of the Fifth Cavalry, under Lieutenant-Colonel Carr, were thrown out from Fort Laramie to Sage Creek, June 24, near the point where the Indian trail from the agencies to Powder River crosses that creek.

Captain Stanton and Lieutenant Maguire of the Engineers accompany, as I have stated, these expeditions, and though their surveying parties are small, it is expected that they will cover by their reconnaissances a large portion of the partially explored country comprised within the limits of the campaign, and will be enabled to make many important corrections to the maps of Northern Wyoming.

The engineer officers attached to the department headquarters are very zealous in the performance of their duties, but their operations are much circumscribed by the very limited facilities they have for executing work of an extended character. In collecting topographical information in the Territories, they have hitherto been compelled to rely to a great extent upon the itineraries kept by the officers and soldiers of the line engaged in scouting after Indian or Mexican marauders. These itineraries being kept by persons usually averse to duties foreign to their proper sphere, are necessarily imperfect and inaccurate, as the marches are long and the records entered hastily, and the engineer officers at department headquarters hesitate to use them except with great care and caution.

The only sketches of scouts or campaigns, in which any great confidence is placed, are those executed by the engineer officers themselves, or by assistants especially selected from among the junior officers of the line, whose attainments and disposition fit them for such duty, and by the enlisted men of the engineers detached from the battalion and assigned to duty in the departments.

The services of these enlisted men in this capacity cannot be too highly estimated, and it would be well if their number could be so increased that every engineer officer serving at department headquarters could have at least four; so that a small party well trained could enter the field with every scouting party or expedition that is sent out during the season. I desire to particularly call your attention to this subject.

The engineer's office at headquarters Department of Texas has been in charge during the year of Lieut. William Hoffman, Eleventh United States Infantry. He has shown great interest in his work, and has given full and entire satisfaction to this office and to his department commander. He is at present at Fort Concho determining the longitude of that post, and the office is temporarily in the charge of Lieut. Hugh G. Brown, Twelfth Infantry, whose annual report is forwarded herewith.

I submit his report without modification, that you may have a clear idea of the manifold duties assigned to the officers at department headquarters, and of the importance of the officers and the office in the estimate of the department commanders.

As has been customary heretofore, I leave the engineer operations carried on in the Departments of Dakota, the Platte, and the Missouri to be reported upon by the officers in charge of the offices, repectively.

Amount required for surveys under direction of this Office during the fiscal year ending June 30, 1878, $6,000.

Very respectfully, your obedient servant,

GEORGE L. GILLESPIE,
Major of Engineers,
Chief Engineer Military Division of the Missouri.

Brig. Gen. A. A. HUMPHREYS,
Chief of Engineers United States Army.

Bloody Knife

21

ANNUAL REPORT OF THE CHIEF OF ENGINEERS FOR THE FISCAL YEAR ENDING JUNE 30, 1876
APPENDIX 00

A Crow Scout

APPENDIX O O.

ANNUAL REPORT OF LIEUTENANT EDWARD MAGUIRE, CORPS OF ENGINEERS, FOR THE FISCAL YEAR ENDING JUNE 30, 1876.

EXPLORATIONS AND SURVEYS IN THE DEPARTMENT OF DAKOTA.

CAMP ON THE YELLOWSTONE RIVER,
NEAR THE MOUTH OF THE BIG HORN RIVER,
July 10, 1876.

GENERAL: I have the honor to submit the following report of operations in the Department of Dakota from the date of my assignment to duty as chief engineer of the department to the close of the fiscal year ending June 30, 1876:

In obedience to orders received from the Adjutant-General's Office, I reported in person to Brig. Gen. A. H. Terry, at Saint Paul, Minn., on the evening of May 8, and was assigned to duty vice Capt. Wm. Ludlow, Corps of Engineers, United States Army, relieved. In compliance with orders from headquarters Department of Dakota, I left Saint Paul early on the morning of the 10th, and proceeded to Fort Abraham Lincoln, Dakota Territory, to join the troops about to take the field against the hostile Sioux. Mr. W. H. Wood, assistant engineer, with the detachment of enlisted men, had preceded me some days. On arriving at Fort Lincoln, I learned from the commanding general that, unless the services of my assistant were necessary, it was desirable that he should not accompany the column. As his services would have been simply a convenience to me, and in no respect a necessity, I directed him to return to Saint Paul, where he has remained. The detachment of the battalion of engineers, consisting of Sergeant Wilson and Privates Goslin and Culligan, has accompanied me on the expedition, and has performed most excellent service. Sergeant Becker, with two privates, had, previous to my assignment, been ordered to Montana to accompany the column under command of Colonel Gibbon, Seventh Infantry.

After a detention of a few days near Fort Lincoln, due to rain, we finally broke camp at 5 a. m., May 17, and the march westward was

25

commenced. The column was commanded by Brig. Gen. A. H. Terry, and was composed of the following troops: The Seventh Cavalry, commanded by Lieut. Col. G. A. Custer; a battalion of infantry, commanded by Capt. L. H. Sanger, Seventeenth Infantry; headquarters' guard, consisting of one company of the Sixth Infantry, commanded by Capt. Stephen Baker; a battery of three ½-inch Gatling guns, commanded by Second Lieut. W. H. Low, Twentieth Infantry; 45 Indian scouts, guides, and interpreters, under the command of Second Lieut. C. A. Varnum, Seventh Cavalry; the wagon and pack-trains and herd, with their numerous attachés. There was a total of 50 officers, 968 enlisted men, 190 civilian employés, and 1,694 animals.

I was furnished with a four-mule ambulance for the transportation of my instruments and men. To the wheels of this ambulance were attached the odometers.

The column reached Powder River without having seen an Indian, nor even a trace of recent origin. The only difficulties encountered, with the exception of a snow-storm, which commenced on the night of the 31st of May and lasted until the 3d of June, were those offered by the nature of the country to the passage of a heavily-loaded train. There was not a day that bridging was not necessary; but the journey through Davis Creek to the Little Missouri, through the Bad Lands immediately west of the latter stream, and then the descent into the valley of the Powder, demanded almost incessant bridging and road-making. We reached Powder River late in the evening of June 7. From this camp, Major Reno, Seventh Cavalry, with six companies of his regiment, was sent on a scout up Powder River to the forks, thence across to the Rosebud, and back to the mouth of the Tongue. On June 11, we marched down the valley of the Powder, and reached the Yellowstone, where a depot was established under command of Major Moore, Sixth Infantry. Leaving the wagon-train at this point, Lieutenant-Colonel Custer, with the troops and pack-train, proceeded to the mouth of Tongue River. General Terry and staff went on the steamboat to the same place, there meeting Reno, who reported that he had found a fresh heavy Indian trail, leaving the Rosebud in a westerly direction. The whole command was then moved up the Yellowstone to the mouth of the Rosebud, where we met Gibbon's column. At this point, a definite plan of campaign was decided upon; and, as this plan is clearly set forth in the letter of instruction furnished to Custer, I insert it in full:

CAMP AT MOUTH OF ROSEBUD RIVER,
June 22, 1876.

COLONEL: The brigadier-general commanding directs that as soon as your regiment can be made ready for the march, you proceed up the Rosebud in pursuit of the Indians whose trail was discovered by Major Reno a few days since.

It is of course impossible to give you any definite instructions in regard to this movement, and, were it not impossible to do so, the department commander places too much confidence in your zeal, energy, and ability to wish to impose upon you precise orders which might hamper your action when nearly in contact with the enemy. He will, however, indicate to you his own views of what your action should be, and he desires that you should conform to them unless you shall see sufficient reason for departing from them. He thinks that you should proceed up the Rosebud until you ascertain definitely the direction in which the trail above spoken of leads; should it be found (as it appears to be almost certain that it will be found) to turn toward the Little Big Horn, he thinks that you should still proceed southward perhaps as far as the headwaters of the Tongue, and then turn toward the Little Big Horn, feeling constantly, however, to your left, so as to preclude the possibility of the escape of the Indians to the south or southeast by passing around your left flank.

The column of Colonel Gibbon is now in motion for the mouth of the Big Horn; as soon as it reaches that point, it will cross the Yellowstone and move up at least as far as the forks of the Big and Little Big Horns.

Of course, its future movements must be controlled by circumstances as they arise; but it is hoped that the Indians, if upon the Little Big Horn, may be so nearly inclosed by the two columns that their escape will be impossible. The department commander desires that on your way up the Rosebud you should thoroughly examine the upper part of Tulloch's Creek, and that you should endeavor to send a scout through to Colonel Gibbon's column with information of the result of your examination. The lower part of this creek will be examined by a detachment from Colonel Gibbon's command. The supply-steamer will be pushed up the Big Horn as far as the forks if the river is found to be navigable for that distance, and the department commander (who will accompany the column of Colonel Gibbon) desires you to report to him there not later than the expiration of the time for which your troops are rationed, unless, in the mean time, you receive further orders.

Respectfully, &c.,

E. W. SMITH,
Captain Eighteenth Infantry, Acting Assistant Adjutant-General.
Lieutenant-Colonel CUSTER,
Seventh Cavalry.

These instructions were supplemented by verbal information to Custer, that he could expect to find Gibbon's column at the mouth of the Little Big Horn not later than the 26th.

Pursuant to these instructions, Custer took up his line of march about noon on the 22d of June. His command (counting officers, enlisted men, and civilians) numbered nearly 650 mounted men. Both man and beast were in excellent condition, and there was not one of the command who was not filled with high hopes of success. Upon Custer's departure, General Terry and staff proceeded up the Yellowstone with Gibbon's column, and when near the mouth of the Big Horn the command was crossed to the right bank of the former stream. Gibbon's column, as now constituted, consisted of four companies of the Second Cavalry, five companies of the Seventh Infantry, and Lieutenant Low's Gatling Battery, amounting in all (including the civilian employés) to 377 fighting men. The night of June 24 we passed in camp on Tulloch's Creek. The next day we crossed the divide between Tulloch's Creek and the Big Horn, and reached the latter stream after a severe march of twenty-two miles. The country was exceedingly rough, hill after hill and ravine after ravine, with but little grass and plenty of the ubiquitous sage and cactus. The soil was alkaline, and the air was filled with dust, clogging up the nostrils, ears, and throat. In addition to this, the day was very warm, and not a drop of water to be obtained on the march. The infantry had understood that we were to follow Tulloch's Creek, and knowing that in that case they could obtain water at any time they did not fill their canteens. The consequence was that they suffered terribly, and numbers of men toward the close of the march dropped on the way, utterly exhausted. The refreshing sight of the Big Horn finally gladdened their hearts, and those left on the road having been brought in, they remained in camp that night. General Terry, taking the cavalry, pushed on, and a most wearisome and disheartening march we made of it. The night was black, and a cold rain drenched us. Besides this, we were obliged to cross a very rough country; and the descent and ascent of steep declivities, with no other guide than an occasional white horse, (if so lucky as to get directly behind one,) was anything but pleasant. The Indian scouts finally found a pool of alkaline water after a march of 12 miles, and we encamped in the mud for the short remaining portion of the night. About 11 o'clock the following morning (June 26) we were joined by the infantry near the mouth of the Little Big Horn, and we then proceeded up the

27

valley of that river. We went into camp that night only after the infantry had made a march of more than 50 miles in two days. The next morning the march was resumed, and we soon sighted two teepees in the valley. These teepees were filled with dead warriors, and were all that remained standing of a large Indian village. We found the ground strewn with skins, robes, camp-equipage, &c., indicating that the village had been hastily removed. The cavalry-saddles and dead horses lying around gave us the first inkling of the fact that there had been a fight, and that the troops had been worsted; but we were not prepared for the whole truth. As we passed on, we were met by Lieutenant Wallace, of the Seventh Cavalry, who informed us that Major Reno, with the remnant of seven companies, was intrenched on the bluffs across the river, where he had sustained a siege for nearly two days. We ascended the steep bluffs, and the welcome we received was such as to move even the most callous. Officers and men relieved their surcharged natures by hysterical shouts and tears. The question then arose on all sides, "Where is Custer?" The reply came only too soon. About 3 miles below Reno's position, we found the hills covered with the dead bodies of officers and men.

Of Custer's fight we at present know nothing, and can only surmise. We must be content with the knowledge gleaned from the appearance of the field, that they died as only brave men can die, and that this battle, slaughter as it was, was fought with a gallantry and desperation of which the "Charge of the Light Brigade" cannot boast. The bodies, with but few exceptions, were frightfully mutilated, and horrors stared us in the face at every step.

I proceed to give the details of Custer's march from the Rosebud, and of the battle, as I have been able to collect them up to the present time. On the 22d they marched 12 miles; on the 23d they marched 35 miles; on the 24th they marched from 5 a. m. till 8 p. m., or about 45 miles; they then rested for four hours. At 12 they started again and proceeded 10 miles. They were then about 23 miles from the village. They reached the village about 2 p. m. on the 25th. They had made a march of 78 miles in a day and a half, and, Captain Benteen tells me, without a drop of water. At some distance from the village, Custer made his disposition of the regiment. He ordered Benteen, with three companies, to move to the left and scour the country for Indians. He ordered Reno, with three companies, to advance parallel with his (Custer's) own command. When the village was sighted, he ordered Reno to charge with his three companies, telling him that he would be supported. Reno crossed the river at the point A, (see sketch herewith,) and moved down the woods at C without encountering much opposition. On reaching this latter point, the men were dismounted and deployed as skirmishers on the line indicated on the sketch. The Indians immediately swarmed around them, and Reno, finding that they were getting in his rear in large numbers, remounted his command and charged through them in retreat to the bluffs on the opposite side of the river. There were Indians on all sides of them, and Lieutenant McIntosh and several enlisted men were actually pulled from their horses and butchered. The command, with some loss, including Lieutenant Hodgson, reached the bluffs, and, being joined by Benteen and his command, they succeeded in keeping the Indians off. Benteen had received an order from Custer to hurry up, as the village had been struck, and in moving up he saw Reno's retreat, and joined him on the bluffs as quickly as possible. The Indians were all around them, and kept up an incessant fire of unerring accuracy. In the mean time, Custer had gone down stream and attempted to make a crossing at the point B, but was met by an overpowering force, and the troops retreated to the hills in rear in order to procure a more defensible position. From the position of the dead bodies on the field, I conclude that they retreated on the two lines marked on the sketch to concentrate at E, which was the highest point of the ground. At the hill D a stand was undoubtedly made by the company under command of Lieutenant Calhoun to protect the men passing up to E. Lieutenants Calhoun and Crittenden were killed on this hill. Captain Keogh was killed about half-way up the slope to E. The column which retreated along the line B H E must have been dismounted, and, fighting along the whole distance, a portion of its men, taking to the ravine H for shelter, must have been surrounded by the Indians. There were twenty-eight bodies found in this ravine. From H to E stretched a line of dead men with skirmish intervals. The crest E was literally covered with dead officers and men. Here we found General Custer and his brother, Captain Custer, Captain Yates, Lieutenant Smith, Lieutenant Cook, and Lieutenant Riley. The Indians must have been present in overwhelming numbers, for this part of the fight did not, from all accounts, last over two or three hours.

As night came on, the attack on Reno ceased, and the troops were enabled to intrench. The attack was renewed early on the morning of the 26th, and continued until late in the afternoon, when the Indians, seeing Gibbon's column advancing in the distance left Reno, and, packing up their village, moved off toward the Big Horn Mountains. The number of Indians is estimated to have been fully 3,000 warriors, and they marched off with all the precision of movement and regularity of formation of the best-drilled soldiers. The officers tell me that they (the Indians) fought with the utmost bravery and coolness, and that they were well drilled and disciplined. Volleys were fired by them at the commands "Ready! Aim!! Fire!!!"

The casualties of the Seventh Cavalry are as follows:

Killed.—Lieut. Col. G. A. Custer, Seventh Cavalry; Capt. M. W. Keogh, Seventh Cavalry; Capt. G. W. Yates, Seventh Cavalry; Capt. T. W. Custer, Seventh Cavalry; Lieut. W. W. Cook, Seventh Cavalry; Lieut. A. E. Smith, Seventh Cavalry; Lieut. D. McIntosh, Seventh Cavalry; Lieut. J. Calhoun, Seventh Cavalry; Lieut. J. E. Porter, Seventh Cavalry; Lieut. B. H. Hodgson, Seventh Cavalry; Lieut. H. M. Harrington, Seventh Cavalry; Lieut. J. C. Sturgis, Seventh Cavalry; Lieut. W. V. W. Riley, Seventh Cavalry; Asst. Surg. G. E. Lord; Act. Asst. Surg. DeWolf; Lieut. J. J. Crittenden, Twentieth Infantry— 16 officers; 252 enlisted men; 9 civilian employés: 277 killed; 59 wounded. The number of Indians killed and wounded is not known.

We remained two days on the field to bury the dead and burn the material left by the Indians, and then returned to the boat with the wounded, who have all been sent to Fort Lincoln. We are here waiting in camp for instructions.

There are some conclusions which force themselves upon the mind as indubitable. They are as follows:

1st. The number of Indians was underestimated at the outset of the campaign.

2d. The courage, skill, and, in short, the general fighting ability of the Indians has heretofore been underestimated and scoffed at. It has been forgotten that the Indian traders, by furnishing the Indians with the best breech-loading arms, and all the ammunition they desire, have totally changed the problem of Indian warfare. Sitting Bull has displayed the best of generalship in this campaign. He has kept his troops well in hand, and, moving on interior lines, he has beaten us in detail.

3d. The Indians are the best irregular cavalry in the world, and are superior in horsemanship and marksmanship to our soldiers, besides being better armed. Our regiments of cavalry are composed of men about three-fourths of whom are recruits, who have never fought with Indians. They are never drilled at firing on horseback, and the consequence is that the horses are as unused to fighting as the men themselves, and become unruly in action.

4th. The carbine has not a sufficiently long effective range, and, considering it simply as a weapon for close encounters, it has not the advantages of a magazine-gun.

The trail has been kept, and observations with the sextant have been made whenever practicable.

Very respectfully, your obedient servant,

EDW. MAGUIRE,
First Lieutenant Corps of Engineers,
Chief Engineer, Department of Dakota.

Brig. Gen. A. A. HUMPHREYS,
Chief of Engineers, U. S. A.

Buffalo Head-Dress

CUSTER'S BATTLE-FIELD

(June 25ᵗʰ 1876)

Surveyed and drawn under the personal supervision

of

LIEUT. EDWARD MAGUIRE

Corps of Engineers U.S.A.

by

Sergeant Charles Becker

Co."D" Battalion of Engineers

———————•———————

Note :- *The figures on the map are those of the stakes driven into the ground to mark the graves.*

1	Capt. M.W. Keogh , 7ᵗʰ Cav.	7	Capt. G.W. Yates	7ᵗʰ Cav.
2		8	Lieut. W. Van W. Reily	7ᵗʰ Cav.
3	Lieut. J. Calhoun 7ᵗʰ Cav.	9	Lieut. A.E. Smith	7ᵗʰ Cav.
4	Lieut. J. J. Crittenden 20ᵗʰ Inf.	10	Lieut. W.W. Cooke	7ᵗʰ Cav.
5	Lt. Col. G. A. Custer 7ᵗʰ Cav.	11	Mr. W. B. Custer .	
6	Capt. T.W. Custer 7ᵗʰ Cav	12	Mr. Reed	

Scale of Miles.

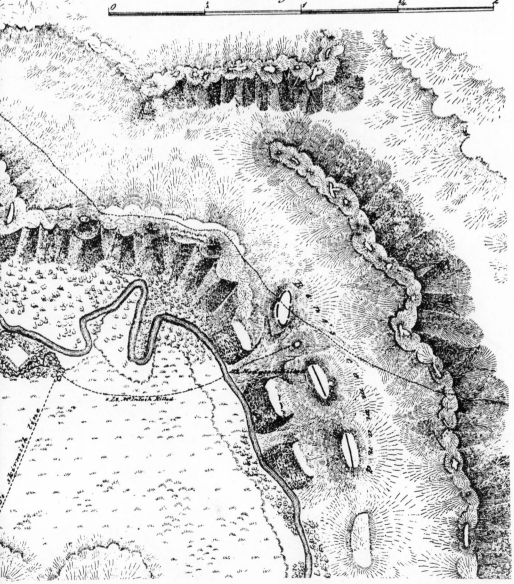

ANNUAL REPORT OF THE CHIEF OF ENGINEERS FOR THE FISCAL YEAR ENDING JUNE 30, 1877
APPENDIX PP

A Sioux Warrior

APPENDIX PP.

ANNUAL REPORT OF LIEUTENANT EDWARD MAGUIRE, CORPS OF ENGINEERS, FOR THE FISCAL YEAR ENDING JUNE 30, 1877.

EXPLORATIONS AND SURVEYS IN THE DEPARTMENT OF DAKOTA.

HEADQUARTERS DEPARTMENT OF DAKOTA,
CHIEF ENGINEER'S OFFICE,
Saint Paul, Minn., June 30, 1877.

GENERAL: I have the honor to submit herewith my annual report for the fiscal year ending June 30, 1877.

At the close of the fiscal year, the engineer detail in this department consisted of myself as engineer officer and a detachment of the battalion of engineers, consisting of two sergeants and four privates. One private was discharged July 14, 1876, in consequence of the expiration of his term of service, but with this one exception the detachment served with the troops in the field till September 7, 1876, when the campaign having virtually terminated, it returned to Saint Paul. One sergeant was, January 8, 1877, transferred to the Department of the Platte at the request of the engineer officer of the Division of the Missouri. While in the field the attention of the detachment was devoted to topographical work and the collection of such information as was possible. In addition to the topographical work, I was engaged in the superintendence of the bridging and crossings of streams and in such road-making as was found to be necessary in order to allow the passage of the train. A full report of last summer's work was submitted to the Brigadier General commanding this department, and a copy of it was forwarded to the Chief of Engineers.

Since the return to this city the office work has consisted in the arrangement, compilation, and plotting of the notes taken last summer, in the performance of such duties as were found necessary in the routine operations of the department, and in collecting such information relating to this department as could be obtained. There have been numerous calls for maps, tracings, and information of a varied nature, not only from military sources but from citizens interested in the country west of the Missouri River, from the superintendent of Indian affairs in this district, and from steamboat-men.

In addition to the above-mentioned work I have furnished working-drawings and specifications for and superintended the construction of trestle-bridge material to be used during the coming campaign.

An appropriation of $2,500 having been made for the improvement of the road from Springfield, Dak., to White Swan, Dak., I received orders to examine and report upon the said route. This duty was performed.

Upon the recommendation of the Quartermaster-General the sum of $10,000 was set aside from the appropriation for transportation of the Army to be expended in the improvement of the Yellowstone River. As the engineer officer of this department I was placed in charge of the work, but with instructions to confine the work to the three points known as Wolf, Baker, and Buffalo Rapids. As the appropriation expired with the fiscal year it became necessary for me to make a contract with each employé by which he agreed, for and in consideration of a certain sum, to remove the obstructions to navigation in the Yellowstone by the 1st of November; and should the work be finished before that time, there should be deducted from that sum an amount equivalent to pay for the number of days between the date of cessation of work and the 1st of November, at the rate of so much per day.

There is still much topographical work to be done in this department, but it is impossible at present to furnish an estimate of the amount which can be accomplished during the next fiscal year. The approaching campaign and the construction of the two large posts on the Yellowstone and Big Horn absorb all the attention and troops in this department. It is to be hoped, as expressed in a letter from this office to the Chief of Engineers, dated the 11th instant, "that the Indian problem will receive such a solution this summer that it will be possible next spring to fill in some of the gaps now existing on the maps."

Upon my application to the department commander two officers (Lieut. L. R. Hare, Seventh Cavalry, and Lieut. O. F. Long, Fifth Infantry,) have been detailed as acting engineer officers to accompany the troops serving in the field. Their notes will be plotted when received, and it is hoped that new information will be gained.

Orders have been issued for the survey of Tongue River reservation, and the survey will be made, other duties permitting.

The entire office work for the year has been well performed by the different enlisted men of the detachment.

Very respectfully, your obedient servant,

EDW. MAGUIRE,
First Lieutenant of Engineers.

The CHIEF OF ENGINEERS
United States Army.

EXPEDITION AGAINST THE HOSTILE SIOUX INDIANS IN THE SUMMER OF 1876.

HEADQUARTERS DEPARTMENT OF DAKOTA,
CHIEF ENGINEER'S OFFICE,
Saint Paul, Minn., March 9, 1877.

GENERAL: I have the honor to forward by to-day's mail a copy of the report submitted by me to the Brigadier General commanding this Department.

As will be seen from the report and the map, the line of march* was generally over portions of the country which had been traversed before and upon the nature of which other reports had been submitted. I have expressed my views concerning that region simply because men differ in their ideas of the quality of things, and any opinion which, though when considered by itself may be of little importance, yet when compared with or added to others, aids in forming true estimates.

There is still much work to be done in this department in the way of reconnaissances, but the unsettled condition of Indian affairs, with the consequent drain upon the different posts for troops to serve in active operations against the hostiles, will preclude all idea of obtaining an

---

* Map on file in Engineer Department, Washington, D. C.

escort large enough to furnish adequate protection during the coming season.

Colonel Miles, Fifth Infantry, with a command of about 2,400 men, will commence operations this year, but my experience last summer taught me that very little work could be done on a military expedition, and as the two new reservations, one at Tongue River, 20 miles square, and the other at the mouth of the Little Big Horn, or Custer River, must be surveyed, I have concluded to start up the Yellowstone about May 1, for the purpose of laying out these reservations.

Very respectfully, your obedient servant,

EDW. MAGUIRE,
First Lieutenant Corps of Engineers,
Chief Engineer Department of Dakota.

Brig. Gen. A. A. HUMPHREYS,
Chief of Engineers U. S. A.

REPORT.

HEADQUARTERS DEPARTMENT OF DAKOTA,
CHIEF ENGINEER'S OFFICE.

SIR : I have the honor to submit the following report :

In obedience to Special Orders No. 80, War Department, Adjutant-General's Office, April 21, 1876, I reported for duty at these headquarters May 8, 1876, relieving Capt. William Ludlow, Corps of Engineers, of his duties as chief engineer of this department; and in compliance with Special Orders No. 64, Headquarters Department of Dakota, dated May 9, 1876, I proceeded to Fort Abraham Lincoln, May 10, to join the expedition against the hostile Sioux.

After a delay of a few days, due to rain, the column finally started from the encampment at 5 a. m., May 17, and commenced its march into the land of the turbulent Dakotas.

The morning was raw and cold, and a heavy mist hung over the whole region round about. It gradually rose, however, as we passed Fort Lincoln, and when we reached the foot of the long ascent leading to the prairie above, it was a very beautiful sight, that of the gradual fading-out of the mist-bows and the rolling upward of the mist.

The column took up the line of march almost due west for Heart River. The route was over a rolling prairie, which was found to be in fair condition for the wagon-train. This was surprising, as after the heavy rain it was expected that the ground would be very soft ; but the train experienced no difficulty, and at half past one in the afternoon, after a march of 13½ miles, we encamped on Heart River. The camp was established in the bottom, which is about 500 feet square, and was fenced in on three sides by high bluffs, the fourth side being bounded by the gentle slope leading to the prairie we had just traversed. Quite a number of rattlesnakes, from 2 to 2½ feet long, were killed in the camp. The grass was good and plentiful, and there was no lack of wood. A slight rain fell during the night. The water of the Heart was the first we had seen after leaving Fort Lincoln. The river is so named from a prominent butte which is supposed to present the appearance of a gigantic heart.

The Indian scouts furnished much amusement. They were all, with one exception, members of the tribe called Arickarees. This one exception was Bloody Knife, a half Sioux, the hero of many fights.

The Arickarees were formerly a large and war-like tribe, living on Grand River, but small-pox and other diseases have brought them to their present state. They are of medium size and quite dark. Judging from the council held with them by Col. G. A. Custer they are not without a sort of rude eloquence. They had at all times a dirty appearance, and when mounted they looked not unlike antiquated negro washerwomen. They appeared to be a sedate class of men, even the younger ones scarcely ever smiling. They paid but little attention to their personal appearance, and I saw but few and slight attempts at ornamentation of any kind. They acknowledge the existence of one Supreme Being. They also worship the "Mother," who has especial charge of them, and who, on leaving them ages ago, left them an ear of corn as a legacy. Their legends state that this Mother led them into the heart of a mountain and drove in for them various kinds of game. After a time one of the tribe, while exploring, crawled out into this country. On his report they enlarged somewhat the hole, and a portion of the race came forth into this land; but finally, a woman who was enormously big with child could not pass through, and the hole is closed to this day, a portion of the race remaining in the mountain. They have no established form of worship. They make use of offerings, and these offerings placed on the top of a pole in the prairie are held sacred by all, even hostile tribes, and never disturbed.

There is some chastity among them, but it is not general. Courtship and marriage among them are simply a bargain, the lover giving the father the number of ponies he demands. This number varies with the social and political standing of the father. There is no marriage ceremony. In taking a wife the husband is entitled to his sisters-in-law who live with and work for him, and are disposed of in marriage by him. There is seldom any disagreement among the wives, and each treats the others' children as her own.

Their divorce-law is as a law without essence; that is to say, a man may put away his wife at will and she returns to her parents or relatives.

Their language contains about seven hundred and fifty words. Their composition is crude, their most definite rule of grammatical construction being that for distinguishing the genders. Masculine is changed into feminine by prefixing an *S*.

They can count up to one thousand, but beyond that they must resort to sticks. Their term for twenty signifies a man, from the fact that a man has ten fingers and ten toes.

Their rulers or chiefs are elected, and are generally chosen with a view to generosity, courage, and intellect.

They have numerous legends and songs. The latter, as with all primitive people, are usually of battle or the chase.

They have the reputation of being very brave, and, indeed, well-known officers of the Army are willing to testify to their character in this respect. Yet, the whole time they were with us they could not be induced to go any distance in advance of the troops. Before the column left Fort Lincoln they said that we would meet a great many Indians, and, acknowledging their claims to being considered a brave tribe, the only theory, and it is thought the true one, to account for their apparent cowardice, was the fact that they knew that there were more hostiles in the field than were supposed to be, and yet had no precise knowledge of where these hostiles would be encountered.

Their appetites are gross. They eat the intestines of animals either cooked or raw, and their favorite morsels are a fœtus of an antelope, elk, or deer, and the raw liver taken warm from the freshly-killed animal.

The next morning (18th) the command moved again, crossing Heart River. The Heart at this point is about 30 yards wide, 3 feet deep, with a fairly firm sandy bed and a slight current. The water was clear and good. A great deal of work was required in corduroying the bank to enable the train to cross, and it was only after a delay of three hours that the head of the column commenced its march for the Sweetbriar, on a branch of which we encamped at 1.45 p. m., after a journey of $10\frac{3}{4}$ miles. Camp was established on a plateau of about 70 acres, 50 feet above the creek. This branch of the Sweetbriar is about 10 feet wide and 4 feet deep, with a soft, muddy bed. It contains quite a number of small fish. The quantity of wood was small, and the grass fair. We were greeted on our arrival with a severe rain-storm which lasted about twenty minutes. The rain continued to fall at intervals of half an hour or so during the remainder of the day. The country between the Heart and this camp is covered with a well-defined drift containing numbers of bowlders, (often found to be arranged in almost perfect circles on the summits of the hillocks,) quartzose, feldspathic and siliceous limestones. On this march we caught our first glimpse of the " bad lands." They were of small extent.

The next day's march of $13\frac{1}{2}$ miles brought us to Crow's Nest, or Buzzard's Roost Butte. The first portion of the route lay over an exceedingly rough country covered with drift. After struggling over a distance of $1\frac{1}{4}$ miles we arrived on the banks of the Sweetbriar. It was found to be a rushing torrent fully 50 feet wide, and much over 10 feet in depth. To cross it with the means at hand was impossible, so it was determined to go southward and turn the stream. This was done, and skirting the valley we passed out into an open, flat, and marshy prairie, in a northwesterly direction towards " Crow's Nest." The ground was very soft and interspersed with fragments of slate, and the last $4\frac{1}{2}$ miles were passed over a swamp, double teams being necessary for each wagon. At noon a terrible storm arose. The rain came down as in sheets, while for twenty minutes hail five-eighths of an inch in diameter descended with great violence. Fortunately none of the herd were stampeded, but darkness fell upon us before the last wagon was parked. " Crow's Nest" consists of two peaks, the eastern one being considerably taller than the other. It is so called from the fact that large numbers of crows formerly built their nests and brooded there. Twin Buttes are plainly visible from the eastern peak bearing $254\frac{1}{2}°$ and $255\frac{1}{2}°$. The only water at this camp was that in coulées and " buffalo-wallows." There was no wood easily accessible, and the grass was poor. A large portion of the command were unable to cook supper or breakfast. The bridge was laid once during this march.

At 5 the next morning I left camp with Reynolds, the guide, and ten Indian scouts, to look for a crossing of the Big Muddy Creek. Numbers of antelope were seen. A crossing was found, but returning we met the command, which had moved at 7.30 a. m., and it was decided to turn the stream. During the journey a branch of Muddy Creek was crossed by a bridge. After a march of $9\frac{1}{2}$ miles the command encamped on another branch of the Big Muddy Creek at 1.30 p. m. The grass along the route was thin and the ground soft, but the train encountered but few and slight difficulties. A heavy rain fell during the night.

The following day the creek was crossed by a bridge. The stream is about 9 feet in width and $1\frac{1}{2}$ feet deep. The day opened foggy and rainy. The first portion of the route was nearly northwest toward Big-

Butte, then turning west the march was along the eastern edge of a line of bluffs overlooking an extensive area of bad lands, in the center of which are situated "Twin Buttes," or "Maiden's Breasts," so called from their appearance. Camp was established on another branch of the Big Muddy, crossed by bridge at 3.30 p. m., after a march of 13½ miles.

"Cherry Ridge," a long, prominent, and well-timbered range of hills, was visible all day. In addition, numerous buttes were in view during the march, among which were "Wolf's Den" and "Big Butte."

The grass was fair, but the soil was often rocky. There was no timber nearer than 2 miles from camp, and that was but a pocket of small growth.

Breaking camp the next morning, the route lay nearly southwest over a low swamp, which proved to be the headwaters of the Big Muddy. Crossing this swamp, we ascended the divide on the south side of the Big Muddy Valley, the course then turning westward over a firm and finely-grassed country intersected by well-wooded ravines. From this divide the timbered valley of the Muddy could be seen to the south. Reaching the headwaters of a branch of Knife River, we proceeded along the left bank for about 6 miles, and then turning southwest of the valley the road led up a steep hill covered with sage and cactus, there being little or no other vegetation. Large alkaline patches were prominent features of the country. Moving around the summit of the hill, we again descended to the valley of the stream, ("Thin-faced Woman's Creek,") and crossed the latter by bridge. The creek is well wooded; the banks are steep, and it is about 20 feet wide and 12 feet in depth. There was no water at the crossing, but a sufficient quantity was obtained from pools a short distance from camp. A few elk were seen during the march.

Starting at 5.30 the next morning, and passing Young Men's Butte about 8.20, we encamped at 8.40 a. m. near the springs which form the headwaters of another branch of Knife River. There was plenty of good water, wood, and grass. The valley of Knife River is visible for 30 miles from this point. It is well timbered and of considerable width. Elk, black-tail deer, and antelope were seen during the day.

Leaving the camp near Young Men's Butte, we crossed the divide between Knife River and a branch of Heart River, and encamped on the latter a short distance from the river itself. The main stream receives the branch about 1½ miles from this camp. The branch is about 30 feet wide and 1 foot in depth, with a hard, gravelly bed. The current is swift, and the water is clear but alkaline, and contains quite a number of small fish. The grass around camp was good, and, like the wood, plentiful. A great many elk and one lynx were seen in this region. During this march we encountered for the first time limited fields of a species of primrose. The flowers were very beautiful, and as they were crushed under the horses feet they gave forth a protest of the most delicate and welcome odor.

On the morning of May 25 we forded the branch of the Heart, and, crossing the divide, encamped on what is called North Fork of Heart River. The grass in and around camp was good; there was plenty of wood and fair water. The bridge was laid twice during the march.

Having crossed the North Fork by bridge, we ascended a long and easy slope to an alkaline plain covered with cactus and prickly pears. After a march of about 5 miles, the North Fork was crossed again by bridge. The stream at this point is well timbered, and its course can be seen for fully 12 miles. After crossing several tributaries, the command finally encamped on one of the latter about 2 o'clock in the afternoon. The grass was excellent, but there was no wood. The weather was very warm, and the mosquitoes troublesome. Millions of young grasshoppers were seen covering the ground. The bridge was laid three times during the day. We were visited by a heavy rain-storm at night.

The next morning opened up quite foggy, but, breaking camp at the usual hour, the command proceeded in a south-southwest direction for nearly 7 miles, when we came in full view of the bad lands of the Little Missouri. These bad lands, as seen from a distance, present a very striking and picturesque appearance, forcibly reminding one of the ruins of some great city destroyed by fire. This effect is heightened by occasional patches of brilliant red clay, which glisten in the sunlight like beacon-fires. Upon a near approach the beauty of the scene vanishes into thin air. One finds but deep and tortuous ravines flanked by almost perpendicular bluffs of alkaline clay. In addition to the bluffs, there are numerous solitary formations, usually conical in shape, and some of these have layers or bands very distinctly marked, as with a brush. The surface of the conical formations is quite hard, but detached pieces of the clay offer but slight resistance to being crushed to an impalpable powder. Different varieties of clay, argillaceous limestones, and friable sandstones are encountered. Beds of lignite appear at almost every step, and occasionally a burning bed is to be seen. The clays are of divers shades, running through black, brown, red, yellow, blue, and gray to pure white. Often the ground and hill-sides are strewn with slag-like masses, which bear strong evidences of having been fused. Some of them have a vitreous luster, others looking very much like bog iron-ore.

The lignite is of an impure variety, sometimes of a dead black color, with a conchoidal fracture, and resembling cannel-coal; at other times it is brown, with a decided vegetable structure. In the descent to the valley of Powder River, where a road had been cut in the side hill, there was found a bed of lignite. Specimens taken from it broke freely in laminæ, and the fracture showed numerous projections like black shells of a small size imbedded in the lignite. These raised shell-like portions were black, and of a bright vitreous luster, while the matrix, if it may be so termed, was of a dull black color, with a slightly brownish tinge. The lignite does not burn well. It is difficult of ignition, and a white ash is produced by combustion.

The valleys of the streams appear to be all of the same nature, varying simply in extent. The following section of the banks of the Yellow-stone, near the mouth of Powder River, furnishes a type of the general formation of the whole section.

The drift consists of various kinds of siliceous pebbles and stones, often containing beautiful specimens of moss and fortification agates. Silicified wood is common. The clay is of different shades of yellow, blue, and gray, some being of dazzling white. The sandstone is usually of a light-yellowish color, but is quite often found in dislodged masses on the bluffs of a dark rusty or brown color. It is quite soft and can be broken readily by hand. With the exception of drift, and now and then small quantities of shale or indurated clay, this sandstone was the only kind seen during the whole season.

From the point where we first caught sight of the bad lands the course was turned nearly due south, and having marched a distance of about 5 miles, a halt was ordered to determine our position.

It is with great pleasure that I can testify to the accuracy and reliability of the maps furnished by the Engineer Department.

The descent to the valley of Davis' Creek was accomplished without much difficulty. We found plenty of wood, some water which was quite alkaline, and some grass of a poor quality.

The march to the Little Missouri was resumed the next day. Davis' Creek is a very tortuous one, with high perpendicular banks. It is generally skirted with cottonwood, (some of large size,) willow-brush, and sage-brush of small growth. Plenty of good grass was found all the way. The bed of the stream varies in width from about 15 to 70 feet, the bottom being a miry, sandy earth, with occasionally a slight layer of gravel. The water was generally yellow and alkaline. The slopes and peaks of the valley are covered with a light growth of grass. One of the guides stated that when he passed down this valley with General Sully, in 1864, there was no vegetable growth; and Lieutenant Chance, Seventeenth Infantry, states that in 1872 no work was required to cross the train. In a distance of 8 miles, ten crossings were made, at the expense of much time and labor. As we drew near to the Little Missouri the aspect of the country changed for the better. The hills had a thicker and brighter covering of grass. The timber and brush became more luxuriant, and now and then were found fine springs of clear cold water. We were greatly troubled with mosquitoes until the parking of the train at the Little Missouri, where we arrived about 9 a. m., May 29. In the march down the valley of Davis' Creek, twelve crossings in all were constructed. The camp was established in a plain bounded on three sides by high hills, and having between it and the river a belt of fine timber about 200 yards in width. Game abounds in this section of the country and the river is well stocked with pan-fish. The river at high-water stage is about 200 yards wide from bank to bank. At the time we crossed, it was about 100 feet in width and from 2 to 3 feet deep, with a hard gravel bottom. The portions of the bed not covered with water were very soft and required much work to make them passable for the train.

Leaving the Little Missouri on the morning of May 31, the route lay in the bed of a small creek for about half a mile and then led over the bluffs. This latter portion of the route was very difficult of passage and required much and extensive work in the way of cuttings. The train, however, passed with but two upsets, and, considering the nature of the road, with remarkable speed. We reached the base of the more eastern of Sentinel Buttes about 7 miles from camp, and skirting this butte we passed over a very rough but well-grassed country and descended through a deep and difficult ravine to an open valley through which ran a stream of then small proportions on which we encamped. Rain fell during the evening, but changed into snow, and at 3 a. m. the next day several inches of snow had fallen, and the storm was severe. The little stream of the day before had swollen to quite important dimensions. Wood was scarce and not easily accessible. The animals suffered from exposure and want of grass. Two Big Horn sheep were killed by Reynolds on the road to this camp.

We left this camp on the morning of June 3, and a cold and disagreeable march of about 6 miles brought us out into a beautiful rolling prairie full of game. Before reaching the prairie we passed numbers of well-wooded ravines. Here we met scouts sent by the commanding officer of the Montana column, who brought information that their column had seen several parties of Indians, numbering from about twenty to fifty. These Indians were bold enough to assemble on the bluffs on the south side of the Yellowstone and dare the troops on the other side to an encounter. After a march of 25 miles, the longest yet made, we encamped on Beaver Creek. Beaver Creek at this point is about 30 feet wide with a depth varying from 1 to 6 feet, and the water is cool and clear. The banks are covered with a thick growth of brush. The bed of the creek is soft and muddy. There was wood in plenty and the grazing was excellent.

The next day, moving almost due south, we crossed a low "divide," from which rose here and there bare rugged buttes capped with masses of rusty sandstone, into the valley of a tributary of Beaver Creek. Crossing the stream by bridge we passed over a rolling, well-grassed prairie to another branch of Beaver Creek, which was found to be timbered, but the water was in pools. Thence we moved in a southerly direction over a barren country to a rocky "divide," along this divide for about 3 miles, and then changing the route to west of south, we encamped on Beaver Creek. The water here was in pools. Plenty of wood and good grass were obtained. Antelope and rabbits were the only game seen during the day, but large numbers of these were passed.

Bridging the creek early the next morning, the command crossed a rolling country, which had a fair soil and a good growth of grass on the higher portions. It was, however, intersected by numerous "coulées" and ravines. Reaching the "bad lands" at the head of Cabin Creek, we encountered a steep descent to the valley. Great difficulties presented themselves to the advance of the wagon-train. The valley was narrow and of a soft alkaline earth with deep washouts. The ridges or bluffs had a thick growth of small pine. Worrying through this bad-land region, and crossing three different branches of Cabin Creek, we finally reached a beautiful rolling prairie with fine grass. Some pools of snow-water were discovered, and camp established.

The alkaline bottom-lands traversed during the march were strewn with fragments of satin gypsum, which glistened in the sunlight and relieved somewhat the barren aspect of the scene. First-Sergeant Hill, Company B, Seventh Cavalry, informed me that while hunting he had seen a bed of lignite burning. His attention was attracted by seeing smoke issuing from a level spot of alkaline ground. Approaching, he saw a fissure about 10 feet long and 4 feet wide with radial arms. Smoke issued constantly, with now and then a puff of thicker, blacker quality. The earth crumbled and fell into the fissures, the latter gradually enlarging. There was no noise or upheaval.

The march to O'Fallon's Creek was over a country similar to that passed the day before. This creek was found to be about 30 feet wide, with a soft, muddy bed and good clear water. It was well timbered, many of the trees being of large size.

The march of the next day carried us into a region which, it is believed, was never before traversed by a wagon-train. Starting at the usual hour, we ascended the bluffs immediately west of camp, and found before us a very rough and uninteresting country. The land appeared to be entirely worthless. The monotony of the march was rendered still more dreary by a cold, drizzling rain, which lasted until the afternoon. The ascent to the "divide" was long, but gradual. The descent to the valley of the Powder was a difficult and delicate task, but we were more than repaid by the view which was unrolled before us as we reached the summit of one of the hills. The sight was one the remembrance of which will long linger with us. To our left was Powder River Ridge, with its fringe of pine trees. At our feet was the bad-land formation, with its deep, yawning chasms and its various-colored earths, fashioned into weird and fantastic shapes by the rains and floods. Leading up from these were long ravines, with their thick growth of timber, the dark, green hue of which formed a strong and beautiful

85 E

41

contrast to the softer and lighter shade of the grass-covered hills. To the right there stretched out a rolling country backed in the distance by the Yellowstone bluffs, whose rugged outlines stood forth in bold relief.

It was not until 7.20 p. m. that we encamped on the Powder about 20 miles from its mouth. The river at this point is 200 feet wide, and 2 to 3 feet deep. The water was very yellow, carrying a large amount of matter in suspension. The bottom is at places gravelly, with bowlders distributed over it; but at others it is a treacherous quicksand, demanding great caution in crossing. It commenced to rain about 4 p. m., June 9, and continued so to do until noon of the 10th. On the afternoon of the 10th, Major Reno, Seventh Cavalry, with six companies of his regiment, left this camp on a scout. Lieutenant Sturges, Seventh Cavalry, and Lieutenant Kinzie, Twentieth Infantry, were selected to keep a journal and itinerary of the march; but the latter commanded the Gatling detachment, and was too much occupied in keeping the gun with the cavalry to take any bearings. The former unfortunately had his note-book with him at the time he was killed.

We broke camp at 5 a. m., June 11, and commenced the march to the Yellowstone. For the first 5 or 6 miles the road was very rough, being over hilly ground, but after crossing the first creek we ascended to a beautiful plateau about 3 miles long. Two other plateaus, each between 3 and 4 miles in length, were traversed. They were separated by alkaline creeks with steep banks of soft earth. The bottom lands, like the valley of the Powder, were poor in grass, it being very thin and dry.

The ground was covered with sage, cactus, and prairie-dogs' houses. The hilly portion of the road was covered with drift, but this seemed to almost entirely disappear on reaching the plateaux. A march of 20 miles brought us to the northwest extremity of the last plateau, and from this point the Yellowstone and the Powder are both visible. From this plateau we descended to the open land formed by the junction of the valleys of the two rivers. It was found to be very soft, cut up by numerous gullies and abounding in sage, cactus, and rattle-snakes. Passing over the almost swampy portion we finally reached the banks of the Yellowstone, and found a spot sufficiently firm to enable us to establish camp.

The total distance marched up to this time was 318½ miles, with an average day's march of 15.9 miles.

The grass on the plateaus and in the swales leading down to the valleys was very fine. There was but little timber on any of the creeks, and that little was of small size. On the descent to the third creek we found some springs of very cold and clear water, but a decided alkaline taste was developed when the canteens became heated by the sun's rays.

The timber on the Powder diminishes quite rapidly as the valley is descended, but there is a thick grove on the Yellowstone at the mouth of the former stream. We remained in this camp until June 15, on which date Lieutenant-Colonel Custer, with six companies of the Seventh Cavalry and the pack-train, moved up the right bank of the Yellowstone. Lieutenant Wallace, of the Seventh Cavalry, was selected to keep the itinerary of the march. He did so until June 25. His report will be found annexed.

The Brigadier General commanding, with his staff, left the camp and proceeded up the Yellowstone on board of the steamer Far West. The Yellowstone is a river which has been described so often by different persons that any elaborate account of its valley would be but a tautological echo of the words of others. It will be sufficient to give but a general account of the state of the river at the time we ascended it.

The width varied from 200 yards to nearly 2 miles. The latter width was where the stream was divided up into narrow, rapid channels by numbers of islands. The water was very yellow, and held great quantities in mechanical suspension. The current was between 5 and 6 miles.

The first rapids we encountered were about 4½ miles above the mouth of Powder River, and the second about 23 or 24 miles above the same point. The channel was clear of islands until we reached Sunday Creek. Here the river commences to be studded at intervals with very beautiful timbered islands, on many of which we saw deer and elk. The water-level gradually fell during the season, and by the 1st of September the reef at Wolf Rapids was out of water, and impassable by the steamers. Navigation on this stream undoubtedly ceases at that time of the year.

About noon June 16 we arrived at the Seventh Cavalry camp, 2 miles below the mouth of Tongue River. The camp had been established on the site of an Indian burying-ground. We saw here quite a number of bodies. Some were found in trees, and others on the usual scaffolds erected by the Indians. I saw at this place the dead body of an infant about 10 months old in quite a good state of preservation. The skin was about the color of that of an Eyptian mummy, and was as well preserved as any mummy I ever saw. The face had been painted red. The hands were closed and bent upward and backward on the arms. The feet were similarly bent backward on the legs. This was probably due to the wrappings of calico and buffalo skins. The whole body was covered with what appeared to be a salt of lime.

Leaving this place June 20 we arrived at the camp of the Montana column about 11 a. m. the next day. Here we saw for the first time the Crow scouts. They were a very handsome set of men and appeared to be extremely good-natured. They greeted us with smiles and hearty "hows." They are much lighter in color than the Rees, and of larger size. They look very much more like warriors than any Indians I had hitherto seen, and their by no means inartistic dress adds much to their personal appearance. Their language is quite musical, especially when spoken by the women. It is not unlike Spanish in its general sound.

Leaving this camp we steamed up to the camp of the Seventh Cavalry, just below the mouth of the Rosebud. At noon the next day, June 22, Lieutenant-Colonel Custer with his regiment commenced the march which closed in the battle of the Little Big Horn, June 25. The report of Lieutenant Wallace, appended, contains the account of this march.

Early on the morning of the 24th we passed Fort Pease, which is situated on the left bank of the Yellowstone about 6½ miles below the mouth of the Big Horn. It consisted of a stockade with two block-houses, one at the northern and the other at the southern corner. It was established as a trading-post by a man named E. D. Pease, but the Indians continually harassed the garrison and killed quite a number of them. A battalion of the Second Cavalry was ordered to their relief last winter, and the post was abandoned. In the afternoon the troops were transferred to the right bank of the Yellowstone, and the march to the Little Big Horn was commenced.

I ordered Sergeant Wilson, with Private Culligan, to remain on the steamer, which was to ascend the Big Horn, for the purpose of making as accurate a survey as possible of the river, and collecting information in relation to the nature of the country. His report is appended with map.

The first march of 5 miles up the valley of the Big Horn brought us to Tullock's Fork, where we encamped.

At 5 a. m. the next morning the march was resumed. The route for the first 3 miles lay in the valley of the creek. The valley is very narrow, about half-a-mile wide, and of no value. The grass was rank and dry. The bed of the stream is about 30 feet in width. The water was found only in pools, and strongly alkaline. Leaving the valley we passed up and over the divide between this stream and the Big Horn. The country was very rough, with a miserable soil. It was a meshwork of ravines with steep sides. Pine trees were sparsedly scattered over the hills, and the ravines were thickly timbered. The grass was thin and short, and associated with large quantities of cactus and isolated patches of sage-brush. Outcroppings of sandstone were frequent, and every now and then we saw dislodged masses of this stone which had been weather-worn into curious and somewhat artistic shapes. Here and there we observed conical-shaped peaks of purely white alkaline earth entirely destitute of vegetation. As we drew nearer to the valley of the Big Horn the accidents of the land became much more decided. The "divide" became a sinuous backbone and the ravines much deeper and more ramiform. The sandstone occurred more frequently and in larger quantities. From this divide the snow-capped Big Horn Mountains and cañon and Pryor's Mountain were plainly visible, and at the foot of these the valley of the Big Horn gradually sloped down to the stream. That section of the country appeared to be much more open and extensive than any we had previously seen, and it it said to be a fine agricultural region. The whole surface of the divide was covered with drift, which contained many beautiful specimens of agates. The descent to the valley of the Big Horn was very precipitous and uncomfortably difficult. The sun seemed to concentrate its rays in this valley, and to absolutely pour down its heat. In addition, the air was thick with dust which seemed to overcome the senses. It was only when the sharp rattle of the snakes aroused the almost slumbering troopers that there appeared to be any life left in the column. The infantry particularly had a very severe march, as there was no water to be obtained. The latter portion of the journey was down the valley of a dry creek, and, after a march of 22 miles, we reached the beautiful and refreshing Big Horn. The river at this point was about 200 yards wide, with a swift current of clear, cool water. It contained islands which, like those of the Yellowstone, were thickly timbered, and had a carpeting of most excellent grass. Resting here for a short time, the command moved up the valley for a distance of about a mile and a half, when the infantry encamped in the thickly-timbered bottom. The Brigadier-General commanding with the cavalry pushed on, and a very disagreeable march we made of it. The night was cold and wet, and so dark that nothing could be seen at any distance in front of us. After much difficulty we succeeded in finding a creek which contained a pool of alkaline water, and the remainder of the night we passed in a slough of mud and disgust.

Breaking camp the next morning, we moved toward the Little Big Horn. Crossing a tributary of the latter stream, we ascended the high bluffs to the plateau above. Here the infantry rejoined us, and here for the first time we heard of Custer's fight. Two of the Crow scouts who had been sent with Custer were brought to the column by Lieutenant Bradley, of the Seventh Infantry. They reported that Custer's command had been "wiped out." This report was not believed at that time, and the command moved on. The country traversed before reaching the valley of the Little Big Horn was that of the usual description of high lands west of the Missouri. Descending to the valley of the Little Big Horn we crossed that river about 9 miles above its mouth. The march was continued up the valley of this stream for a distance of 5½ miles. At this point we first saw hostile Indians. About 7 p. m., on this date, June 26, scouts came in with the report that they had been fired upon. A halt was ordered and on the hills in front of us were seen bodies of mounted men. As well as I could judge by the eye, I should say the nearest were within about 2 miles. They remained standing and regarding us intently. They were formed in regular order with one man a short distance in advance. They were at first supposed to be Custer's men, but Lieutenant Roe of the Second Cavalry was sent with one company to reconnoiter, and, on showing a white flag for a parley, was fired upon. The Indians slowly moved off in the direction of the Big Horn. We went into camp in the middle of the valley of the Little Big Horn, about 9 p. m. This valley is about 1½ miles wide; the soil is good and the grass very fine. There is but little cactus or sage. The stream varies in width from about 30 to 75 yards. The current is rapid; the bottom a fine gravel, and the water beautifully clear and sweet. It is well lined with timber, much of it being of large size. The next morning (June 27) we resumed the march up the valley. In moving over the hills about 2 miles from camp, we crossed the trail made by the Indians the night before. From these hills we saw two teepees in the valley beyond. Continuing the march we soon descended to the valley and arrived at the teepees, which were found to contain the dead bodies of Indians, and which were all that remained of what had been a large Indian village. Information was soon brought to us by Lieutenant Wallace that Major Reno with a portion of the Seventh Cavalry was intrenched on the bluffs. After a march of about 9 miles we encamped in the valley at the foot of the bluffs, which had been the site of a siege for nearly two days. We remained in this camp until the evening of the next day when the command was moved down the valley a distance of about 4½ miles.

The next day a survey of the field was made, and in the afternoon the command again moved with the wounded in the direction of the mouth of the Little Big Horn. News having been received that the steamer was at the mouth of the river, a night march was made, and at 1 a. m. all the wounded were safely and comfortably settled on board.

July 3 found us in camp on the Yellowstone about 3 miles below the mouth of the Big Horn. We remained in this camp until July 22, when the command was moved by Colonel Gibbon to a point a short distance below Fort Pease. At this latter camp the mosquitoes were almost intolerable. On the night of July 14 we were visited by a severe storm, and about 3 a. m. of the 15th the camp was flooded, the water being about a foot in depth.

On the 27th of July the command was moved to a camp opposite the Rosebud where Gibbon's command arrived July 30. In this camp we remained until August 6, on which date the forces, with the exception of the guard for the supply-camp, were crossed to the right bank of the Yellowstone. During this time the re-enforcements, consisting of six companies of the Fifth and Twenty-second Regiments of Infantry each, arrived. In the mean time, also, the battery had been changed, two 3-inch rifles and one Napoleon having been substituted for the Gatlings.

On August 7 we experienced the warmest weather of the season, the thermometer reaching 110° in the shade.

At 5 a. m., August 8, the command commenced its march up the valley of the Rosebud. The stream is well timbered near its mouth, but the grass is poor, and the water was unfit for use. As we advanced up the valley it became narrower and thickly timbered, with plenty of grass, but not of a very good quality. There was but little water in the stream and that was bad along the whole distance traveled by us. The valley consists of alternations of bad lands and narrow reaches of bottom-lands covered with grass, rose-bushes, juniper, and cottonwood. Great quantities of dead timber were found strewn over the ground. The first day's march was severe as the weather was very warm. The next day we were visited by a very cold rain, but August 10 was delightfully cool and pleasant. We passed the sites of three old Indian camps. During this march of 36½ miles twenty-one artificial crossings were constructed and much road-cutting was also necessary.

About noon, August 10, we met the command from the Department of the Platte, and the two forces encamped together that night on the Rosebud.

At 11.30 a. m., August 11, the two commands started on the Indian trail. The wagon-train was sent back to the supply-camp on the Yellowstone, and the pack-mules were again resorted to.

Leaving the valley of the Rosebud and ascending the hills, we found before us an excellent grazing country. The soil was poor, being often of a decided red, giving up clouds of dust; and yet the grass was fine and of most luxurious growth. The usual covering of gravel was present, and the descent to the Tongue was very steep and difficult, the earth being very loose and full of pebbles, bowlders, and detached pieces of shale. The Tongue was crossed after a march of 10 miles in an almost due easterly direction. The river was at this point about knee-deep, beautifully clear, and with a firm gravel-bed and rapid current. The water was cold and sweet.

A march of a few miles down the valley brought us to the camping-place. The grass was very rich and in profusion, and there was plenty of cottonwood interspersed here and there with ash of small size. A heavy and continuous rain fell during the night, and as no tents were allowed everything was drenched. The rain continued until about noon the next day, when the mules were packed with their soaked loads, and the journey down the valley of the Tongue was recommenced. For a distance of about 10 miles along the route the valley is not only picturesque and varied as to its scenery, but of excellent quality as to its soil. The grass was the finest that had yet been seen by us, and while the valley itself is capable of being converted into fine gardens, the grazing upon the hills and high lands made it appear to be, with the exception of the Yellowstone, the most desirable portion of that section of the country. The only game were ducks, geese, and sage-fowl. This was probably due to the fact that the Indians had passed up and down the valley. There was some pine on the hills and in the ravines.

The trail which we had been following was large and the evidences of trains having passed were marked and numerous, but they were not, as afterwards proved, of very recent date.

At a distance of about 13 miles the nature of the valley had gradually changed. The timber had become of poorer quality and much more scarce. The soil became of much less value; the ground was cut up by deep and frequently occurring ravines, and the banks of the river became higher and steeper. The usual accompaniments of uninteresting land, sage and cactus, appeared in unwelcome frequency and profusion. Large amounts of lignite were seen in the deep washouts, and at times the road became rather dangerous on account of the subterranean passages leading from these washouts to the river. The rain continued all night.

The sun shone brightly the next morning, Sunday, August 13, but it again rained during the night. The nature of the valley was similar to that already described.

The next day's march brought us to our camp on Pumpkin Creek, a tributary of the Tongue. The valley of this creek is of the same description as that of the Tongue; only being one of the third order, it is smaller. The stream was well wooded. The bed was hard gravel, but in consequence of the late rains the water was simply liquid mud. Fortunately springs were discovered. Rain fell during the night.

The next day the route lay over a very broken and sterile country; in fact for some miles it was of the pure and unadulterated "bad-land" nature. Crossing the divide we traveled along the valley of a small creek, a tributary of the Mizpah, and thence we descended to the valley of Powder River, striking the latter just where it receives Mizpah Creek. It rained for four hours that afternoon.

In consequence of the poor condition of the horses, both commands left this camp the next day and marched down to the Yellowstone, arriving there on the afternoon of August 17. We found that the Indians had burned much of the grass.

We remained near the mouth of the Powder in a very disagreeable camp on the bare sand until August 25. During that time we were visited by two cold and severe rain-storms, which flooded the infantry camp.

August 25, we marched up the valley of the Powder again to find the Indian trail and follow it. That evening one of the scouts brought news that the boats had been fired into at Glendive Creek. The next morning the command from the Department of the Platte followed the Indian trail. The Brigadier-General commanding this Department, accompanied by his staff and one company of the Second Cavalry, returned to the boats at the mouth of the Powder. The remainder of the troops, under command of Colonel Gibbon, marched down to a point on the Yellowstone about 2 miles below the mouth of O'Tallon's Creek, where they were crossed to the north side of the river by the steamers which had descended the stream for this purpose. About dusk the same day, August 27, the command moved up the valley of a dry creek, and encamped, without wood or water, after a march of $6\frac{1}{2}$ miles.

The next morning we crossed in an almost due northerly direction to Bad Route Creek, where delightful water was found, and we were enabled to break our fast.

Moving out from this halting-place, we followed up the "divide" of Bad Route Creek. The grazing was good, but the ground appeared parched and dry. There was very little water, and no timber was seen except on the stream and its tributaries. At a distance of about 13 miles from our camp we halted at the headwaters of one of these tributaries. Here we found the grass very fresh and green, and the ground sown with flowers of divers and beautiful colors. The rose-bushes with their bright-red berries, the large cottonwood, and the straight ash, added their charms and the comfort of shade to the scene. Springs of clear, cold water were discovered. A farther march of 8 miles brought us again to Bad Route Creek, where we found excellent water in pools, plenty of wood, and good grass. During this last part of the day's march all who were mounted were attacked by swarms of winged ants. Strange to say, the infantry were not troubled by them.

The next day, August 29, we traveled northward towards the Missouri-Yellowstone "divide." When near the "divide," we ran into a herd of between 2,000 and 3,000 buffalo. Great numbers of antelope also were seen.

Upon reaching Clear Creek we turned southeast, and after a march of about 7 miles down the valley of the creek we encamped near some pools of most villainous water. Attempts were made by digging to obtain water which would be free from any taste or odor of the buffalo, but only partial success was attained. Up to this point the country had been a most excellent grazing one, and is easily practicable for a wagon-train, with the exception of a very narrow stretch of "bad-lands," about 8 miles from the Yellowstone. But even this could readily be made so. It is believed that a wagon-train could travel northeast from the Yellowstone to the Missouri without trouble, saving, perhaps, that to be encountered at the bluffs of the Missouri. One very delightful change which we experienced in crossing this section was the almost-total absence of sage or cactus.

Leaving Clear Creek and traveling in a direction a little north of east we crossed the small streams which unite to form Spring Creek. We found in them very good water in pools. Leaving these latter streams the country gradually changed, the alkaline formation became more apparent, the grazing became more scarce and of inferior quality. Positively defined bad-lands made their appearance as we neared Deer Creek, and extended to the creek itself. The upper portion of this creek is very narrow, with low bottom-lands of slight width. The stream had a reddish hue, due to vegetable matter in the bed. The timber on the creek commences about 2 miles below where we encamped. There were quantities of bullberries growing on the banks. These berries are about the size and of the color of currants, and have very nearly the same taste. At that time (before frost) they had quite an astringent, acid taste. The bush is a thorn, with olive-green, elongated elliptical-shaped leaves. The bush grows as high as 20 feet, but the average height is about 10 feet. These berries furnished us at that time with an acid which satisfied a craving that had possessed us for some days.

The next day's march was down the valley of Deer Creek. This valley is very confined and utterly worthless, except in spots, where grazing is fair; but even here the spear-grass is abundant. The bench is narrow, and the bad-lands commence on each side at the edge of the bench. The only timber is cottonwood and ash, and very little of these, except within about 3 miles of the Yellowstone, where the stream commences to be thickly timbered. The bed is gravel and clay. The water was found in pools, but was not unpleasant except near the Yellowstone. Sage and cactus were found in profusion. A few ducks but no other game of any description were seen. Rattlesnakes infested the whole valley. The command remained in camp opposite Glendive Creek until September 6, when the Fifth Infantry were sent to Tongue River, and the Montana column commenced its homeward march.

The Brigadier General commanding, with his staff, arrived at Fort Buford September 7, and receiving orders to return to Saint Paul, my connection with the troops in the field ceased on that date.

JOURNAL OF THE MARCHES MADE BY THE FORCES UNDER COLONEL JOHN GIBBON, COMMANDING THE EXPEDITION DOWN THE YELLOWSTONE, BETWEEN THE 1ST DAY OF APRIL AND THE 25TH DAY OF SEPTEMBER, 1876, BY LIEUTENANT E. J. M'CLERNAND, SECOND CAVALRY, ACTING ENGINEER OFFICER.

April 1.—At 9 o'clock the four companies (F, G, H, and L, Second Cavalry) left Fort Ellis, Mont. They are preceded several days by six companies of the Seventh Infantry, which are already some distance down the Yellowstone, as is also the main supply-train. The object of this movement of the troops is a campaign against the hostile bands of Sioux, known to hunt and camp along the Lower Yellowstone and its tributaries. Stealing parties from these tribes raid the settlements in this vicinity every summer, killing defenseless persons who are so unfortunate as to fall in with them, and generally succeeding in running off a number of horses and mules. Owing to the melting snows, the roads are in a frightful condition, and so great is the difficulty in getting our train along that, although we work until after sunset, we only succeed in making seven miles. Our camp is on a little stream, a short distance above where it joins Middle Creek. The ground is saturated by melting snow, patches of which still exist. To-day's march has brought us in the midst of the hills forming the little divide between the headwaters of the East Gallatin and the Yellowstone Rivers. These hills, besides being picturesque, are exceedingly fertile, growing in places luxuriant bunch-grass, in others dense pine forests. The formation of the divide is usually sandstone, with the strata upturned at a large angle. In this divide, farther to the south, coal of a very fair quality has been found, and not far from this limestone. From the summit of a hill just back of camp one procures a fine view of the beautiful Gallatin Valley, with its rolling foot-hills and girdle of snow-capped peaks.

2d.—Continue our march in the direction of the Yellowstone. A short distance from camp we reach and cross Middle Creek, a clear stream running in a small but pretty valley, between high and gently-sloping hills, covered with fine grass. From here the road ascends a high hill, and soon reaches a point where the divide falls precipitously toward the Yellowstone. Passing from here down a steep hill, we reach, at its foot, Billman's Creek, 10 miles from Fort Ellis. A short distance on, the condition of the roads again compelled us to go into camp, after having marched only a few miles.

3d.—To-day we find the roads greatly improved, due to the fact that the snow never lies so long on this, the eastern side of the divide, as it does on the west, being carried away and evaporated by the high winds which prevail along the valley of the Yellowstone. We follow Billman's Creek through a natural pass between two high and almost parallel ridges, down the sides of which course innumerable little streams; those from the north crossing our road at short intervals on their way to Billman's Creek. In this pass and along the hill-sides the bunch-grass grows with the most lavish luxuriance. Twenty-one miles from Fort Ellis, Fleshman's Creek, a clear, cold stream, flowing from the northwest, is reached. Crossing this and proceeding on a short distance, we pass down the left bank of that river to "Benson's Landing," the head of Mackinaw-boat navigation. This valley is quite extensive, but being covered with loose gravel mixing with the soil, it is not very fertile, while the high winds which so frequently blow down the river make it an unpleasant place to reside. About three miles from Benson's, Shields' River joins the Yellowstone. It is distant from Fort Ellis 29.45 miles, and is a bold, rapid stream, flowing over small granite bowlders, and, rising on the northwest side of Crazy Mountain, it runs through an extensive and fertile section of country, which for some years past has furnished pasture for large herds of cattle. During the afternoon a wet and windy snow-storm came up and continued into the night.

4th.—We remain in camp to-day, awaiting the arrival of several wagons still detained by the heavy roads near Middle Creek.

5th.—Leaving Shields' River, our road crosses a spur of Sheep Mountain, which mountain presents a vertical face of basaltic rock to the Yellowstone.

A march of 7 miles brings us to a bottom on the Yellowstone, opposite the Old Crow agency. This valley, several miles in length and more than a mile wide, is very fertile. Leaving this, the road turns to the left and crosses a range of high hills; on the summit of one of these gypsum of a fine quality lies in sight. From here one commands an extensive view of the surrounding country. Crazy Mountain, lying just back of Sheep Mountain, is detached from the main range, and standing alone it seems to serve as a rallying point for the clouds, great masses of which almost always hover around the tops of its lofty peaks. Thousands of springs trickle down its rugged sides and are the sources of numerous streams. The altitude of Crazy Mountain is about 10,000 feet. To the south, across the Yellowstone, lies a range of high and rugged lava peaks, usually called the Yellowstone Range, whose summits "stand out in bold relief against the sky." Forty-four and one-half miles from Ellis, we reach Hot Spring Creek, on the banks of which, a short distance above the road, are several large and very warm sulphur springs. Three and a quarter miles on, the road crosses Duck Creek, running clear and cold from Crazy Mountain, and 1¼ miles farther reaches the Yellowstone. Crossing here at a

86 E

tolerably good ford, we go into camp on the river. The camp is in a fine and large valley covered with good grass. Along the river the cottonwood trees grow to a great size. Distance traveled during the day, 19.60 miles.

6th.—To-day about noon we reach and cross the Big Boulder, 62.83 miles from Fort Ellis. This is a large and rapid stream, rising in a very high range of granite mountains to the south. Near its mouth it flows over large bowlders, hence its name. Fifteen miles above its mouth it is formed by three forks, each of which is filled with fine trout. These forks run through pretty little valleys, which are favorite resorts for elk. The road, still continuing down the valley of the Yellowstone, reaches, 7½ miles from the Boulder, Little Deer Creek, now dry. From here to Big Deer Creek, about two miles, lies as fine a piece of bottom-land as can be found anywhere. Having marched 21 miles, we encamped on Big Deer Creek.

7th.—Soon after leaving camp, we pass by what is known as the Point of Rocks. This is a high and vertical wall, nearly half a mile in length, and showing plainly the marks left by the river in times past, when it was thirty feet above its present level. A little less than 8 miles from camp, we cross Bridger Creek; its source is in an exceedingly broken country, but near its mouth it flows through a pretty little valley thickly wooded. Soon after crossing the last-named stream, we reach a point where the valley opens out finely, possessing rich black soil, and growing heavy grass. The Yellowstone is bordered by a fine growth of large cottonwood trees, and the foot-hills to the south are covered with pine timber. The country to the north, across the river, is very broken. After marching 20 miles, we encamped on the Yellowstone.

8th.—Moving down the valley 2 miles, the river is forded, to avoid some steep and broken bluffs which it washes on the south bank. This is one of the best crossings on the Yellowstone. Passing along the north bank a few miles, through a drenching rain, we reach the infantry camp, situated on the Yellowstone, 96.79 miles from Ellis. This command arrived here on the 6th, and has succeeded in catching a great number of fine trout. The cavalry are not slow in following their example and supplying themselves liberally with this delicious food.

9th.—Both commands move out about the same time, marching down the valley. Upon arriving at Countryman's Ranch, the train and the cavalry are crossed to the south side, while the infantry continue along the north bank over a range of rough hills. Something less than two miles from Countryman's Ranch lies the Stillwater River; it is a fine large mountain stream, flowing over large bowlders, and filled with trout. Along its banks grow large pines, in a bottom varying in width from one-half a mile to a mile. After passing over two small bottoms on the Yellowstone, separated by a high hill, it again becomes imperative to ford the river. The bed is here composed of large rocks, rendering the fording difficult and even dangerous. Soon after crossing we go into camp, in a pretty spot at the head of one of the largest valleys on the Yellowstone.

10th.—The command remains in camp while the train is sent to the Crow agency, situated on Rosebud Creek, a tributary of the Stillwater. It is 20 miles from camp. The train is to bring down supplies that have been left there. During the evening a furious snow-storm prevails, and at the agency it falls to a depth of 18 inches.

11th.—Most of the train arrives late in the evening. It is but little exaggeration to say the command is living upon fine trout caught in the Yellowstone.

12th.—The day is spent in loading the train for a forward movement.

13th.—Captain Logan, Seventh Infantry, is left with his company to guard such supplies as cannot be carried. The other companies move out as one command, and begin in earnest the campaign at 7 a. m. After marching two hours the range of mountains back of the Old Crow agency come in sight. They are covered with snow and present a grand appearance. We are traveling through a large valley of considerable fertility, and varying in width from 1 to 2 miles. The south side of this bottom is washed by the Yellowstone, while on the north it is hemmed in by steep sandstone bluffs 100 feet high, and rising gradually from the top to the little divide between here and the Musselshell River. On the south side of the Yellowstone the bluffs present a precipitous front, but a little way back break into rolling hills covered with fine grass. The roads are heavy on account of the recent snow, and the train moves slowly. At 3 p. m., having made 11.25 miles, we go into camp on the Yellowstone.

14th.—Breaking camp at 7 a. m., we continue to march through the same valley passed along yesterday. The width increases to 6 miles, but in other respects there is little change. In places the soil is slightly alkaline, and the last snow has made it quite soft. We encamp on the Yellowstone at 3.30 p. m. Distance traveled during the day, 14.18 miles. The bluffs across the river are growing darker, presenting a lignite appearance. A short distance above camp, Clark's Fork joins the Yellowstone, coming from the granite mountains to the southwest; it is rising and the water is of a light brown color, and in quantity seems to be about half as much as the Yellowstone. Along the banks of both grow cottonwood, and at their confluence there is quite a forest. For more than a mile above their junction these two streams run almost parallel; the bearing up Clark's Fork being south 33° west, and up the Yellowstone southwest. A high wind continues to blow all night.

15th.—Starting at 6.45 a. m., we reach, 2¼ miles from camp, Cañon Creek, which is now dry; it has its source near what are known as the Lakes. These are the remains of what have formerly been large lakes, near the summit of the divide between here and the Musselshell, and which now are important water-holes to any one traveling along that divide. A little way and we pass through some large sage-brush, about the first seen. To the north the bluffs present a vertical face, and running nearly 9 miles along the valley, look like a wall built by man to serve as a huge fortification; ten and a half miles from camp this wall reaches the Yellowstone, and there makes a sharp angle with the bluffs running along the river. In this angle is a break, affording an opportunity to ascend the plateau. From this elevated prairie the Red Buttes, sometimes called Bull Mountain, can be seen lying 12° east of north. Passing along this table-land about 6 miles, we reach a valley on the Yellowstone and go into camp, just below "Baker's battle-ground," at 6 p. m. Distance traveled during the day, 17.35 miles.

16th.—Break camp at 9.35 a. m.; about 4 miles below camp we cross the Yellowstone, to take advantage of a large valley on the south side; the ford proves to be deep and swift. Lieutenant Schofield, Second Cavalry, missing the ford a few feet, comes very nearly being drowned. On the south side a continuation of the sandstone bluffs seen since leaving Captain Logan's camp still faces the river; but, stopping abruptly here, and receding from the stream, gives place to an extensive valley. A little way below, on the north side, is the commencement of a long range of broken and barren hills. A distance of nearly 7 miles from camp brings us to Pryor's Creek. This creek, rising in a large mountain of the same name, lying to the south, is swollen by the melting snows, and runs a stream of muddy water 10 yards in width and over 2 feet deep. After crossing, we follow it down to its mouth and camp on the Yellowstone, at 3.30 p. m., having marched 7.07 miles. The river-water is becoming very muddy, due probably to the rise in Clark's Fork. Since passing the mouth of that stream, few if any trout have been caught. A band of elk were seen to-day and several killed.

17th.—Starting at 8 a. m., we march down the valley, intending to camp near Pompey's Pillar. After marching three miles, a halt was made to wait for the train.

The surrounding country is very beautiful. The valley itself is one of the finest to be seen on the Yellowstone, varying in width from 1 to 6 miles, and averaging about 2¼; it extends for miles along the river, and contains perhaps 70,000 acres of arable land, all of which lies favorable for irrigation from either Pryor's Creek or the Yellowstone. It grows fine grass, and in places large sage-brush. The scenery is varied and extensive. To the southwest can be seen the lofty Yellowstone Range, covered with snow; to the north and northwest the bluff country toward the Musselshell stretches away as a vast plateau. To the south and east the gently-rolling hills are lost in the far distance in the granite ranges of the Big Horn and Pryor's Mountain. The valley descends in gentle declivities from the foot-hills, and bears north 40° east. Along the Yellowstone cottonwood timber grows with great luxuriance. To convince one that this valley has a bright future, it is only necessary to remember that the river flowing along its entire front is navigable two months in the year for Upper Missouri River steamboats. Eight and fifteen-hundredths miles from camp, Cachewood or Arrow Creek is reached, and at the crossing is dry, but half a mile above sufficient water, probably snow-water, is found for the animals. The day is very warm and threatens rain; toward evening we gradually approach the river, and reach it just below Pompey's Pillar. A little way below this, camp is placed, about sunset, inside of a semi-circle of cottonwood trees; distance marched, 15.80 miles. Accompanied by Dr. Paulding, I rode to the foot of the pillar, and fastening our horses we easily ascended along its northeast side; indeed here the ascent is so good that one of the scouts reached the summit mounted on a little mule. This rock, named in 1806 by Captain Clark, lies on the south bank of the river, a few yards from the water. It is 160 feet high and 200 in diameter. The soil on the top varies in depth from 1 to 4 feet. The rock is a gritty sandstone. Great blocks that have broken loose lie scattered around its base, and on the east side a huge rock, nearly as high as the pillar, and 5 or 6 yards in diameter, appears ready to fall. On all sides except the east the rock has vertical faces, and is cylindrical in shape. Having reached the summit the view is very grand, especially to the east, south, and west. On the north bank of the river the view is somewhat limited by the bold, rugged sandstone bluffs, about the same height as the pillar, and to which it has undoubtedly been formerly attached. A few miles back these bluffs break into a rolling country, studded with a stubby growth of pine, and presenting a most barren and uninviting appearance. These hills, extending to the Musselshell River, and running along the Yellowstone 40 miles, constitute one of its poorest sections. In a direction north 55° west is seen a range of high, red-looking hills, the Red Buttes. South 64° west lie the snowy peaks on the head of the Stillwater, 60 miles away. About 10 miles down the river, on each side, lies a range of high, rough hills, running almost north and south, and covered on this side with a growth of small pines. The valley is seen merging itself into the foot-hills to the south, and these in their turn rise to Pryor's Mountain. The storm that threatened us to-day has cleared away, and the clear atmosphere enables one to see many distant objects of interest, too numerous to mention.

18th.—We remained in camp awaiting the return of several scouts sent last night to the mouth of the Little Big Horn River to prospect for a Sioux village. A high wind has been blowing all the afternoon, and continues now late in the evening, almost burying us in the great clouds of sand it sends before it. The scouts return, having failed to discover any signs of hostile Indians.

19th.—Starting at 7.30 a. m., a few minute's march brings us to Fly Creek, 1½ miles; the banks are steep and generally soft; the water stands in holes. The valley now narrows and is badly cut up by ravines, but a mile on again opens out nicely; the wind still continues to blow and drive clouds of sand along the river. Ten and a half miles from camp a range of bluffs abruptly terminate the valley, rendering it necessary to cross the river with the train. Leaving the valley we have been traveling in for thirty miles, and fording the river where it is 580 feet wide and 3½ deep, we pass along the north bank 2½ miles and then return to the south side. The ford is 632 feet wide and 3 feet deep; the valley we now enter is narrow and by no means pretty, although the soil is fertile. The rolling foot-hills seen above give place here to steep bluffs of sandstone, scantily covered with scrubby pine timber, and besides being poorly watered produce but little grass. At 4.45 p. m. we encamped on the Yellowstone in a semicircle of large cotton-wood trees. Distance marched during the day 18.60 miles.

20th.—Starting at 7.40 a. m., we continue to pass along the river. The bottom is mostly covered with sage-brush, and for the first 7 miles grows poor grass; after that it improves. Nine and eight-hundredths miles from camp a high range of hills lying this side of the Big Horn River presents a steep face to the valley we are in, forcing us to cross the river. Some difficulty is experienced in finding a ford, and when one is selected the animals can scarcely cross without swimming; the river is evidently rising. After crossing, our road passes for 1½ miles through a sage-brush bottom, and then gains a high plateau. Moving along this elevated ground we pass the mouth of the Big Horn River, and obtain a view of its valley for a long distance. Four miles over this plateau brings us to the head of the Fort Pease Valley; here the grass is luxuriant, and the river-bank is grown up with large cottonwoods and heavy brush; many of the trees are 2½ or 3 feet in diameter, and show plainly by the short distance of the limbs from the ground that this end of the valley has filled up several feet in recent years. This is explained by the fact that two large ravines in the hills to the north do not continue their course to the river, and thus after a hard rain the loose material brought from the hills is scattered promiscuously over the bottom. Having marched 17.17 miles, we encamped in a grassy spot at 4.45 p. m.

21st.—This morning instructions via Fort Ellis are received, ordering us into camp at Fort Pease, there to await further orders. The same mail brings information that the troops from the other directions will not be able to take the field for some time. We move on to Fort Pease, 2.02 miles, and 215.32 miles from Fort Ellis. The command is put in camp immediately outside of the fort.

22d.—The day is passed in policing Fort Pease, something it stands in great need of. The fort, built of rough cottonwood logs, is about 75 feet square, with a bastion on the northeast and southwest corners, erected in June, 1875, by a party of citizens. It was intended as a headquarters for "Wolfers," but the Indians made life there a burden, and it was abandoned in February. It is situated in a valley about 10 miles long, and varying in width from one-half to two miles. The soil is fertile and grass good. Steep bluffs hem it in on the north, and those to the south across the river are very precipitous and extremely broken.

23d.—Remain in camp. Captain Freeman, Seventh Infantry, starts with his company and the train, to bring down supplies left at Captain Logan's camp. To avoid trouble in crossing the river, he is ordered to keep the north bank.

24th.—H and F Companies, Second Cavalry, under command of Captain Ball, receive orders for a seven days' scout, via the Big Horn, Fort Smith, and Tullock's Fork. I am ordered to report to Captain Ball. Starting about noon, the two companies march up the river to a point just above the mouth of the Big Horn, and cross at a good ford 5½ miles from Fort Pease. This distance is estimated from the time of march, as, indeed, all distances on this scout must be. Remaining in camp until 6 p. m., to avoid being seen, and then starting in a direction south 35° west, we soon ascend the bluffs, and reach a high ridge or "backbone." The Big Horn River and its valley is to our left, and just beyond it a picturesque but broken and worthless country. Directly ahead, about five miles away, lies a low wooded bluff, and in the far distance can be seen the Big Horn Mountains, which running east and west terminate the landscape like a huge white wall. For 11 miles our course is south 45° west, and passes through a very broken country; in several places the water-channels draining into the Yellowstone and Big Horn Rivers almost join on the summit of the "divide." Here and there the ridge is sparsely covered with small pines. Frequently it is necessary to wind around and around to cross a deep ravine or turn a precipice. Our Indian guide, however, is equal to the emergency, and wins the admiration of all by the masterly manner in which he guides us through this broken country in the darkness of night. After 11 miles our course is southeast through barren hills. At 11.30 p. m. we encamp on a tortuous little stream, with water standing in pools. The Indians call this Wood Creek. The grass is poor, and consequently the horses get but little to eat. Distance from the Yellowstone, 16 miles; from Fort Pease, 21½ miles.

25th.—Starting at 9.15 a. m., one of our scouts informed us we could travel during the morning and be well concealed; in this he soon proved to be mistaken. An hour's march through high, rough hills, in a southeasterly direction, brings us to the valley of the Big Horn; this stretches away for miles, a little west of south. It proves to be large and fertile, gaining a width in places of 4 miles. It is poorly supplied with creeks, but could be irrigated from the river. A portion of it grows sage-bush and cactus. Buffalo and antelope are seen in the valley and on the foot-hills. At 1.20 p. m. a halt is made on the Big Horn, and the animals turned out to graze. Distance marched during the morning 16 miles; distance from fort 37½ miles. While here a band of elk quietly walk in among the horses, and graze with them for several minutes. At 6.40 p. m. we continue our march up the valley, and in 35 minutes reach the mouth of the Little Big Horn River, coming in from the southeast on the opposite side through a green and pretty bottom. There is a great abundance of cottonwood timber on each stream, but especially on the Big Horn. The pine on the surrounding sandstone bluffs is of a poor quality. The valley of the Big Horn at this point is broad and fertile. After marching 4½ hours (14½ miles) the valley is terminated by high bluffs; it is too dark to see if there is a bottom on the opposite side, but as a general rule in this country, the bluffs lie opposite valleys. A mile and a half farther on, at 11.30 p. m., we turn to the left and camp on the river in a small cove formed by the hills. Distance marched during the day 32 miles; distance from Fort Pease 53½.

26th.—Six a. m. finds all ready to move. Crossing the river just above camp, where the water is 2½ feet deep, we march a mile and a half, and halt on the river-bank in a fine valley; the grass is good, and we determine to remain several hours to permit our animals to feed. The valley, which is here more than a mile in width, can be seen extending in a direction 7° west of south, to the very foot of the Big Horn Mountains, 25 miles or more away. In it the grass seems to be everywhere good. The river runs about one-half as much water as the Yellowstone, and on the opposite side washes steep sandstone about 100 feet high. While resting here buffalo can be seen feeding in the valley and foot-hills in all directions, in little bands of from ten to thirty. Some of them coming within a few yards of camp enables us to procure meat with little trouble. At 1.30 p. m. our march is continued; the valley increases in width to between four and five miles. At a distance of six miles from camp we arrive opposite the mouth of Beauvais Creek, running in a direction 4° south of east, through a pretty and well-timbered bottom. Twenty minutes later Rotten Grass Creek, coming from the southeast, is crossed, running in a ravine 12 feet deep, with steep banks and a muddy bottom. The stream is 10 feet wide and a foot and a half deep. On its south bank the grass is heavy enough to make hay. Fifteen miles from our last resting-place the valley narrows to 400 or 500 yards. but a short distance on again becomes more than a mile wide. At 6.05 p. m. we reach and cross Soap Creek near its mouth. Like Rotten Grass its banks are steep, but the bottom is much harder; the water is clear and cold. At 6.15 p. m. we go into camp on the Big Horn, having marched during the day 20½ miles. Distance from Pease 74 miles. As the grass is good, Captain Ball decides to remain here all night and next day, to recruit our horses and pack-mules, many of them being very weak. All day we have been traveling through a magnificent valley, averaging about 2½ miles wide, with a rich black loam soil, producing luxuriant grass, which is bright and green. The foot-hills, too, grow more fertile. The sandstone formation around Pease, here gives place to granite, always the herald of better and more plentiful wood, water, and grass. Altogether it is the finest piece of tillable land I have seen in Montana; not a stone, cactus or sage-brush is to be found in the valley, and water is everywhere abundant.

27th.—We move in the afternoon at 5.15 through the "Hayfields" of old Fort C. F. Smith, in a direction south 39° west, and after marching 3 miles, reach that place, abandoned in 1868. Most of the walls are still standing, built of adobes on stone foundations. The roofs. however, are all destroyed; the flag-staff lies across the parade-ground, and from the manner in which it is cut, we supposed it was felled by Indians. The cemetery is least injured of all, and the monument erected to the late Lieutenant Sternberg and fifteen soldiers and citizens is but little defaced, the corners having been chipped away in several places with a hatchet. This monument, standing alone in the wilderness and erected by sorrowing friends, was the last token of love for those who slept here beneath the sod, waiting long, and perhaps in vain, for the country they served to avenge their death. It is built of limestone, which I suppose was found some place in the mountains lying 2 or 3 miles to the south. These mountains are covered with fine large pines, which could be easily floated down the river, if needed for building in either of the two valleys of the Big Horn. The Big Horn Cañon, looking very deep and of a red color, is about 3 miles above the fort. The location of this post is inferior, in every respect, to many places down the valley. The weather is cool and threatens rain. Near the fort we see the camp made a few days ago by a large party of citizens on their way to the Black Hills. Leaving Smith at 5.05 p. m., and intending to travel during the night in a general direction southeast, we move along the old Phil. Kearney road to where it crosses the head of Soap Creek, and a little way on ascend what was known in the days of Fort Smith as the Big Hill. Soon after reaching the top of this, we leave the road to our right, and cross several very miry streams, probably branches of Soap Creek. The course selected takes us through beautiful high rolling hills, covered with fine grass. At midnight a halt is made on Rotten Grass Creek, where the water and grass are good. Small timber grows along the banks of the stream, which flows through a pretty though narrow bottom, apparently extending all the way to the valley of the Big Horn. Distance travelled since leaving last camp, 18 miles. Distance from Fort Pease, 92 miles.

28th.—Saddling up and starting at 9.25 a. m., we move in a direction 60° east of north, and at 10.10 a. m. reach a small tributary of Rotten Grass, with good wood, but poor and little water. We pass up this creek a short distance, and then over high rolling hills thickly carpeted with grass. Large game trails cross the country in all directions, but so far this morning we have only seen a band of antelope. At 11 o'clock we are at the top of a high divide, and turning north 71° east pass down a little creek, along which are seen a number of white-tail deer. Buffalo are in sight again. At noon having marched 7½ miles, a fine stream is reached and a halt made. Here we find hard-wood (ash) growing, something I have never before seen in Montana. As numerous little creeks join this one, we name it "Many Stream Creek." The valley is about a half a mile wide, and runs a little west of north. The belt of country we are now traveling in is as fine a grazing district as can be found anywhere, combining hills and valleys, with everywhere a perfect mass of the most nutritious grasses. Numerous streams, fed by the melting snows of the Big Horn Mountains, furnish clear and pure water at short intervals. Besides, the country is alive with game; buffalo, elk, deer, and antelope are seen in great numbers. It is a hunter's paradise. At 2 p. m. we are again in the saddle; traveling north 39° east, brings us at 3.25 p. m. to a small creek running north 45° east. This we follow down three miles to where it joins another running north 71° east; crossing the latter and passing down its north bank four miles, we arrive opposite the mouth of a creek entering from the south; the two combined run a nice stream. The Indians call this Long Creek, but on the map it is named Grass Lodge. Along the banks there are ash and cottonwood timber growing in a valley three-quarters of a mile broad. At 6 p. m. we reach a large stream issuing from a little bottom almost hidden by the hills. This is the Little Big Horn River. Turning to the left we move one mile down the left bank, and unsaddle in a pleasant and strong camp. On the opposite side of the river are high and broken sandstone bluffs, but on this side is a beautiful and extensive valley more than a mile wide. In the soil, like that in the upper valley of the Big Horn, not a pebble is found; it has a gentle slope to the river, and is everywhere covered with good grass. The river-water is clear and cold, a fact that renders it very agreeable, as the day has been warm. Ash timber grows along the banks in great abundance. Distance marched during the day, 21¼ miles; since leaving Fort Pease, 113¼.

29th.—This morning we start at 8.45, and continue our march down the left bank, in a direction about 5° west of north. On the right bank the high bluffs are badly cut up with deep ravines. A few miles from camp we see where a large Sioux village was last summer. The valley increases in width, and, if possible, in beauty. At 11.25 we reach a point where the river washes the hills near Custer's battle-ground, on its west, but a short way on again turns to the right, and leaves a second beautiful and extensive valley on its left. Near this point we cross the river twice; it is about 15 yards wide and 18 inches deep, with a good but not a swift current. At 12.45 we halt to noon. Distance traveled this morning, 12 miles. Wolf Mountains, lying to the east, have been in sight nearly all morning, and directly up the river can be seen the mountains of the Big Horn. The bearing down the valley is north 3° west. We move in the afternoon at 2.30 6 miles down the river; then turning to the right and crossing it we leave the Little Big Horn and its pretty valley. Our course is northeast. Passing into the hills, we are soon in the midst of a very broken country. After 3 miles our course changes 15° more east, and at a distance of 5 miles from the Little Big Horn we reach one of the tributaries of Tullock's Fork, and are disappointed in finding it dry. Turning to the left, we follow down this dry gully, intending to halt as soon as we find water. A little way on we see a small buffalo-herd, and kill five of them. 8.45 p. m. brings us to a miserable little creek, coming in on the right, in which the buffalo have been recently wallowing, and near which they have eaten off all the grass. Making a virtue of necessity, we go into camp, having marched 15 miles since noon, and 27 miles during the day; since leaving Fort Pease, 140¼.

30th.—Getting off at 5.15 a. m., we march down the left bank of Tullock's Fork, bearing north 6° west. The sandstone formation has once more replaced the granite, and the country is poorer. On each side are rough, barren, and poorly-watered hills, many of them looking but little better than the Missouri River bad lands. At 8 a. m., having marched 9 miles and finding good grass, we halt and turn the animals out to graze. Ash grows in the bottom, which is a half a mile wide. The water, standing in pools, is cold and tolerably good, although not clear. Moving again at half past 12, our route lies down the creek, bearing north 14° west, but 3 miles on changes almost due north. Small pine timber begins to appear on the hills, and on the sandstone spurs running down from Little Wolf Mountains. Buffalo have been around us all day, and quite a number of deer are seen. At 4 p. m., after marching 11 miles, we halt for the night. Distance marched during the day, 20 miles; since leaving Fort Pease, 160¼. We have now nearly completed our scout, and no fresh Indian signs have been discovered. Many of our horses and mules are very weak, several having already been abandoned.

May 1st.—We start this morning at 7.15, and continue down the creek, bearing north 16° west until 8.30 a. m., when it changes north 23° west, and a half an hour later (nearly 2 miles) north 28° west. As the creek is very crooked, we cross it often. The bottom grows good grass, large cottonwoods and ash; it is bordered on each side with broken bluffs, covered with scattering pine timber. Deep ravines, looking as if in wet seasons they carry great quantities of water, put in frequently on either side. After marching 12 miles we reach the mouth of Tullock's Fork, emptying into the Big Horn about a mile above the junction of the latter stream with the Yellowstone. Passing through a small valley on these two rivers, we cross the Yellowstone 2¼ miles below the mouth of the Big Horn. The ford is 4 feet deep, and as the current is very swift, it is crossed with great difficulty. Two miles farther on we rejoin the command at Fort Pease, at 3 p. m. Distance marched on the scout, 178 miles. The command remains in camp here until the 10th.

On the night of the 2d and 3d the Crow scouts, who, contrary to orders, failed to tie up their ponies, had them stolen by a small party of Sioux from down the river. On the 7th a Mackinaw boat arrives from "Benson's," three days out. On the 8th Captain Freeman and Captain Logan reach us with supplies we left behind.

10th.—To-day we commence to move down the river, intending to travel slowly until General Terry is heard from. Breaking camp at 8.30 a. m., the command moves down the valley; three miles on there is a bad ravine running from the hills to the river. It is from 15 to 20 feet deep and 25 wide, with a muddy bottom and vertical sides of soft earth; two miles farther there is another. It is evident that they serve as important water-channels for the hills to the north. Although dry now, the train is greatly delayed in crossing them. The valley between them is broad and fertile, and the cottonwood timber along the river very dense. The steep sandstone bluffs to the north are becoming of easier ascent. On the opposite side of the Yellowstone the broken hills, covered with scrubby pine, begin to recede from the river. These hills, although by no means fertile, are picturesque. After traveling 7 miles our road turns to the left and ascends the bluffs, and, having reached the top, we find ourselves on an extensive plateau. Due east can be seen a sharp-pointed butte, a very prominent landmark. to which I give the name Cayote Butte. The guide, Mich. Bouyer, informs me it stands on the east side of the Great Porcupine, just where this stream enters the Yellowstone Valley. To the north, in the direction of the Musselshell and the Dry Fork of the Missouri, the country is sterile and barren. The course of the Yellowstone, seen for a great distance, is a little north of east. On its south bank lies a large valley. There is much gravel in the soil along the plateau, and the grass is poor. A deep ravine runs through it, about 12 miles from Fort Pease, in which there is water standing in pools. It soon begins to rain in torrents, but, thanks to the gravelly soil, this does not make the ground very soft. About 6 p. m. we turn to the right, and, passing down a ravine, reach the Yellowstone, on which we go into camp, among large cottonwoods, at 7.30 p. m.; distance, 16¾ miles. The general bearing of to-day's march is north 60° east. Captain Clifford, who, with his company of the Seventh Infantry, came down the river in three small boats found at Fort Pease, arrives safely.

11th.—Remain in camp.

12th.—Starting at 7.20 a. m., a few minutes march brings us to "Froze-to-Death Creek," so named by the Crows, because nine of their tribe once froze to death near it. There is but little water in it, and that is poor; it has a narrow bottom, in which there is some timber. On each side are "bad lands," containing many fossils, mostly mussels. Just beyond this creek the valley increases in width, and finally becomes nearly 3 miles wide; it grows large sage brush, but the grass is generally poor. The hills to the north look sterile and broken. Seven and a quarter miles from camp it becomes necessary to take to the hills. Crossing a dry creek along the banks of which are a great many fossiliferous sandstone rocks, and passing through some barren hills, we gain a high and large plateau, 11 miles from camp. From here one obtains an extensive view. In every direction can be seen an elevated country, broken here and there by cragged sandstone bluffs and buttes; occasionally by a little bottom on the Yellowstone, and sometimes by the river itself. In this numerous islands, heavily wooded, begin to appear. At

5.30 p. m. we encamp on the Yellowstone, in a pretty spot surrounded by cottonwood groves. Distance marched during the day, 18.90 miles. On a bar in the river, which, by the way, is rising, are the carcasses of eight buffaloes; doubtless they broke through the ice last winter during the passage of a large herd.

13th.—Remain in camp; a scouting party is sent to the Rosebud, and returns without seeing any signs of Indians.

14th.—Breaking camp at 7.45 a. m., our route lies through a little bottom bordered on the north by the ceaseless bluffs of sandstone in horizontal layers; 3.7 miles from camp we reach and cross the Great Porcupine, in which there is a little water, tolerably good. Its banks are generally steep and its bottom soft. At this point the valley is broad and fertile, and grows dense timber along the river. Nine miles from camp our guide discovers a fine spring, which we dig out and name after him, (Bouyer.) Here the bluffs circling around run down to the river, a fact that causes us to pass once more into the hills. Traveling along the bed of a dry creek, we reach after much winding the top, but a half a mile on pass down another ravine, so narrow in places that it scarcely permits a wagon to pass. From the cut banks seen along here, it is evident there have been several drift periods, (of gravel,) covering the country from 2 to 5 feet deep. At the mouth of this creek, 12.10 miles from camp, a fine band of elk approach within a few feet of us. Turning to the left and following along the river, we pass through a sage-brush bottom, and go into camp on the Yellowstone at 4.45 p. m., nearly a mile above the Little Porcupine. Distance marched during the day, 16.97 miles. Our camp, situated in a bend of the river, is a good one. The valley, which is nearly two miles wide, is skirted on the north by sandstone bluffs, many of them having a flat top, which caused Lewis and Clarke to call the Little Porcupine "Table Creek." The sandstone formation exists everywhere in this section, and the layers are almost always horizontal. Most of the streams from the north run dry while passing through the arid hills. Two hours after going into camp a rain-storm completely floods the camp; this is followed by a severe hail-storm, which stampeded the herd.

15th.—Remained in camp. The Little Porcupine, swollen by yesterday's rain, runs a stream of very filthy water 30 feet wide and 18 inches deep. We remain in this camp until the 20th. On the 17th a movement is started against a Sioux village which has been discovered on Tongue River, but on account of being discovered before the crossing is completed, and the difficulty of making the horses swim the river, the movement is abandoned.

20th.—This afternoon some of the scouts report the Sioux crossing in large numbers at the mouth of the Rosebud Creek. Leaving a small party to guard the train, the rest of the command moves down the valley, crosses the Little Porcupine, then on through a large valley to a point opposite the Rosebud. The report about the crossing is now found to be a mistake. About a mile below the Little Porcupine is one of those deep ravines which one sees so often along this portion of the Yellowstone. The valley is about 3 miles wide, and, if irrigated, would produce fine crops. Across the river, which is skirted by heavy timber, in a direction south 17° east, are the Big Wolf Mountains, a bunch of low sandstone peaks; still farther to the east can be seen a line of broken hills lying this side of Tongue River. Having marched 8.66 miles, camp is made on the river between 2 and 3 miles below the mouth of the Rosebud. The command remains in this camp until the 5th day of June awaiting supplies and news from the troops that are to come up the river. Indians hover around from time to time, but scamper off upon the first signs of pursuit. During the first few days the weather is very warm; then it turns cold and snows, and again clears up and is pleasant. The river rises nearly 5 feet, and is 250 yards wide. The Indian village is supposed to have moved to the Rosebud some 15 or 20 miles above its mouth.

June 5th—This morning the movement down the river is continued. Breaking camp at 9 a. m., we march down the valley, and about 2½ miles from camp cross a deep ravine which we have bridged. Farther on the soil is alkaline and soft. Having traveled 9 miles, we reach a point where the valley is terminated by a steep hill which cannot be turned. As it is too late in the day to attempt to cross it, we encamp on the river in a beautiful spot at 1.45 p. m. Several bears are seen, and one killed. The day has been exceedingly warm, but in the evening, as full moon rises, it is pleasant, and the camp extremely pretty.

6th.—Starting at 7.40 a. m., 20 minutes' march brings us to the foot of the "Steep Hill;" it is only 275 yards long, but is covered with loose gravel, and so steep that it takes us 3 hours to get the train up. Having reached the top, the rough and barren hills can be seen extending for miles to the north. Bearing to the left, we soon begin to descend along a small creek, in the banks of which lignite is cropping out between layers of sandstone; 5.69 miles from camp we again reach the Yellowstone and its valley. Passing through a sage-brush bottom, along heavy timber, and over deep ravines, we encamp on the Yellowstone, among large cottonwoods, at 4 p. m., having marched 10.54 miles. The evening is pleasant, but during the day there have been occasional showers.

7th.—We start this morning at 7.40 and continue our course along the river. The march is not a pleasant one, for the day is dark and cloudy, with a stiff and cold breeze blowing. The ground is literally covered with cactus, the largest I have ever seen, and through this the men and animals pick their way carefully, but not without pain. The valley is 13 or 14 miles in length, and over 4 in breadth, and, if irrigated from the river, would doubtless make fine farms. Seven and three-fourths miles from camp our road crosses a dry creek, just where it issues from the hills, and a short way on ascends the bluffs, gaining a magnificent plateau. The grass, unlike that on most of the table-lands we have passed over, is very fine. The soil is black, rich, and entirely free from pebbles; it can be seen stretching away for miles to the north, and finally runs itself out in a rough-looking divide. In the afternoon we pass the mouth of Tongue River, coming in on the opposite side, and flowing through a large and fertile valley, thickly timbered. Our elevated position enables us to see up it about 12 miles, when it turns to the southwest, after which it is hidden by the hills, looking rough and barren. To the east the very broken divide this side of Powder River is plainly in sight. Some difficulty is experienced in finding a place to get the train down to the river, but finally a little bottom about 3 miles below Tongue River is selected, and we go into camp at 7.10 p. m., after a march of 21¼ miles.

8th.—Last night the river rose 6 inches; the morning is cool and pleasant. Moving at 7.40 a. m., we pull up a long hill, and crossing over a narrow ridge descend into the valley of Sunday Creek, in which the water is a half a foot deep, but is not good. Distance, 2.89 miles. The bottom is from a half a mile to a mile in width, and grows good grass and some timber. Following down this creek nearly four miles, and then turning to the left, we cross over a low pass and reach a fine, large valley on the Yellowstone. The grass grows luxuriantly, and is heavy enough to cut for hay. At 3 p. m., having marched 10½ miles, a halt is made for two hours and the animals turned out to graze. Buffalo Rapids are just below us; they are caused by a ledge of sandstone running across the river at an angle with the channel of about 60°, and by loose bowlders below this. At present there is plenty of water on them to permit the passage of any boat on the Upper Missouri. At 5 p. m., the march is resumed and continued until 8 p. m., when we encamp on the Yellowstone; near camp is one of those deep ravines so common in the valleys between here and Fort Pease. At this point another sandstone reef runs across the river; it is not, however, so bad as the one above. But little timber grows along the river in this valley, which in other respects is one of the finest on the Yellowstone. It is about 5 miles wide and 11 in length, and is everywhere covered with thick green grass. Distance marched during the day, 16.15 miles. Distance from Fort Ellis, 334.32 miles.

9th.—General Terry arrives this morning on the steamboat Far West, and returns down the river after a stay of less than two hours. General Custer is on Powder River, and is to move up, while we, taking the back trail, are to take a position opposite the mouth of Rosebud Creek. During the afternoon there is a heavy rain-storm, which continues into the night.

10th.—The rain continues until 8 a. m. The ravine mentioned as being just below camp, and which was dry yesterday, now runs a stream 12 feet deep and 15 wide; this explains the many deep cuts seen in the bottoms between here and Fort Pease. Rains falling in the bad lands back of these valleys penetrate the soil only about 6 or 8 inches, when a kind of paste is formed which turns water like a roof. The water descending through the narrow ravines among the hills strikes the valleys with great force and cuts deep channels for itself, the sides of which are as steep as the walls of a room. I have seen the rains pour down in torrents among these bad lands, and although one raises great masses of mud at each step, yet just beneath this, at the depth of six or eight inches, a fine dust, not unfrequently red like brick-dust, is scattered by the wind. The command returns from here to a point about four miles below the mouth of the Rosebud, the cavalry going first, preceding the infantry one day. The late rains have made the roads very soft, and in addition to this there is great difficulty in getting over Sunday Creek, and on the plateau beyond this creek, which on the 8th had scarcely any water, is now, the 11th, a river 50 yards wide and from 3 to 6 feet deep. The marches of the cavalry were estimated, those of the infantry were measured, and are as follows, viz:

On the 11th, 9.23 miles; on the 12th, 15.6; on the 13th, 13.16; on the 14th, 11.88; total, 49.87 miles.

We remain in camp here (4 miles below the Rosebud) until the 21st. Most of the time the weather is very warm. The river, already high, continues to rise. On the 17th the Crow scouts report a big dust on the Rosebud, and shortly afterward a number of horsemen on the opposite bank of the Yellowstone, 2½ miles above. By means of signals, General Gibbon learns it is Colonel Reno with six companies of the Seventh Cavalry. The river is so broad that we have to use field-glasses to read the signals. They have been scouting on Powder and Tongue Rivers, and on Rosebud Creek. No Indians have been seen, but a large trail leading towar

Colonel Reno returns down the river to-morrow to rejoin his regiment, supposed to be near Tongue River.

On the 21st, the *Far West*, with General Terry on board, arrives; orders are given us to proceed at once to Fort Pease. This movement has been in part anticipated, as we are all packed and ready to start. At 9.45 a. m. the march is commenced. While passing the mouth of the Rosebud a big dust is seen in the direction of Big Wolf Mountains, and soon General Custer's long line of cavalry comes into sight. Having marched 18.95 miles, we go into camp on the Yellowstone, at 7.45 p. m., in the lower end of the Great Porcupine Valley. The tents are scarcely pitched when a severe hail-storm sets in; the hail-stones, which are half as large as an egg nearly drive the horses frantic. At midnight Lieutenant Low reaches us with a battery of Gatling guns; he came from Fort Lincoln with General Custer. The country from here to Fort Pease having been already described, it is unnecessary to give the journal in full here. The cavalry and infantry march separately; the marches of the former are estimated, and those of the infantry measured. They are as follows, viz:

On the 22d, 20.73; on the 23d, 21.04; on the 24th, 3.76, (2¼ miles above Pease.) Total distance since leaving camp on the morning of the 21st, 64.48 miles.

June 24th.—The *Far West* arrives at 6 a. m. General Terry is aboard, and intends to accompany our column. One company of infantry is left to guard the train, the rest of the command begins crossing immediately. By 5.30 p. m. we are in camp on Tullock's Fork, near the mouth, and 4.02 miles from our camp of this morning. General Gibbon is so sick that he is obliged to remain on the boat, which is to run up the Big Horn, and meet us if possible at the mouth of the Little Big Horn. The plan of the campaign seems to be for us to move to the Little Big Horn, and thus get below the village supposed to be on that stream, while General Custer strikes them from above. Both commands have left their wagons, and are traveling with pack-animals.

25th.—Starting at 5.45 a. m., we move up Tullock's Fork 3.3 miles, when it is decided to turn to the right along a dry creek, and ascend the ridge between here and the Big Horn. Having reached the summit, it becomes absolutely necessary to follow it, although it is narrow and very crooked. The entire divide is composed of sandstone, usually in horizontal strata. Rough ravines, hundreds of feet deep, and filled with scrubby pine, run back almost to the summit from both the Big Horn and Tullock's Fork. The day is excessively warm, and the infantry toiling along over the broken country, suffer much for water, which cannot be found any place along the divide. After marching 21.35 miles, and passing down a hill where the Gatling guns have to be lowered by hand, the Big Horn is reached, enabling men and animals to quench their intense thirst. Halting here a few minutes we again take up the march, and climbing over a high hill reach a pretty bottom on the Big Horn. Here a halt is made among noble cottonwood trees. Distance marched during the day, 23.65 miles. On the opposite side of the river, the large valley mentioned in the journal of April 25th, begins to open out. At 4.30 p. m. the rain begins to fall heavily, but General Terry decides to push on with the cavalry and battery, desiring to get in the immediate vicinity of the Little Big Horn as soon as possible. The infantry being completely exhausted by the day's march, which has been a severe one, is to remain in camp, and follow in the morning. At 5.15 p. m., we are again in the saddle and continuing our march up the Big Horn. After leaving the little bottom, in which we have been resting, our course lies over rough hills and across deep ravines. Night comes on very dark, and the rain continues to fall heavily until 10.30 p. m. It is with difficulty that the parts of the command in rear can see to follow those in advance. The battery especially has great difficulty in keeping up. At midnight we halt on a ravine, where there is a little water standing in holes, and near which the grass is tolerably good. There is some wood here, but to prevent all risk of signaling our approach, no fires are lighted. Distance marched since leaving the infantry, 12.10 miles; during the day, 35.75.

26th.—Starting at 9.15 a. m., we go but a short way, when Lieutenant Bradley, in charge of the scouts, brings in word that two of our Crows who were sent with General Custer, are on the opposite side of the Big Horn, and say that General Custer was badly beaten yesterday and killed in a fight about 18 miles from here on the Little Big Horn, which river is now but a short distance in our front. Up this stream a big smoke can be seen; but the report of the Crows not being generally believed, it is supposed to be caused by Custer burning the village. A halt is made to await the infantry, and about this time General Gibbon arrives from the boat, which he reports is coming up the Big Horn without difficulty, with 160 tons of freight. The hills around us are barren and broken, growing little else but cactus. The infantry having arrived, the march is resumed. After marching 10.35 miles, the infantry having made 18.85, a halt is made on the Little Big Horn, in a pretty spot covered with fine grass, and surrounded with beautiful groves of cottonwood and ash. The river is about 20 yards wide, and 2½ feet deep. At 5 p. m. the march is resumed. Passing along the west bank of the Little Big Horn, our route lies through a beautiful valley carpeted with fine grass. After marching about 5 miles, twelve or fifteen ponies are picked up, and shortly afterward several Indians are seen hovering around our front. A long line looking like cavalry, and three or four miles on our right and front is seen, by several officers through their glasses. One officer also sees something on the hills to the left looking like buffalo lying down. Night comes on before anything definite can be determined, but it is evident that General Custer has not been entirely successful. Having marched 6¾ miles from our last resting place, we go into camp at 8 p. m., in the middle of a grassy and pretty valley. Distance marched during the day by the infantry, 29.10 miles; by the cavalry, 17 miles. Whatever the result of the fight has been, every one anticipates another one to-morrow.

27th.—The night passed away quietly. Making an early start, we go but a short way when two tepees are seen through the timber, and crossing a narrow sandstone point (mentioned in the journal of April 29) we see just in front of us where a very large village was yesterday. The fate of Custer is now more puzzling than ever. We are not left much longer in suspense. Lieutenant Bradley sends in word he has counted one hundred and ninety-six dead cavalrymen lying on the hills to the left. What the officer saw yesterday looking like buffalo lying down are dead comrades and their horses. Soon two officers reach us from Colonel Reno, and tell us of their part of the action. "Where is Custer?" is asked them. "The last we saw of him he was going down that high bluff toward the lower end of the village. We do not know where he is now." They are told "We have found him." The Indians evidently left in a great hurry, leaving several lodges standing, and great numbers of buffalo-robes, blankets, tepee-poles, camp utensils, together with great quantities of dried meat and 50 or 60 ponies. After marching 8¾ miles we encamp on the Little Big Horn near Colonel Reno's position, which is on a high and steep bluff. The field and its incidents have been described too often to bear repetition here. An official map of it has been made by the chief engineer officer of the department. The fight taking place here reminds me of a taunt left by one of our Crow scouts not more than 3 or 4 miles up the valley during our scout over this same ground on the 29th of last April. Taking an abandoned hard-bread box and a piece of charcoal he covered it with a lot of drawings, which he said would tell the Sioux that we meant to clear them out, and then sticking a handful of green grass in the cracks, he added, "and this will tell them we are going to do it this summer." It is a little strange, considering the hundreds of miles we have marched over, that this taunt should have been left almost on the very spot where the one desperate fight of the campaign took place.

28th.—Most of the day is passed in burying the dead, bringing the wounded down from "Reno's Hill," and making hand-litters for them. At 6.30 p. m. the movement for the mouth of the Little Big Horn is commenced, but the difficulty of carrying the wounded by hand is so great that although the march is continued until midnight we only make 4.64 miles, and then go into camp on the river near what was the north end of the village.

29th.—Last night's experience having demonstrated the inefficiency of hand-litters, mule-litters are constructed to-day. A portion of the command is employed in burning the plunder found in the Indian camp, and as there are many wagon-loads of it the work takes most of the day. At 5 p. m. the march is resumed. Upon leaving camp it was only intended to proceed during the evening a few miles, but meeting two couriers 3 miles from camp, who inform us the boat is at the mouth of the Little Big Horn, it is decided to push on. After following the valley marched through on the afternoon of the 26th, for several miles, we turn to the left across some rolling hills and finally gain an elevated plateau. This plateau grows large cactus, and as the night is dark, it is very annoying to men and horses. The steamboat is reached after marching 14.9 miles. On account of the darkness it is only after much difficulty that a trail can be found leading down to the bottom near the boat. About 1 o'clock fires are built along a ravine, and by this means the wounded are gotten down and put aboard at 1.30 a. m. The *Far West* has been several miles farther up the Big Horn, and is now lying in that river, about half a mile above the mouth of the Little Big Horn.

30th.—The boat leaves about noon for our supply-camp, and General Terry being aboard, the command falls to General Gibbon. At 5 p. m. the entire command, including the Seventh Cavalry, cross the Little Big Horn and go into camp on its north bank, near the mouth, in a pretty camp among large cottonwood trees. From here to the supply-camp the route followed is nearly the same as the one used on our way up a few days ago. The following are the distances marched, (approximated.)

July 1st.—Start at 5 a. m., march 20 miles, and camp on the Big Horn, where the infantry camped the night of the 25th.

2d.—Started at 4.30 a. m., march 23 miles, and crossing the Yellowstone on the boat, go into camp where we left the train. We remain in this camp until the 22d, waiting for re-enforcements and supplies. During this time the river falls about 4 feet. Part of the time the weather is very warm.

.22d.—The command is moved to-day 4.38 miles down the river, to a camp where there is fine grass. The mosquitoes, however, nearly eat us up. We remain in this camp until the 27th. On the 24th there is a hard rain, and by next day the river has

risen nearly a foot. On the 25th General Crook is heard from. He is on Goose Creek, awaiting re-enforcements.

27th.—This morning at 11 o'clock camp is moved down the valley 4.06 miles to the second ravine mentioned in the journal of May 10th. The grass here is superb; the water, however, is poor. From this last camp we move to the mouth of the Rosebud, finding the roads good all the way, but the weather excessively warm. The following are the marches made, viz:

28th.—Start at 5.30 a. m., march 16.44 miles, and go into camp on the Yellowstone at 2 p. m.

29th.—Start at 5.15 a. m., march 22.9 miles, and camp on the Yellowstone at 4 p. m., about a mile from Bouyer's Spring.

30th.—Start at 5 a. m., march 15.1 miles, and camp on the Yellowstone, opposite the mouth of the Rosebud. Here we find four companies of the Sixth Infantry, two of the Seventeenth, and one of the Seventh Cavalry. The command remains in this vicinity until August 8th, awaiting supplies and re-enforcements. The river has fallen about 8 feet below high-water mark, and the boats commence to have trouble in shallow water.

On August 3d General Gibbon's command crosses the Yellowstone, and goes into camp on the south bank, on a high bench surrounded by still higher hills.

On the 7th the heat is terrible, the thermometer marking 116° in a tent. In the evening everything is ready to move next morning, about 1,700 strong.

For the purpose of abbreviating this paper, which has become already longer than originally intended, the journal form will be abandoned whenever convenient. The following are the marches made up the Rosebud, viz:

August 8th.—Start at 5 a. m., march 9 miles, and camp on the Rosebud at 3 p. m., among large cottonwood trees.

9th.—Start at 5 a. m., march 10.91 miles, and camp at 5 p. m., where a very large Indian village has been some time during the spring.

10th.—Start at 5 a. m., march 15 miles, and camp with General Crook's command on Rosebud Creek.

Soon after leaving camp on the morning of the 8th we crossed the Rosebud, which is a miserable little creek about 15 feet wide, with muddy banks, and a soft bottom. In the lower part the water stands in pools. The valley, which is usually about one-half or three-quarters of a mile wide, grows good grass and quite a quantity of cottonwood timber. It is bordered on each side by sandstone bluffs, in which the strata is commonly horizontal. As we proceed up the stream the valley increases a little in width, while the timber diminishes in size. The water improves, and about 18 miles from the mouth begins to run. The creek, in the lower part especially, is very crooked, and the many crossings greatly delay our large trains.

On the 9th an exceedingly cold rain sets in, and continues the greater part of the day, but on the morning of the 10th it is again clear and pleasant.

At 11 a. m. of the 10th, those of our Indian scouts who are in advance come rushing back, crying "Sioux," and calling our attention to a large cloud of dust seen rising from behind a hill a few miles up the valley. That the Crows think the time has come at last to meet in fair battle their hated enemy is evident from their excited words and actions. They leap from their ponies and begin stripping for the fight, at the same time daubing their faces with paint. The squaws, even more excited than the men, go hurriedly to work saddling the "war-ponies," and all the time screaming and gesticulating in the wildest manner. A cavalry skirmish-line with one wing resting on the bluffs and the other in the timber is stretched across the valley, the infantry take position on the flanks, and the train is placed in the rectangle thus formed; the position is an admirable one, and the troops are eager and confident.

Soon the arrival of the famous "Buffalo Bill" puts an end to our warlike demonstrations, for he tells us the dust arises from General Crook's column, consisting of 25 companies of cavalry and 10 of infantry. Both commands encamp together on the Rosebud, and officers and men alike compare notes upon the campaign. On such occasions, when the long, tiresome, and continuous marches which have been made are the topic of the conversation, one appreciates the immensity of the country held by a few thousand Sioux—a country large enough to support millions of people. Here it is decided to send the wagon-train back to the Yellowstone under General Miles and his regiment of infantry. Upon reaching the river he is to patrol it on a steamboat, and prevent, if possible, the Sioux from crossing and escaping to the north. All the rest are to follow a tepee-trail found by General Crook's scouts, leading toward Tongue River. Fifteen days' rations are put on the pack-mules, and the march commenced. From this point on the Rosebud it is only 10 miles to Tongue River. The trail leads over a high divide which presents a steep face toward each stream, but the eastern side is especially precipitous. On the summit is an elevated and rolling prairie, dotted occasionally by a small grove of pines. In places the sandstone formation has been disturbed by volcanic action, and pieces of lava are scattered over the ground. The grass is magnificent and of a variety known as "bunch-grass." A smell of sulphur coming from a ravine attracted attention to it, and going there I found a seam of coal on fire.

Tongue River is a fine stream, 75 yards wide and 2 feet deep; it has a rocky bottom and the water is clear and good. We marched down this river nearly 50 miles, still following the Indian trail. The greater part of the distance there is a little bottom on one side or the other, varying in width from one-half a mile to a mile, and always covered with the most luxuriant buffalo-grass. The hills on each side are very broken; in places they are of various colors, usually red. Where we reached the river there is a quantity of timber, cottonwood and ash, but about 25 miles down it becomes quite scarce, until just below the mouth of Pumpkin Vine Creek, where there is a great abundance. At this point there is an extensive and fertile valley, bordered by rolling hills. The citizen-scouts claim the trail is growing much fresher, and that it is only five days old when we reach Pumpkin Vine Creek; our Crows, however, maintain that it is at least nine.

The trail turns off to Pumpkin Vine, a short distance above where this muddy little creek joins Tongue River, and, following along it 6 or 7 miles through a country alternating with valley and bench land, crosses over to Powder River.

The divide lying west of this river is the roughest I have ever seen. It is composed of bad-land hills separated by yawning ravines hundreds of feet deep. Many of these hills are entirely destitute of any grass; even cactus refuses to grow on them.

Descending from this divide we reach a little bottom on Turtle or Mizpah Creek, in which the water is muddy and poor. This is doubtless due to the recent rains which have fallen almost incessantly for the past five days.

From where we cross Turtle Creek it is but a short distance to Powder River, which is about 100 yards wide and 2 feet deep. The water running over a sandy bottom is tolerably good, although by no means clear. The trail turned down this river and followed it to a point about 18 miles above its mouth, then turned to the right in the direction of the Little Missouri.

It being generally conceded that the Crows were right about the age of the trail, and that the Sioux are nearly two weeks ahead of us, we continue on down the river to the Yellowstone for the purpose of getting supplies.

The valley of Powder River is generally misrepresented; it is not all a hideous waste. We passed through several large and fertile bottoms growing fine buffalo-grass. In many places this has been burnt off by the Sioux, intending by this means to secure their retreat; and had it not been for the many heavy rains in the past two weeks they doubtless would have succeeded in making it an almost impossibility to pursue them. As it is, many of General Crook's cavalry-horses are on their last legs. The bluffs on each side are very precipitous and often present a bad-land face, yet on top they are generally covered with good grass. Large cottonwood timber grows almost everywhere along the banks.

The river seems extremely sensible to every rain, rising and falling in rainy weather sometimes twice a day with a variation of at least 18 inches. Its bottom is everywhere soft, and in places quicksand.

The following are the distances marched each day since leaving the Rosebud on the 11th:

August 11th.—Start at noon, march 12.45 miles, and camp on Tongue River. During the evening there is a severe rain-storm.

12th.—Start at noon, march 12.64 miles, over heavy roads; camp on Tongue River at 6 p. m.; during the day there have been occasional showers.

13th.—Start at 7 a. m., march 24 miles, and camp on Tongue River at 6 p. m.; during the afternoon and evening there is a hard rain.

14th.—Start at 5 a. m., march 14 miles, and camp on Pumpkin Vine Creek,

15th.—Start at 5.40 a. m., march 20.28 miles, and camp on Powder River at 3 p. m.

16th.—Start at 5.55 a. m., march 19 miles, and camp on Powder River at 3.30 p. m.

17th.—An early start, march 24.10 miles, and camp on the Yellowstone, near the mouth of Powder River. We remained in this last camp until the 25th, getting supplies, and recruiting the strength of the men and animals.

The weather is very rainy, causing a rise in the Yellowstone of over a foot. In this river, about 2½ miles below the mouth of Powder River, are the Wolf Rapids, offering, just before the rise mentioned, considerable difficulty to steamboat navigation. The expense of making them navigable at all seasons when the river is low would be very little, either by removing the obstructing rock or by building a wing-dam so as to utilize all the water.

The valley on the Yellowstone at this point is large and fertile, and hemmed in by rolling and grassy hills. On the opposite side there are a mass of bad lands, back of a little bottom.

On the morning of the 24th, General Crook's command starts up Powder River to pick up and follow the Indian trail. The command belonging to the Department of Dakota followed the next day, and, marching 17.1 miles, goes into camp, part on the river and the rest on a little creek. This evening Buffalo Bill brings news from Lieutenant

Rice, opposite the mouth of Glendive Creek, that the Indians are hovering around there. For fear that they may escape north, General Terry turns in that direction. The next morning, the 26th, General Crook with his command is to follow on along the trail.

Instead of returning to the mouth of Powder River, we move obliquely to the Yellowstone, over a high hilly country, where the grass has been lately burnt off, and reach the river just above O'Fallon's Creek, and camp there. Distance 22.4 miles.

The grass along the route has evidently been very fine. The hills are entirely destitute of timber, and are only suitable for pasturage.

O'Fallon's Creek, swollen by the recent rains, is 30 feet wide and nearly 3 feet deep. Crossing the Yellowstone about 6 miles below our camp of last night, we set out on a long march toward the Missouri divide.

Leaving the river at 6.40 p. m., on the evening of the 27th, we proceed a short distance down the stream, and then turn to the left and follow a large buffalo-trail leading a little west of north, through pretty hills covered with good grass. The moon is about half full, and the weather being fine, the march is an exceedingly pleasant one. After traveling 6.25 miles, a halt is made on the prairie for the night.

The following are the distances made on each day of the march, from here to a point opposite the mouth of Glendive:

August 28th.—Start at 5 a. m., march 20.95 miles, and camp on Bad Route Creek.

29th.—Make an early start, march 17.36 miles, and camp on Rush Creek.

30th.—March 17.50 miles, and camp on Deer Creek.

31st.—March 13.26 miles, and camp on the Yellowstone, near the mouth of Deer Creek.

I have always heard the country passed over during these marches described as a bad-land waste, but such an idea is a very great mistake; it is one of the finest grazing districts in the world. In all the distance traveled, about 70 miles, not more than 10 took us through a poor country, and that was on the lower end of Deer Creek. Our course was first northwest to the head of Bad Route, then northeast to Deer Creek, and thence down that creek, running southeast, to the Yellowstone. The country is a series of long waving hills, thickly carpeted with magnificent grass, and separated by valleys which descend from them in gentle declivities. There was some difficulty in finding water, and yet we always had enough. I do not doubt but that our ignorance of the country accounts better for our trouble in finding water than its scarcity does. When compared with districts around the base of a granite mountain it cannot be called a well-watered country; yet 1,200 men, not one of whom knew the ground, marched through it with as many animals, and never wanted for water. The pebble-drift scattered over the elevated prairies farther up the river, and which causes the grass to be thin, entirely disappears here. It is destined to be some day a favorite stock country, for certainly it is capable of furnishing pasturage for immense herds of cattle.

Antelope and buffalo were seen in great numbers. On the 29th, striking a large buffalo herd, a grand hunt took place. Permission being given to many to join in the sport added additional excitement to the chase. About a dozen were killed, making many a man look well pleased at the prospect of plenty of fresh meat. Just after this hunt the Second Cavalry was ordered to cross the divide in the direction of the Dry Fork, and then turn and travel east. The object of this movement is to examine the trails on the northern slope.

The officers represent the country as a good one. The battalion returned the next morning without having seen any fresh Indian signs. Upon our arrival at Glendive we were pretty well convinced that the Indians had gone to the Little Missouri, having broken up into small parties. This opinion was strengthened three days later upon the return of the Seventh Cavalry, which left us on the head of Deer Creek and scouted down to the mouth of the Yellowstone without seeing a fresh trail. The country across the Yellowstone is a high rolling prairie, apparently growing good grass.

The mouth of Glendive Creek lies about a mile above camp; on each side of it there is a little bottom. Along this portion of the Yellowstone there is but little timber, indeed it is scarce all the way below Tongue River. A few miles back from the river small but straight cottonwood and ash timber is found, but not in sufficient quantities to be of much service. At one camp, the night of the 29th, we were obliged to use buffalo chips.

The river has fallen so much that the boats have great difficulty in navigating it, and it is believed that, unless some of the troops are sent home, it will be impossible to supply the Tongue River post. As the Montana troops have the greatest distance to march, they are ordered to return home and start on the morning of September 6.

The country from Deer Creek to York's River is much the same as that traveled over on our scout out towards the divide.

Our route, upon starting, takes us through a fair and large valley on the Yellowstone, opposite the "stockade" built by General Stanley in 1873. I observed while passing through this bottom that Turtle Creek is laid down wrong on the maps. It joins the Yellowstone 5.92 miles from Deer Creek (measured along the wagon-road) and not near the "stockade."

West of York's River the country grows rapidly rougher, and following down Custer's

Creek one travels through a hideous mass of bad-lands. The utter waste of such a country passes the understanding of those who have not seen it. Huge hills of sandy clay and earth-like ashes, entirely destitute of grass, brush, or even cactus, which would be a fitting companion, lie thrown together in all imaginable shapes. Some a hundred feet high are not any wider at the base, and only an inch or two thick at the summit. In places the gray sandy clay, looking almost like sandstone, but so soft that one can mold it in the hand like mud, stands with sides almost vertical.

When one begins to wonder why these hills do not follow the laws of gravity and fall, he concludes that it is because every thing around is utterly without law or order. In other places little mounds of chalky clay, nearly pure white, are carved out by the winds and water into the most fantastic shapes. Various shapes and various kinds of earth are tumbled together in one confused mass. From the mouth of this creek we proceed on to Union Creek, where we turned back on the 10th of last June.

In the hills, a short way up the river from Custer Creek, I observed several fine seams of coal, and not far from this volcanic rock scattered around.

On the bad-lands, 9.92 miles from Custer Creek, we made a camp in a little bottom on the river, on the opposite side of which is a large and beautiful terraced valley. The next day we reached Union Creek, after marching about 8 miles, and from there followed our old trail from Fort Ellis with three exceptions; one was just above Fort Pease. Upon arriving at the ford, 8 miles above that place, we found we could not cross the river without wetting every thing in the wagons; this forced us to take the rough hills mentioned previously in this journal as lying opposite Pompey's Pillar. We did not strike the old trail again until within 3 or 4 miles of Baker's battle-ground. The district thus passed over, about 60 miles by the wagon-road and 40 in a straight line, is a poorly watered and barren waste. In all this distance we crossed but one running creek, Willow Creek, about 15 miles above Fort Pease. The second place was from the supply camp to countryman's ranch, again finding the river too deep for the wagons.

Passing into the hills to the north, we soon reached White Beaver Creek, and then passed over high rolling hills, covered with good grass, and in many places with fine forests. Sweet Grass Creek, a clear mountain stream, is also crossed just below Big Timber. The infantry turned to the north to reach Camp Baker and Fort Shaw, via the Forks of the Musselshell. The cavalry reached Fort Ellis on the 29th day of September. The infantry reached Camp Baker on October 2d, and Fort Shaw on the 6th.

The following are the distances marched each day on way from Glendive Creek. home, viz:

September 6th.—Started at 10.30 a. m., marched 13.96 miles, and camped at 3.30 p. m. on a ravine putting into the Yellowstone not far above the stockade. Here we found water in holes.

7th.—Start at 6 a. m., march 6 miles to Rush Creek; to Bad Route Creek, 18.26, (here we noon;) to camp, 6.30 p. m., on a dry ravine, 25.12 miles. Hard rain, lasting from 3 p. m. until midnight.

8th.—Start at 7.15 a. m., march 15.32 miles, and camp on York's River at 1.30 p. m. Occasional showers during the day.

9th.—Start at 6 a. m., march about 15 miles to Custer Creek, and 26.97 miles to camp at 5 p. m. at the mouth of Custer Creek; the roads are very heavy.

10th.—Start at 12.20 p. m., march 9.92 miles, and camp on the Yellowstone at 4 p. m.

11th.—Start at 7.20 a. m., march 21.8 miles, and camp on Sandy Creek.

12th.—Start at 7.45 a. m., march 5.4 miles and camp on the Yellowstone just above and across the river from the new post.

13th.—Start at 7 a. m., march 20.67 miles, and camp on the Yellowstone at 2.30 p. m.

14th.—Start at 7 a. m., march 21.68 miles, and camp on the Yellowstone at 3.15 p. m., at the mouth of the Little Porcupine. The water in this creek is now clear and good.

15th.—Start at 7 a. m., march 16.76 miles, and camp on the Yellowstone, above the Great Porcupine.

16th.—Start at 7 a. m., march 18.57 miles, and camp on the Yellowstone, above "Froze-to-Death Creek."

17th.—Start at 7.05 a. m., march 23.72 miles, and camp on the Yellowstone, 7 miles above Fort Pease, at 4 p. m.

18th.—Remained in camp.

19th.—Start at 7 a. m., march 25.18 miles, and camp on a ravine, where water stands in holes, at 5.30 p. m.

20th.—Start at 6.30 a. m., march 7.9 miles to the Yellowstone, opposite Pompey's Pillar, and then on to camp on the river. Total distance, 30.62 miles. The wagons did not arrive until 7.30 p. m.

21st.—Start at 9 a. m., and camp just above Baker's battle-ground. Distance, 10.29 miles.

22d.—Start at 6.45 a. m., march 22.75 miles, and camp on the Yellowstone at 3.30 p. m., a little ways above the mouth of Clark's Fork.

23d.—Start at 7 a. m., march 20.52 miles, and camp on the Yellowstone at 2.15 p. m. at the old supply camp.

24th.—Start at 7 a. m., march 20.66 miles, and camp on the Yellowstone at 4 p. m.

25th.—Start at 7.15 a. m.; take the back trail for 2.17 miles. From camp to White Beaver Creek it was 8.27 miles, and to camp, near some small springs, 16.70 miles.

26th.—Start at 7.05 a. m.; after marching 8.87 miles we reach Sweet Grass Creek, and 17.56 miles brings us to the Big Timber.

The infantry turns to the north about 1 mile below the last-named creek. The cavalry crosses the Big Timber, and goes into camp on the Yellowstone. Total distance, 18.63 miles.

27th.—Start at 6.35 a. m., march 14.09 miles, when we reach Gage's Ford, where we noon. Duck Creek is 1.20 miles farther, or 15.29 from this morning's camp. Warm Spring Creek, 18.54, and camp on the Yellowstone, near Countryman's old ranch, 25.64 miles.

28th.—From camp to Shields's River, 8 miles, and to camp on Billman's Creek, 26.6 miles.

29th.—To Fort Ellis, 11.28 miles.

Total, from the camp opposite Glendive Creek to Fort Ellis, 448.76 miles.

The following are the marches made by the infantry on their way from the Yellowstone to Fort Shaw:

September 26th.—From camp to camp on White Otter Creek, 21.99 miles.

27th.—From camp to camp on Sweet Grass Creek, 20 miles.

28th.—From camp to camp on Big Creek, 23.72 miles.

29th.—From camp to camp on Musselshell River, 21⅞ miles.

30th.—From camp to camp on Six-Mile Creek, 25 miles.

October 1st.—From camp to camp at Warm Spring, 7½ miles.

2d.—From camp to camp at Camp Baker, 16.9 miles.

3d—From camp to camp on Cottonwood Creek, 19.5 miles.

4th.—From camp to camp on creek between Hough Creek, 18⅛ miles.

5th.—From camp to camp on the Missouri at the ford, 24 miles.

6th.—From camp to camp at Fort Shaw, 20⅛ miles.

Total, 218.97 miles.

Total from Glendive Creek to Fort Shaw, 585.58 miles.

Total marched by the united command from Fort Ellis to camp of September 25, 1,288.42 miles.

Total march by the infantry as a battalion from March 17 to October 6, 1,687.39 miles.

Total march by the Second Cavalry as a battalion from April 1 to September 29, 1,393.21 miles.

To the amount marched by the infantry, 208.14 miles wants to be added for the company commanded by Major Freeman, 247.18 for the company commanded by Lieutenant English, and 186.24 miles for Captain Sanno's.

To the amount marched by the cavalry, 306 miles is to be added for F Company, Lieutenant Roe in command; 352.50 for G Company, Captain Wheelan; 404.50 for L, Lieutenant Hamilton; and 388 for H, Captain Ball.

In conclusion, it might be said that the country marched over, taken as a whole, is a good one. Along the Yellowstone and its tributaries are many large and fertile valleys, only waiting for the hand of man to make them bloom with golden crops. Back of these valleys are rolling hills, covered with the most luxuriant and nutritious grasses, and as a grazing district challenging superiority.

The Yellowstone River has been thoroughly tested, and the trial has resulted in proving it navigable. The expenditure of a little money in removing the Wolf and Buffalo Rapids, and confining the water in one channel in several other places, would do away with all difficulty, from the 1st of June until the 1st of October, to a point near the mouth of the Big Horn. The facility with which it can be used for supplying its lower districts, by Mackinaw boats from Benson's, at an expense immensely less than by wagon-trains, has also been proved this last summer.

E. J. McClernand,
Second Lieutenant Second Cavalry,
Acting Engineer Officer, District Montana.

REPORT OF LIEUTENANT GEORGE D. WALLACE, SEVENTH CAVALRY.

Saint Paul, Minn., *January 27, 1877.*

Sir: I have the honor to submit the following report of the march and the country passed over by the Seventh Regiment of Cavalry from the 22d to the 25th of June, 1876:

At 12 m. on the 22d of June, 1876, the Seventh Cavalry, under Lieutenant-Colonel Custer, left camp on the Yellowstone and moved up that stream for 2 miles to the mouth of the Rosebud, then up the Rosebud. We crossed the latter near its mouth. It was a clear running stream, from 3 to 4 feet wide, and about 3 inches deep; bottom gravel, but in many places water standing in pools. Water slightly alkaline. Owing to delays with the pack-train the command moved only about 12 miles that day. We camped on the left bank of the Rosebud, at the base of a steep bluff. We had plenty of wood and water, and grass for our animals. During the greater part of the march the trail followed the high ground, or second bottom, where the soil was poor, the grass thin, and crowded out by sage-brush and cactus. In the lower part of the valley the soil appeared to be good, the grazing fair, the bottom timbered with large cottonwood. Small willows grew thickly along the banks in many places. For the first 8 miles the hills sloped back gradually, but near camp were more abrupt, and covered with stones and cactus. Several deep ravines were crossed during the day. The only serious obstacle to a wagon-train would be the numerous crossings of the bends of the Rosebud. Weather clear, but not unpleasantly warm. No game visible. Plenty of fish in the creek.

June 23, 1876.—Orders were given last night that trumpet-signals would be discontinued, that the stable-guards would wake their respective companies at 3 a. m., and the command would move at 5 a. m. General Custer stated that short marches would be made for the first few days, after that they would be increased. All were ready at the appointed time, and the command moving out we crossed to the right bank of the Rosebud. The bluff being very broken, we had to follow the valley for some distance, crossing the Rosebud five times in 3 miles; thence up the right side for about 10 miles. There we halted, to allow the pack-train to close up. Soon after starting, crossed to the left bank and followed that for 15 miles, and camped on right bank at 4.30 p. m., making a distance of over 30 miles. The last of the pack-train did not get into camp until near sunset. About 5 miles from our last camp we came to the trail made by Major Reno, a few days previous, and a few miles farther on saw the first traces of the Indian camps. They were all old, but everything indicated a large body of Indians. Every bend of the stream bore traces of some old camp, and their ponies had nipped almost every spear of grass. The ground was strewn with broken bones and cuttings from buffalo hides. The country passed over after the first few miles was rolling, and a few deep ravines the only obstacle to hinder the passage of a wagon-train. Soil poor, except along the creek. Grass all eaten up. Plenty of cottonwood along the creek. During the last 5 or 6 miles of the march, the cottonwood timber was gradually replaced by ash and a species of elder. The valley was about one-fourth of a mile wide, and for the last 15 miles the hills were very steep and rocky, sandstone being present. The country back from the hills looked to be very much broken. The hills were covered with a short growth of pines. No game seen during the day; weather warm and clear.

June 24, 1876.—The command moved at 5 a. m. this morning. After we had been on the march about an hour, our Crow scouts came in and reported fresh signs of Indians, but in no great numbers. After a short consultation, General Custer, with an escort of two companies, moved out in advance, the remainder of the command following at a distance of about half a mile. We followed the right bank of the Rosebud; crossed two running tributaries, the first we had seen. At 1 p. m. the command was halted, scouts sent ahead, and the men made coffee. The scouts got back about 4, and reported a fresh camp at the forks of the Rosebud. Everything indicated that the Indians were not more than thirty miles away. At 5 p. m. the command moved out; crossed to left bank of Rosebud; passed through several large camps. The trail now was fresh, and the whole valley scratched up by the trailing lodge-poles. At 7.45 p. m. we encamped on the right bank of Rosebud. Scouts were sent ahead to see which branch of the stream the Indians had followed. Distance marched to-day, about 28 miles. Soil in the valley very good, and in many places grazing very fine. Timber scattering, principally elder and ash. Hills rough and broken, and thickly covered with pines. Weather clear and very warm. About 9 p. m. the scouts returned and reported that the Indians had crossed the divide to the Little Big Horn River. General Custer determined to cross the divide that night, to conceal the command, the next day find out the locality of the village, and attack the following morning at daylight. Orders were given to move at midnight, but we did not get off until near 1 a. m., and, owing to delays on account of pack-train, we had only marched about 8 miles when daylight appeared. We halted, and the men were ordered to make coffee. While waiting here a scout came back from Lieutenant Varnum, who had been sent out the night before. In a note to General Custer, Lieutenant Varnum stated that he could see the smoke of the village about 20 miles away, on the Little Big Horn. The scout pointed out the butte from which the village could be seen. It was about 8 miles ahead.

We moved on, and when near the butte Lieutenant Varnum joined us and reported that the Indians had discovered the command and that he had seen couriers go in the direction of the village. General Custer assembled the officers, told them what he had heard, and said he would move ahead and attack the village without any further delay.

At 12 m., on the 25th, we crossed the divide between the Rosebud and Little Big Horn. From the divide could be seen the valley of the Little Big Horn, and about 15 or 20 miles to the northwest could be seen a light blue cloud, and to practiced eyes showed that our game was near. A small stream starting from the point near where we crossed the divide flowed in the direction of the smoke. After the assignment of battalions was made, General Custer followed down the right bank of this stream, and Major Reno the left. When within three miles of Little Big Horn, Major Reno was ordered across to the right bank and the two columns moved together for some distance, when Major Reno was ordered ahead. He recrossed this stream, moved down it, crossed the Little Big Horn, halted his column, formed line and moved down the valley and commenced the battle of June 25.

In passing from the Rosebud to the Little Big Horn, we followed up the left branch of the first, then up a dry ravine to the crest of the divide; grass short, soil poor, hills low. From the crest to the Little Big Horn the country was broken and the valley narrow; some timber along the little stream we followed down. Distance traveled during the night of the 24th and on the 25th about 6 miles.

I am, sir, very respectfully, your obedient servant,

GEO. D. WALLACE,
First Lieutenant and Adjutant Seventh Cavalry.

The CHIEF ENGINEER
Department of Dakota.

REPORT OF SERGEANT JAMES E. WILSON, BATTALION OF ENGINEERS.

HEADQUARTERS DEPARTMENT OF DAKOTA,
CHIEF ENGINEER'S OFFICE,
Saint Paul, Minn., January 3, 1877.

SIR: I have the honor to submit the following report:

In obedience to orders received from you in the field, I remained on the steamer Far West during its trip up the Big Horn River, for the purpose of making a boat survey, and collecting information in regard to the nature of that stream and the adjacent country.

June 24.—Immediately after the departure of General Terry and staff, at 6.30 p. m., the boat moved up a short distance and wooded, after which it crossed over and tied up on the left bank of the Yellowstone River.

Two Indian curs were seen this evening in close proximity, but were not molested. The escort commanded by Capt. S. Baker and First Lieut. J. Carland, Sixth Infantry, was composed as follows: Company B, Sixth Infantry, to which were attached some soldiers left in charge of property belonging to the absent portion of the command. A few sick men, in charge of Hospital Steward Dale, occupied the rear portion of the cabin-deck. These with first-class private Thomas Culligan and myself of the engineer detachment made up the total commissioned and enlisted on board. The whole fighting force, including the armed civilians on board, did not exceed 60 men.

June 25.—At 12 m. the boat moved up the Yellowstone, and at 12.35 p. m. reached the mouth of the Big Horn. The country on the right bank of the Yellowstone at this point is quite level for a considerable distance, and thickly timbered with cottonwood. The Big Horn is about 150 yards wide at its mouth, with a depth of from 3 to 8 feet. Tullock's Fork enters the Big Horn on its right bank, about 4 miles from its mouth. Reached Josephine Island at 4.50 p. m. It is well timbered, and about three-fourths of a mile long, and situated about 12 miles from the mouth of the river. The river at a point about a mile above Josephine Island spreads out to a width of 500 or 600 yards, causing a shallow channel. The current is swift, and the bed of the river studded with numerous islands and sand-bars.

After a travel of 15 miles the first creek entering the Big Horn on its left bank was reached. About one mile further on the boat tied up, at 8.30 p. m., on the left bank. The current of the Big Horn is much swifter than that of the Yellowstone, with a depth varying from 3 to 8 feet; 5½ feet of water at Josephine Island. Rapid water was encountered on two occasions during the day's travel. The country as we advance becomes richer, the hills on the right bank close gradually in, and the left bank is low, thickly timbered, and well grassed. Game appeared to be abundant in the valley, as we saw a herd of 8 elk on the right bank in the afternoon. Passed many old Indian encampments. Heavy rain fell during the night. Pine timber was obtained at the point where the boat was tied up. Maximum thermometer, 91°; minimum thermometer, 63°. Bearings were taken by prismatic compass; the rate of the boat carefully noted whenever a change was observed, and at intervals not greater than 10 minutes. Whenever rapids were encountered the distance to the end of the course was estimated. Readings of the barometer and thermometer were taken each day. Mean solar chronometer 1362, Arnold and Dent furnished the time. The means used to ascertain the rate of the boat were as follows: By selecting two objects near the river immediately in line, and keeping them in line by walking toward the stern of the boat. The rate of the walk determined the rate of the boat.

June 26.—Started at 3.30 a. m. Two hours later reached a creek entering the Big Horn on its right bank, and a short distance further on we encountered the first rapids. Here a long delay was occasioned. At 1 p. m. the hills on the right bank closed in up to the water's edge, rising to a height of 150 feet, and in some places to 200 feet. The river valley on the left bank still low and thickly timbered with cottonwood, the hills on the right sparsely timbered with pine. Passed General Terry's camp, of June 25, at 9.30 a. m.; fires still smoldering. Tied up on the west side of a large island near the right bank at 9 p. m., after an estimated travel of 29 miles. The day was beautiful and clear, and the country passed through extremely rich and fertile. No game, however, was seen to-day. The Big Horn Mountains were in view about 75 miles to the south and towering to the clouds. As we ascended the river the channel became narrower and deeper and more easily navigated. The ridge of hills on the right bank extended for a distance of 8 miles. They are all washed and of a dark color; bare and destitute of any vegetation, excepting some small quantities of pine in the cañons and ravines. At 8 p. m. the clouds toward the west looked dark and threatening, but they soon cleared away. Maximum thermometer, 70°; minimum thermometer, 60°. Rapid water was encountered many times. Old Indian encampments were met with at nearly every bend of the river. Concerning the fertility of this region, Mr. Hall, an experienced western farmer, stated that he would rather have a farm on the Big Horn River than any other place he knew of. Mr. Hall was on board the Far West during the trip, and the further the boat ascended the more profuse was he in his praises of the country.

June 27.—Boat started at 3.30 a. m., but at 6 a. m. very little had been accomplished, owing to the shallowness of the channel and swiftness of the current. Two chutes were tried without success. An ascent of the third was, however, accomplished after considerable trouble and delay. A little further on the site of Fort C. F. Smith became visible about 35 miles distant. The second ridge of high hills on the right bank was reached at 9 a. m., rising to a greater height, but bearing the same appearance, except that this ridge is more broken, and two of its peaks rise to a height of fully 300 feet above the water's edge. Mountain-sheep, 15 in number, were seen on this ridge. Ridge about 3 miles long. The valley on the left bank bears the same rich, park-like appearance, the scenery splendid, and the river studded with large, beautiful, heavily-timbered islands.

A short distance above the southern extremity of the second ridge, the Little Big Horn River enters the Big Horn on its right bank. This point was reached at 10 a. m. The valley of the Little Big Horn is well timbered, and about 1¼ miles wide at this point. Near the mouth of the stream are many dangerous quagmires. A delay of two hours was experienced here while Captain Baker and his company proceeded to the summit of the ridge of bluffs on the south side of the Little Big Horn Valley for the purpose of reconnoitering. Started at 12.35 p. m., and continued up the Big Horn River; travel slow and very difficult, and the water very rapid.

About 2.30 p. m. the third ridge of hills on the right bank was reached, bearing the same appearance as the others and of the same height as the second ridge. Allowing the river to be about 3,300 feet above sea-level, then the respective altitudes of the three ridges would be 3,500, 3,600 and 3,600 feet. This is a rough estimate, but I think an approximate one. Above the upper ridge the river-channel becomes wider and much cut up with small islands. At 5.30 p. m. Sitting Bull's Rapids were reached, and one hour occupied in ascending them. Very soon afterward a series of rapids were encountered, extending in quick succession a distance of fully 3 miles, over which it was found impossible to force a passage. The boat accordingly dropped to the foot of these rapids and tied up on the right bank at 8.30 p. m., after an estimated travel of 21 miles. Total estimated distance from the mouth of the Big Horn River about 66 miles.

From Sitting Bull's Rapids the hills on the right bank wheel sharply away from the river, and from our present camping-place a good view on both sides is obtainable. Elk abound in this part of the country, their favorite resorts being the grassy and well-shaded islands along the river. During the day's travel, similar features to those of yesterday presented themselves. Maximum thermometer, 76°; minimum thermometer, 63°.

June 28.—The ascension of the rapids was again tried this morning but without success, and consequently the further navigation of the river was abandoned. The passage back to the mouth of the Little Big Horn was made in a very short time—the current forcing the boat right around so that the stern led the way on many occasions, and the downward run accomplished in a whirling, revolving manner, by reason of which the boat must have sustained considerable damage. Remained at the mouth of the Little Big Horn all day.

An Indian scout named "Curley" (known to have been with General Custer) arrived about noon with information of a battle, but there being no interpreter on board very little reliable information was obtained. He wore an exceedingly dejected countenance, but his appetite proved to be in first-rate order. Elk and deer killed here. Good fishing.

June 29.—Three scouts arrived during the day with the news of the disastrous battle of the Little Big Horn. The Far West was immediately barricaded, and preparations made to receive the wounded on board. At 10 p. m. the van of General Terry's command arrived. The main column with the wounded did not arrive until 1 a. m., June 30

I am, sir, very respectfully, your obedient servant,

JAMES E. WILSON,
Sergeant of Engineers.

Lieut. E. MAGUIRE,
   Corps of Engineers, U. S. A., Chief Engineer Department of Dakota.

Gall

HOUSE OF REPRESENTATIVES
EXECUTIVE DOCUMENT NO. 1,
PART 2
44th CONGRESS, 2nd SESSION

The Death of Charley Reynolds

REPORT OF LIEUT. GEN. P. H. SHERIDAN.

NOTE.—The reason this report is not printed in the usual place is because it was not received in time.

No. 1.

HEADQUARTERS MILITARY DIVISION OF THE MISSOURI,
New Orleans, La., November 25, 1876.

GENERAL: I have the honor to submit, for the information of the General of the Army, a brief report of the events occurring in the Military Division of the Missouri since my last annual report.

The division covers a large extent of territory, reaching from the eastern line of Illinois to Nevada, and from the line of the British possessions to the Gulf of Mexico, embracing within these limits three-fourths of all our Indian population.

For the convenience of administration, it is divided into five military departments, named as follows:

Department of Dakota, embracing the State of Minnesota and Territories of Montana and Dakota;

Department of the Platte, embracing the States of Iowa and Nebraska, the Territories of Wyoming and Utah, and so much of the Territory of Idaho as lies east of a line formed by the extension of the western boundary of Utah to the northeastern boundary of Idaho;

Department of the Missouri, embracing the States of Illinois, Missouri, Kansas, Colorado, the Indian Territory, and the Territory of New Mexico;

Department of Texas, embracing the State of Texas; and the

Department of the Gulf, embracing the States of Louisiana, Arkansas, Mississippi, Alabama, and those portions of Tennessee and Kentucky lying west of the Tennessee River;

Commanded, respectively, by Brig. Gens. Alfred H. Terry, George Crook, John Pope, Edward O. C. Ord, and Christopher C. Augur.

These departments are units of administration, each department commander being alone responsible for the administration and executive working of his department, and for economy in the expenditure of public money and the discipline of the troops.

The duties of the division commander are supervisory and corrective. He adjusts the wants of each department, and transfers the troops from one department to another to meet any new condition which may arise and to correct any abuses of administration and executive management.

The troops in the Department of Texas have been constantly on the alert to meet the depredations of Indians from Mexico and from Mexican cattle-thieves along the Rio Grande, but I am happy to state that both these causes of complaint have greatly diminished, and, with the increase of our cavalry regiments authorized by Congress last session, we hope to remove all anxiety by giving full protection. For the operation of the troops, I respectfully refer you to the report of Brig. Gen. E. O. C. Ord, commanding the department.

The Department of the Missouri has been entirely quiet since the campaign of 1874–'75, when the hostile Indians were dismounted and disarmed and the worst leaders sent to Florida. For a detailed account of the affairs of the department, I refer to the report of Brig. Gen. John Pope, accompanying.

In the Department of the Gulf no events have occurred other than those incident to the disturbed condition of affairs arising from the political contests of this year. The department has been somewhat changed, by taking from it the Gulf posts of Florida and adding to it Alabama and those portions of Kentucky and Tennessee which lie west of the Tennessee River.

In the Departments of Dakota and the Platte serious Indian troubles have existed, which have been attended by some disasters, much labor, and considerable expense, but there is a fair prospect of a complete settlement by the defeat and surrender of all the hostile Indians, with their arms, ponies, men, women, and children, before the winter is over.

On the 9th of November, 1875, United States Indian Inspector E. C. Watkins reported to the Commissioner of Indian Affairs the attitude of certain wild and hostile Indians in Dakota, Montana, and Wyoming, composed of a small band of thirty or forty lodges, under Sitting Bull, who had been an out-and-out anti-agency Indian, and the bands of other chiefs and headmen under Crazy Horse, an Ogallalla Sioux, belonging formerly to the Red Cloud agency, numbering about one hundred and twenty lodges. Mr. Watkins stated that these hostile bands had never accepted the reservation policy of the Government, were continually making war on the Arickarees, Mandans, Gros Ventres, Assinaboines, Blackfeet, Piegans, Crows, and other friendly tribes, as well as upon frontier settlers and emigrants, and recommended that the Government send troops to operate against them and reduce them to subjection. The report of Inspecter Watkins, with the views of the Commissioner of Indian Affairs and the recommendation of the honorable Secretary of the Interior, that these Indians be informed that they must remove to a reservation before the 31st of January, 1876, and that, in the event of their refusal to come in by the time specified, they would be turned over to the War Department for punishment, were referred to me by the General of the Army, December 13, 1875.

As Generals Terry and Crook command the departments in which these Indians were located, I submitted the subject to them, and General Terry was of the opinion that Sitting Bull's band was encamped near the mouth of the Little Missouri; that it could be reached by a quick movement, which might be decisive at that season of the year, and that he had sufficient troops to make such a movement. General Crook was of the opinion that operations could be undertaken in his department against the hostiles whenever, in the judgment of the Indian Bureau, such action became necessary.

As the commands of these two officers embraced all the Indians against whom military action was contemplated, and as they felt competent and able to move, I requested that, should operations be determined upon, directions to that effect be communicated as speedily as possible, so that the enemy might be taken at the greatest disadvantage; in other words, in midwinter, when they could not well get out of the way of the troops.

On February 4, 1876, I again stated, by indorsement on a letter of the Commissioner of Indian Affairs, that if it was intended to operate against these Indians, I could safely say that every possibility of success would vanish unless directions were immediately given; saying further that I fully comprehended the difficulties of the country, and that unless they were caught before early spring they could not be caught at all.

On February 7, 1876, authority was received, by indorsement of the General of the Army on letter of the honorable Secretary of the Interior, to commence operations against the hostile Sioux. They were, at that time, Sitting Bull's band, of 30 or 40 lodges, and not exceeding 70 warriors, and Crazy Horse's band, not exceeding 120 lodges, and numbering probably 200 warriors. Meantime General Terry had learned that

72

Sitting Bull's band was on the Dry Fork of the Missouri, some 200 miles farther west, instead of the Little Missouri.

On the 8th of February, the letter of the honorable Secretary of the Interior was referred to General Terry, with directions to take such steps with the forces under his command as would carry out the wishes of the Interior Department and the orders of the General of the Army. No specific directions could be given, as no one knew exactly, and no one could have known where these Indians were, as they might be here to-day and somewhere else to-morrow.

General Terry was also informed that General Crook would operate from the south in the direction of the headwaters of Powder River, Pumpkin Buttes, Tongue River, Rosebud and Big Horn Rivers, where Crazy Horse and his allies frequented, and that departmental lines would be disregarded by the troops until the object requested by the Secretary of the Interior was attained. General Terry was further informed that the operations of himself and General Crook would be made without concert, as the Indian villages are movable and no objective point could be fixed upon, but that, if they should come to any understanding about concerted movements, there would be no objection at division headquarters.

On the same date, February 8, 1876, a copy of the same paper was referred to General Crook, with similar general instructions, informing him also that the operations conducted by General Terry would be communicated to him for his information whenever received at division headquarters.

During the time this correspondence was taking place, from December 12, 1875, to February 4, 1876, efforts were being made by the Interior Department to have these hostile Indians come in and settle down on reservations. Communications had been sent them from various agencies, informing them of the wishes and intentions of the Government, and every inducement held out to them to become peaceable and obedient. The only end gained, however, by all these communications was that of informing the hostiles that troops were to be sent out to compel them to come in.

Immediately on receipt of his instructions, General Crook commenced concentrating the available cavalry of his command at Fort Fetterman, consisting of ten companies, numbering about 50 or 60 men to a company, and this force, with the addition of two companies of infantry, formed an expedition, which moved out from Fort Fetterman on March 1 against the hostiles, who were believed to be located on the headwaters of Powder River, Tongue River, or the Rosebud. On the 17th of March the main portion of the expedition, under the immediate command of Col. J. J. Reynolds, struck an Indian village under Crazy Horse on Powder River, destroying all the lodges, 105 in number, and the ammunition and stores it contained, and killing some of the Indians as well as capturing a large herd of horses.

The success of this attack was to some extent compromised, however, by afterward allowing the Indians to recover their horses by a surprise, on the morning after the engagement. The command had suffered so much from the severity of the weather (the mercury having congealed in the thermometer on several occasions) that it had to return to Fort Fetterman without inflicting any further blow than the burning of one hundred and five lodges or tepees.

The failure to retain the captured horses greatly modified the success of the expedition, and the troops had to be redistributed to their various winter-stations to protect them from the extreme cold.

About the same time that General Crook was making his preparations to move, as just described, General Terry also projected an expedition against Sitting Bull's band, which was then believed, from information he had received, was located on the Little Missouri River, but afterward found to be on the Dry Fork of the Missouri, some two hundred miles farther west. Before, however, the Seventh Cavalry could be concentrated at Fort Abraham Lincoln the season became so inclement—a great number of men being badly frost-bitten in reaching the fort—and the snow so deep that it was thought advisable to abandon the expedition until later in the season. The impracticability of operations against these Indians from Fort Lincoln, on the Missouri River, during the existence of the wild storms of Dakota in the early spring, became pretty well settled by the result already experienced, and satisfied me that the recommendation for the establishment of the two military posts in what is known as the Yellowstone country, made in my last annual report and in my report of 1874, in anticipation of hostilities with the Sioux, was the only view to take of this subject which promised undoubted success, and I again renewed my solicitations for the establishment of the posts at the mouth of Tongue River and the Big Horn. This advice, if adopted, would have given us abundant supplies at convenient points, to operate in the very heart of the country from whence all our troubles came.

For some years it had been apparent to me that the marauding bands who lived in this country, and who formed a nucleus for all the dissatisfied and unmanageable Indians at the Missouri River, Red Cloud and Spotted Tail agencies, would have to be subjugated and made to feel the power of the Government; and as a means to this end I recommended the occupation of the country in which these hostiles roamed by two permanent and large military posts. Had my advice been taken, there would have been no war. These posts would not only have been the means of preventing the assembling of Indians in large bodies in that great buffalo region, but they would have given us depots of supplies and shelter for troops that could, on account of the short distances from these supplies, operate at any season of the year. In addition to these advantages, the troops would have become familiar with the haunts of the Indians, learned the country thoroughly, and would not have been obliged, as they afterward were, to operate blindly in an almost totally unknown region, comprising an area of almost ninety thousand square miles.

Early in the spring, as no change had then been made in the orders, Generals Terry and Crook made preparations to resume the operations, General Crook concentrating at Fort Fetterman fifteen companies of cavalry and five companies of infantry; and on May 29 he marched from that point for Goose Creek, and established his supply-camp there on the 8th of June.

From this camp he moved out toward the headwaters of the Rosebud, on the morning of the 13th of June, and on the 17th his scouts discovered the Indians in large numbers about forty miles north of Goose Creek. A few minutes after this information was received, the command was attacked with considerable desperation. The Indians displayed strong force at all points, and contested the ground with a tenacity which proved they were fighting for time to get their village away. The command finally drove them off, with a loss of 13 Indians killed, left on the field; and on our side, of 9 men killed, one officer and 23 men wounded. The victory was barren of results, however, as, on account of his wounded and a lack of rations for his troops, General Crook was unable to pursue the enemy. The next day he returned to his supply-camp on Goose Creek and awaited re-enforcements and supplies, considering himself too weak to make any movement until additional troops reached him.

It now became apparent that he had not only Crazy Horse and his small band to contend against, but that the hostile force had been augmented by large numbers of the young warriors from the agencies along the Missouri River and the Red Cloud and Spotted Tail agencies in Nebraska, and that the Indian agents at these agencies had concealed the fact of the departure of these warriors; and that, in most cases, they continued to issue rations as though they were present. I had feared such a movement from the agencies, and early in May had asked that power should be given to the military to exercise supervisory control over the agencies and keep in all who were then there and all out who were then out and hostile, but no attention was paid to this representation.

General Terry concentrated at Fort Lincoln the Seventh Cavalry, three Gatling guns, and six companies of infantry, and on the 17th of May marched from that post for the mouth of the Powder River, where he arrived and established his supply-camp on the 7th of June. From this point, Major Marcus A. Reno, Seventh Cavalry, with six companies of that regiment, scouted up the Powder River to its forks, across the country to the Rosebud, and down the Rosebud to its mouth. In the mean time, General Terry moved with his main forces up the south bank of the Yellowstone and formed a junction with Col. John Gibbon's command, consisting of four companies Second Cavalry and six companies of the Seventh Infantry, that had marched eastward along the north bank of the Yellowstone from Fort Ellis, in Montana, to the mouth of the Rosebud.

During Major Reno's scout a large Indian trail was discovered leading up the Rosebud, but as his orders did not contemplate an attack with his small force, it was only followed a sufficient distance to enable him to definitely locate the Indians in the vicinity of the Little Big Horn River. He then returned to the mouth of the Rosebud.

General Terry, now pretty well informed of the locality of the Indians, directed Lieut. Col. George A. Custer to move with the Seventh Cavalry up the Rosebud until he struck the trail discovered by Major Reno, with instructions that he should not follow it directly to the Little Big Horn, but that he should send scouts over it and keep his main force farther south, to prevent the Indians from slipping in between himself and the mountains. He was also to examine the headwaters of Tulloch's Creek as he passed it, and send word to General Terry of what he found there.

Custer moved on the 22d of June, following the trail as soon as he struck it, and after marching about 125 miles from the place of starting, attacked the Indians in their village on the west bank of the Little Big Horn, and about 30 miles above its mouth, between 10 and 12 o'clock on the morning of the 25th of June. In the mean time General Terry moved up the Yellowstone River with Colonel Gibbon's column, arriving at the mouth of the Little Big Horn on June 26.

The attack of General Custer proved disastrous, resulting in the destruction of himself, twelve officers, and five companies of the Seventh Cavalry, and in a heavy loss in killed and wounded to the detachment commanded by Major Reno, whose command of three companies was saved from annihilation by the timely arrival of Major Benteen with four companies, and by intrenching its position on an eminence on the east bank of the river. His position at this point was soon completely enveloped by the Indians, who kept up a constant fire until the approach of General Terry with Gibbon's column, on the evening of June 26.

As much has been said in regard to the misfortune that occurred to General Custer and the portion of his regiment under his immediate command in this action, I wish to express the conviction I have arrived at concerning it. From all the information that has reached me, I am led to believe that the Indians were not aware of the proximity of Custer until he had arrived within about eight or nine miles of their village, and that then their scouts who carried the intelligence back to the valley were so closely followed up by Custer that he arrived on the summit of the divide overlooking the upper portion of the village almost as soon as the scouts reached it. As soon as the news was given, the Indians began to strike their lodges and get their women and children out of the way, a movement they always make under such circumstances. Custer, seeing this, believed the village would escape him if he awaited the arrival of the four companies of his regiment still some miles in his rear. Only about 75 or 100 lodges or tepees could be seen from the summit or divide, and this probably deceived him as to the extent of the village. He therefore directed Major Reno with three companies to cross the river and charge the village, while he with the remaining five companies would gallop down the east bank of the river, behind the bluff, and cut off the retreat of the Indians. Reno crossed and attacked gallantly with his three companies, about 110 men, but the warriors, leaving the women to strike the lodges, fell on Reno's handful of men and drove them back to and over the river with severe loss. About this time Custer reached a point about 3½ or 4 miles down the river, but instead of finding a village of 75 or 100 lodges, he found one of perhaps from 1,500 to 2,000, and swarming with warriors, who brought him to a halt. This, I think, was the first intimation the Indians had of Custer's approach to cut them off, for they at once left Reno and concentrated to meet the new danger. The point where Custer reached the river, on the opposite side of which was the village, was broken into choppy ravines, and the Indians crossing from Reno got between the two commands, and as Custer could not return, he fell back over the broken ground with his tired men and tired horses, (they had ridden about seventy miles with but few halts,) and became, I am afraid, an easy prey to the enemy. Their wild savage yells, overwhelming numbers, and frightening war paraphernalia made it as much as each trooper could do to take care of his horse, thus endangering his own safety and efficiency. If Custer could have reached any position susceptible of defense, he could have defended himself, but none offered itself in the choppy and broken ravines over which he had to pass, and he and his command were lost without leaving any one to tell the tale. As soon as Custer and his gallant officers and men were exterminated, and the scenes of mutilation by the squaws commenced, the warriors returned to renew the attack upon Reno, but he had been joined by Captain Benteen and the four companies of the regiment that were behind when the original attack took place, and the best use had been made of the respite given by the attack on Custer to entrench their position. Reno's command was thus enabled to repulse every attack made by the Indians, until relieved by General Terry on the morning of the 27th, as before mentioned.

Had the Seventh Cavalry been kept together, it is my belief it would have been able to handle the Indians on the Little Big Horn, and under any circumstances it could have at least defended itself; but, separated as it was into three distinct detachments, the Indians had largely the advantage, in addition to their overwhelming numbers. If Custer had not come upon the village so suddenly, the warriors would have gone to meet him, in order to give time to the women and children to get out of the way, as they did with Crook only a few days before, and there would have been, as with Crook, what might be designated a rear-guard fight, a fight to get their valuables out of the way, or, in other words, to cover the escape of their women, children, and lodges.

After the disaster to poor Custer, General Terry withdrew his command to the mouth of the Big Horn, there to refit and await re-enforcements. Additional troops were at once put in motion for General Terry's command, as had already been done for General Crook's, but, as these additional troops had to be collected from all the various stations on the frontier, some of them very remote from railroads, considerable time was consumed before their arrival. During this period the bands which had broken off from the main body of hostiles and the young men at the agencies continued their old and well-known methods of warfare—stealing horses on the frontier and killing small parties of citizens; while the constant communications by the hostiles with the Indians at the agencies made it evident that supplies of food and ammunition were being received. To prevent this, I had deemed it necessary that the military should control the agencies, and, as before mentioned, on the 29th of May requested that the Interior Department would so co-operate with the military as to enable us to carry out the policy of arresting, disarming, and dismounting such of the hostiles as made their appearance at the agencies. On July 18 I renewed this request, and on the 22d the honorable Secretary of the Interior authorized the military to assume control of all the agencies in the Sioux country, but it was too late.

I at once directed the commanding officers at Camps Robinson and Sheridan to take possession at Red Cloud and Spotted Tail agencies, and sent Colonel Mackenzie to Red Cloud with a sufficient force to arrest any hostiles who might come in, and to count and enroll the Indians. A careful count was made by September 1, and it was found that those at Red Cloud numbered 4,760, nearly one-half less than had been reported by the agent. The count at Spotted Tail's agency was less than 5,000, whereas nearly double that number was alleged to be present at their agency, and were issued to.

Troops were also sent to occupy the Missouri River agencies to accomplish the same purposes, and the number of Indians found present was less from one-half to one-third than was reported present and issued to by the agents. It was then easy to see where the small bands, originally out and on whom war was made, got their strength from, as well as their supplies.

Congress having at last passed the bill, late in the session, July 22, authorizing the construction of two posts in the Yellowstone country, preparations were made to build them at once and all the material was prepared as rapidly as possible, but the season had now become so far advanced that it was found impracticable to get this material up the Yellowstone River on account of low water, and the building of them was consequently deferred until next spring, when the work will be speedily done, as the material is now at the mouth of the Yellowstone ready for shipment; but as soon as I found the post could not be built this year, I directed a cantonment to be formed at the mouth of the Tongue River, the place selected for one of the two posts, and a strong garrison to be detailed under the command of Colonel Miles, Fifth Infantry, to occupy it.

On August 3 General Crook had received all the re-enforcements that could be sent him, and all that he wanted, and having received information that the hostiles had moved eastwardly from the Big Horn Mountains, and crossed the Fort C. F. Smith road on the 26th of July, his column moved out on the 5th of August down Tongue River in pursuit. He followed the trail across Powder River and some distance to the east of it, when it separated and became indistinct. He then marched his command southward in the direction of the Black Hills, the command of Captain Mills, Third Cavalry, capturing a village of 35 lodges on the morning of September 17, killing a number of Indians and capturing a few women and children. For the details of this action I respectfully refer to the report of General Crook.

As soon as I learned from General Crook of his contemplated movement to the Black Hills, and the great need of food and clothing for his command, supplies were pushed out from the Red Cloud agency and Fort Laramie to meet him and to reach Custer City before his arrival there.

General Terry, finding that most of his troops would be engaged in the protecting and forwarding of supplies, and in hutting for the winter, and that would be consuming the supplies sent out, broke up his command, sending Colonel Gibbon back to Montana before the extreme cold weather began, and returned to Fort Lincoln with the Seventh Cavalry. From Fort Lincoln he proceeded down the Missouri River with the Seventh to the Standing Rock and Cheyenne River agencies, dismounting and disarming the Indians at these two points—a policy that had been resolved upon as offering unquestionably a final settlement of all further difficulties with the Sioux.

While this was going on, the hostiles attacked the trains carrying supplies to the Tongue River cantonment, and Col. Nelson A. Miles, Fifth Infantry, marched out his command, and, after an engagement on the 21st of October and a successful pursuit, over 400 lodges of the Missouri River Indians surrendered to him, giving hostages for the delivery of men, women, children, ponies, arms, and ammunition at the Cheyenne River agency on the 2d of December; Sitting Bull, with his band of about 30 lodges, escaping to the north, and, no doubt, to the British possessions.

General Crook, after refitting at Custer City, detailed Colonel Merritt, Fifth Cavalry, to make a scout down to the forks of Cheyenne River, and thence in to the Red Cloud agency, where it had been resolved to disarm and dismount the Indians; but before Colonel Merritt's arrival, it was found necessary to direct Colonel Mackenzie, Fourth Cavalry, to perform this duty, and it was successfully accomplished without firing a shot.

With the view of continuing operations during the winter, I had directed the establishment of a cantonment at old Fort Reno, and had ordered that a considerable amount of supplies of forage and rations be sent there, and as soon as the Indians at the Red Cloud agency were dismounted and disarmed, General Crook re-organized a new column to operate from Reno. This column is now in the field, under Colonel Mackenzie, and accompanied by General Crook, and I anticipate the very best results from it.

The surrender of the Indians from the Missouri River agencies to Colonel Miles on the 27th of October, numbering, in men, women, and children at least 2,000, and the escape of Sitting Bull with his small band to the north, leaves now out and hostile only the Northern Cheyennes and the band of Crazy Horse and his allies from the Red Cloud agency, and it is against these Indians that General Crook is now operating, and when these are killed, captured, or surrendered, the Sioux war will be at an end, and I think all future trouble with them, as it is intended to put most of them on foot, and a Sioux on foot is a Sioux warrior no longer.

If the posts on the Yellowstone had been established according to my recommendation, there would have been no war. If the Indian Bureau had turned over to the military the control of the agencies before the troops took the field, as I had represented, it would not have assumed the magnitude that it did. But it seems to have required some disaster like that which happened to Custer before good judgment or common sense could be exercised on this subject.

The operations against these Indians during the summer were the same as summer campaigns against them generally are, and not much success can attend them other than preventing the Indians from accumulating winter-supplies, and the demoralizing effects that result to the men, women, and children from being constantly harassed, and when winter comes they are but ill-prepared to pass over it safely.

The undersigned has no good evidence to show that Sitting Bull was the leader of the hostile Indians during the summer; on the contrary, it is more than probable he was in that respect quite insignificant, as he has never had but a few followers, and is old, and very much crippled by disease. His reputation was accidental, and I am inclined to believe he is totally unconscious of it, as he never did anything to acquire it. Sitting Bull, as I have said further back in this report, had only 30 or 40 lodges of the Uncpapa band of Sioux, not exceeding 70 warriors. He was an anti-agency Indian—that is, he never came in to any of the agencies, or to any of the councils of his tribe whose agency is at Standing Rock, on the Missouri River; and some of his followers, strange to say, were so wild as to have never seen a white man's face until the past summer. They were hostile out and out, and always had been. When the Interior Department requested the military to commence operations against the hostiles, (which embraced Crazy Horse and his allies and Sitting Bull and his small band,) the request was to "make war on Sitting Bull and other hostile Indians." And the name of Sitting Bull and the word "hostile" became synonymous, and whenever the name "Sitting Bull" was read it was understood by me to mean hostile Indians; and by this confusion, and by the aid of newspaper-correspondents, Sitting Bull in person became a great leader, when it is known he has never been more than an insignificant warrior, with a few thieving followers. I believe Crazy Horse's band and the Northern Cheyennes have done nearly all the fighting, especially the Northern Cheyennes, and I doubt if there was any special or distinguished leader.

The troops did as well as could be done during the summer, and certainly as well as I expected; for long experience has taught me how difficult it is to catch an Indian in the summer season. They were, however, harassed, and prevented from accumulating supplies for the winter, and no doubt the balance will be caught when the cold weather comes on.

I recommend that the whole Sioux Nation be established on the Missouri River, between Standing Rock and Fort Randall. They can be cheaply fed there, and can be sufficiently isolated to be controlled. To take so many wild Indians to the Indian Territory would be a difficult undertaking at this time, and would, in my opinion, be attended with the worst results to those now there, as well as to the Sioux. They should go gradually, from time to time, and when the Indians there are ready to receive them.

I have been obliged to delay this report to await the report of General Terry, which is not yet in, until I could delay no longer on account of the near approach of the day when Congress meets; and now, when

I do submit it, I am obliged to write it here, and have not been able to make it as full as it should be on account of the absence of data now in my office at Chicago.

Very respectfully, your obedient servant,

P. H. SHERIDAN.
Lieutenant-General, Commanding.

Brig. Gen. E. D. TOWNSEND,
Adjutant-General of the Army, Washington, D. C.

Rain-in-the-Face

No. 3.—REPORT OF GENERAL TERRY.

HEADQUARTERS, DEPARTMENT OF DAKOTA,
Saint Paul, Minn., November 21, 1876.

SIR: In obedience to the instructions which I have received from the Lieutenant-General commanding, I have the honor to submit the following report of the military operations which have taken place in this department during the past year.

This report will necessarily be imperfect, for, with the exception of a very few days, I have been personally in the field from the 9th of May until now. During my absence from Saint Paul many changes were made in the distribution of the troops, and many orders were necessarily issued from these headquarters, of which I am as yet imperfectly informed. It is, therefore, impossible for me to make a full and detailed report in time to meet the requirements of the orders which I have received.

My last annual report was made on the 12th day of November, 1875. At that time the force in the department consisted of the following troops:

Four companies of the Second Cavalry.

Nine companies of the Seventh Cavalry.

The First Regiment of Infantry.

The Sixth Regiment of Infantry.

The Seventh Regiment of Infantry.

The Seventeenth Regiment of Infantry.

The Twentieth Regiment of Infantry.

The force was at that date distributed as follows:

At Fort Snelling, Minn., the regimental headquarters, and Companies C and H of the Twentieth Infantry.

At Fort Ripley, Minn., Companies B and G of the Twentieth Infantry.

At Fort Pembina, Dak., Companies D, F, and I of the Twentieth Infantry.

At Fort Totten, Dak., Companies E and L of the Seventh Cavalry, and Companies E and K of the Twentieth Infantry.

At Fort Seward, Dak., Company A of the Twentieth Infantry.

At Fort Abercrombie, Dak., the regimental headquarters, and Companies A and F of the Seventeenth Infantry.

At Fort Wadsworth, Dak., Companies B and C of the Seventeenth Infantry.

At Fort Shaw, Mont., the regimental headquarters, and Companies A, B, D, G, I, and K of the Seventh Infantry.

At Fort Ellis, Mont., Companies F, G, H, and L of the Second Cavalry, and Company C of the Seventh Infantry.

At Fort Benton, Mont., Company F of the Seventh Infantry.

At Camp Baker, Mont., Companies E and H of the Seventh Infantry.

At Fort Buford, Dak., the regimental headquarters, and Companies C, D, E, F, and G of the Sixth Infantry.

At Fort Abraham Lincoln, Dak., the regimental headquarters, and Companies A, C, D, F, and I of the Seventh Cavalry, Company B of the Sixth Infantry, and Company G of the Seventeenth Infantry.

At Fort Rice, Dak., Companies H and M of the Seventh Cavalry, and Company D of the Seventeenth Infantry.

At Fort Stevenson, Dak., Companies H and K of the Sixth Infantry.

At Camp Hancock, Dak., Company H of the Seventeenth Infantry.

At Standing Rock, Dak., Companies A and I of the Sixth Infantry, and Company E of the Seventeenth Infantry.

At Fort Randall, Dak., the regimental headquarters, and Companies C, D, G, I, and K of the First Infantry.

At Fort Sully, Dak., Companies B, E, F, and H of the First Infantry.

At Cheyenne Agency, Dak., Companies I and K of the Seventeenth Infantry.

At Lower Brulé Agency, Dak., Company A of the First Infantry.

This force was increased in April, 1876, by three companies (B, G, and K) of the Seventh Cavalry, by transfer from the Department of the Gulf; in July, 1876, by six companies (E, F, G, H, I, and K) of the Twenty-second Infantry, from the Military Division of the Atlantic; in July and August, 1876, by the Fifth Regiment of Infantry, from the Department of the Missouri; and in August and September, 1876, by the Eleventh Regiment of Infantry, from the Department of Texas.

The following is the present distribution of the troops for winter stations:

At Fort Snelling, Minn., the regimental headquarters, and Company C of the Twentieth Infantry.

At Fort Ripley, Minn., Companies B and G of the Twentieth Infantry.

At Fort Abercrombie, Dak., Company F of the Seventh Cavalry and Company A of the Seventeenth Infantry.

At Fort Sisseton, (formerly Fort Wadsworth, Dak.,) Companies B and C of the Seventeenth Infantry

At Fort Totten, Dak., Company C of the Seventh Cavalry and Company K of the Twentieth Infantry.

At Fort Pembina, Dak., Companies D and F of the Twentieth Infantry.

At Fort Seward, Dak., Company A of the Twentieth Infantry.

At Fort Buford, Dak., the regimental headquarters, and Companies C, D, E, F, G, and I of the Sixth Infantry.

At Fort Abraham Lincoln, Dak., the regimental headquarters, and Companies B, E, G, I, K, and L of the Seventh Cavalry; Company B of the Sixth Infantry, and Companies D and G of the Seventeenth Infantry.

At Fort Rice, Dak., Companies A, D. H, and M of the Seventh Cavalry.

At Fort Stevenson, Dak., Companies H and K of the Sixth Infantry.

At Standing Rock Agency, Dak., Companies G and K of the First Infantry; Company A of the Sixth Infantry; Companies A, B, and H of the Eleventh Infantry; regimental headquarters, and Companies E and F of the Seventeenth Infantry, and Company H of the Twentieth Infantry.

At Camp Hancock, Dak., Company H of the Seventeenth Infantry.

At Fort Randall, Dak., the regimental headquarters, and Companies C, E, and I of the First Infantry.

At Fort Sully, Dak., Companies B, D, F, and H of the First Infantry.

At Lower Brulé Agency, Dak., Company A of the First Infantry; and Companies E and I of the Twentieth Infantry.

At Cheyenne Agency, Dak., the regimental headquarters, and Companies C, D, E, F, G, I, and K of the Eleventh Infantry, and Companies I and K of the Seventeenth Infantry.

At Fort Shaw, Mont., the regimental headquarters, and Companies A, B, G, H, I, and K of the Seventh Infantry.

At Fort Ellis, Mont., Companies F, G, H, and L of the Second Cavalry, and Company C of the Seventh Infantry.

At Fort Benton, Mont., Company F of the Seventh Infantry.

At Camp Baker, Mont., Companies D and E of the Seventh Infantry.

At the cantonment on Tongue River, Mont., the Fifth Regiment of Infantry, and Companies E, G, H, I, and K of the Twenty-second Infantry.

The changes of station from which this distribution resulted are shown by the following-described movements of troops, irrespective of the movements of the force engaged in the campaign against the hostile Sioux:

In November, 1875, Companies D and H of the Seventh Infantry, stationed respectively at Fort Shaw and Camp Baker, Mont., interchanged stations.

In April, 1876, Companies D and G of the Twentieth Infantry changed stations respectively from Forts Pembina and Ripley to Fort Abraham Lincoln, and are now under orders to return each to its former station.

In April, 1876, Companies D and E of the First Infantry stationed respectively at Forts Randall and Sully, interchanged stations.

In May, 1876, Company H, Seventeenth Infantry, changed station from Camp Hancock to Fort Abraham Lincoln, and is now under orders to return to Camp Hancock.

In May, 1876, Company B of the First Infantry changed station from Fort Sully to Fort Rice, and on the 4th instant was ordered to be returned to Fort Sully.

In May, 1876, Company C of the First Infantry changed station from Fort Randall to Fort Sully, and on the 4th instant was ordered to be returned to Fort Randall.

In July, 1876, Company H, Twentieth Infantry, changed station from Fort Snelling to Standing Rock.

In August, 1876, Companies G and K of the First Infantry, stationed at Fort Randall, and Company F of the Seventeenth Infantry, stationed at Fort Abercrombie, changed station to Standing Rock.

In August, 1876, Company E of the Twentieth Infantry changed station from Fort Totten to Fort Abercrombie.

In August, 1876, Company A, Seventeenth Infantry, changed station from Fort Abercrombie to Fort Abraham Lincoln, and is now under orders to return to Fort Abercrombie.

In August, 1876, the regimental headquarters of the Seventeenth Infantry were transferred from Fort Abercrombie to Standing Rock.

In September, 1876, Company E of the Twentieth Infantry changed station from Fort Abercrombie to Lower Brulé Agency.

In September, 1876, Company I of the Twentieth Infantry changed station from Fort Pembina to Lower Brulé Agency.

Company D of the Seventeenth Infantry is now under orders to change station from Fort Rice to Fort Abraham Lincoln.

During August and September, 1876, the ten companies of the Eleventh Regiment of Infantry arrived by detachments at Yankton, Dak., and proceeded to take station as follows: Companies A, B, and H at Standing Rock Agency; Companies C, D, E, F, G, I, and K at Cheyenne Agency.

Forts Shaw, Ellis, Benton, and Camp Baker constitute the district of Montana, with headquarters at Fort Shaw.

Forts Abraham Lincoln, Rice, and Stevenson, Camp Hancock, and Standing Rock constitute the middle district, with headquarters at Fort Abraham Lincoln.

Forts Randall and Sully and Lower Brulé and Cheyenne agencies constitute the southern district, with headquarters at Cheyenne agency.

Forts Snelling, Ripley, Abercrombie, Sisseton, Totten, Pembina, and Buford, and the cantonment on Tongue River, Montana, are independent posts, reporting directly to department headquarters.

The following tables show the strength of the several garrisons at the date of the last returns received at these headquarters. For the cantonment, representing the Fifth Regiment of Infantry and the six companies of the Twenty-second infantry, and for two companies of the Seventh Infantry (C and G) not borne on post returns, only the approximate strength is given, as no recent returns have been received:

District of Montana.

Posts.	Officers.	Enlisted men.
Fort Shaw	24	287
Fort Ellis	17	278
Fort Benton	3	43
Camp Baker	6	82
Total	50	690

Middle District.

Posts.	Officers.	Enlisted men.	Indian scouts.
Fort Abraham Lincoln	40	852	40
Fort Rice	8	87	4
Fort Stevenson	6	92	5
Fort Standing Rock	30	423	7
Total	84	1,454	56

Southern District.

Posts.	Officers.	Enlisted men.	Indian scouts.
Fort Randall	12	127	
Recruits First Infantry		39	
Fort Sully	13	196	3
Cheyenne agency	26	474	6
Lower Brulé agency	9	114	
Total	60	950	9

Independent posts.

Posts.	Officers.	Enlisted men.	Indian scouts.
Fort Snelling	9	63	
Fort Ripley	4	33	
Fort Abercrombie, (detachment accounted for at Fort Seward)			
Fort Sisseton	3	46	6
Fort Totten	3	40	1
Fort Pembina	4	39	
Fort Seward	3	33	
Fort Buford	23	295	6
Cantonment, Tongue River, Montana	55	770	75
Six companies Seventh Cavalry not borne on post returns	18	611	
Two companies Seventeenth Infantry not borne on post returns	6	80	
Total	128	2,010	88

Grand.

Districts, independent posts, &c.	Officers.	Enlisted men.	Indian scouts.
District of Montana	50	690	....
Middle district	84	1,454	56
Southern district	60	950	9
Independent posts, &c	128	2,010	88
Total	322	5,104	153

On the 19th of February I was informed, by a dispatch of that date from Maj. James S. Brisbin, Second Cavalry, commanding the post of Fort Ellis, that he had on the previous day received an appeal for help from a party who had established themselves for the purpose of trade, trapping, and mining at a point near the mouth of the Big Horn, known as Fort Pease. It was stated that fourteen men were holding a stockade against the Indians, who had surrounded them. Major Brisbin proposed to go to their relief. The proposal of Major Brisbin was approved by me, and he was instructed by telegraph to proceed at once to carry it into effect. He marched from Fort Ellis on the 21st of February with four companies of his regiment, and arrived at Fort Pease and relieved the occupants on the 4th of March. It was found that the original party had consisted of forty-six men, of whom six had been killed, and eight wounded, thirteen had escaped by night, and nineteen were found in the stockade and were brought away. No Indians were seen by the troops, but war-lodges were found representing a force of about sixty Sioux who had fled southward.

On the 10th of February last I received from the Lieutenant-General commanding orders to commence operations against the hostile Sioux. At the same time I was informed that similar instructions had been given to Brigadier-General Crook, then as now commanding the Department of the Platte, who would operate from Fort Laramie in the direction of the head-waters of Powder River, Pumpkin Butte, and the Big Horn. Preparations for the movement were immediately commenced, and it was supposed that the troops could be made ready to march early in April. The collection of troops and supplies for the expedition, however, was dependent on the opening of the Northern Pacific Railroad.

That road was opened earlier than is usual in the spring, but severe snow-storms again closed it. Owing to this fact, and to the necessity of waiting for the arrival of troops ordered from the Department of the Gulf to this Department, it was not until the middle of May that all preparations were completed.

The force originally intended for the field consisted of the nine companies of the Seventh Cavalry then in this Department. Companies C and G of the Seventeenth Infantry, Company B of the Sixth Infantry, a battery of Gatling guns; manned by detachments from the Twentieth Infantry, and forty Indian scouts. Subsequently it was increased by the three remaining companies of the Seventh Cavalry, which, on my application, were ordered from the Department of the Gulf to their regiment, in order that they might accompany it into the field.

Lieut.-Col. G. A. Custer, of the Seventh Cavalry, was at first assigned to the command of this force; but under subsequent instructions I assumed the command in person, Lieutenant-Colonel Custer being assigned to the command of his regiment.

On the 27th of February I directed Col. John Gibbon, of the Seventh Infantry, commanding the district of Montana, to prepare for the field all the troops which could be spared from the garrisons in his district, and to be ready to march from Fort Ellis down the valley of the Yellowstone.

These orders were crossed on their way to Montana by a dispatch from Colonel Gibbon, in which he suggested the same movement.

On the 25th of February a telegram was sent to Colonel Gibbon in which he was directed not only to make his preparations, but to move as soon as he should be able. The force available for the movement consisted of four companies of the Second Cavalry and six companies of the Seventh Infantry. It was collected as rapidly as possible, and it started from Fort Ellis on the 3d of April. For the details of Colonel Gibbon's march until he made a junction with the column under my own command, I refer to his report, which is forwarded herewith. It was not intended that this column should seek for and attack the hostile

Sioux independently, unless, indeed, some favorable opportunity should present itself. Its duty was to guard the left bank of the Yellowstone, and, if possible, prevent the Indians from crossing it in case that they should attempt to do so, either in pursuance of their habit of following the herds of buffalo to the north during the summer, or in case they should seek to avoid the troops coming from the south and the east.

This duty was admirably performed. Colonel Gibbon advanced to the mouth of the Rosebud, and from that point kept detachments moving up and down the Yellowstone.

It is of course impossible to say whether the Indians would or would not have crossed the latter stream had not Colonel Gibbon's force occupied its left bank, but my own opinion is that they would have done so.

To supply the forces in the field, subsistence and forage were sent up the Yellowstone, by steamer, to Stanley's stockade, near the mouth of Glendive Creek. With them was sent a guard of three companies of the Sixth Infantry, under command of Major O. H. Moore, of that regiment. The departure of the boats from Fort Lincoln was so timed as to bring them to their destination a short time in advance of the presumed arrival of the troops at the same point.

No train of pack-mules has ever been organized in this department, and the marching columns were necessarily dependent on wagons for the transport of their supplies. There were, however, carried in wagons about 250 pack-saddles to be placed on the mules of the train in an emergency

I arrived personally at Fort Lincoln on the 10th of May. Soon after my arrival I received information from more than one independent source which led me to believe that the main body of the hostile Sioux was on the Little Missouri River, and between that stream and the Yellowstone. I therefore sent to Fort Ellis a telegraphic dispatch, to be forwarded to Colonel Gibbon, directing him to move down the Yellowstone to "Stanley's stockade," to cross the river, and move out on "Stanley's trail" to meet the column from Lincoln. This column marched on the morning of May 17. For some days its progress was slow, for the wagons were heavily laden and recent rains had made the ground extremely soft.

The Little Missouri was reached on May 29. Here a halt was made for a day in order that the valley of the river might be reconnoitered. This was done by Lieutenant-Colonel Custer with a portion of his regiment, but no indications of the recent presence of Indians were discovered. The march was resumed on the 31st; but on the 1st and 2d of June a heavy snow-storm detained the column on the edge of the bad lands which border the left banks of the Little Missouri. On the 3d Beaver Creek was reached. In the morning of that day scouts, sent out by Major Moore from the Yellowstone, brought me dispatches from that officer and from Colonel Gibbon also. From the scouts I learned that there were no traces of Indians between "Stanley's stockade" and Beaver Creek; by the dispatches I was informed that the steamers with supplies had reached their destination, and that Colonel Gibbon, having received the dispatch sent to him from Fort Lincoln, was marching down the Yellowstone. Upon this information I determined to move up Beaver Creek, and thence march directly to Powder River. Orders were therefore sent to Colonel Gibbon to suspend his movements and to Major Moore to send one boat-load of supplies to the mouth of the Powder.

On the morning of the 4th the march was again resumed, our course being up the Beaver. On the 6th we turned again to the west, and in the evening of the 7th reached Powder River at a point about twenty miles from the Yellowstone.

On the 8th, leaving the column in camp, I went with an escort to the mouth of the Powder, and there found the steamer Far West with supplies.

The next day I went on the steamer up the Yellowstone to meet Colonel Gibbon. I met him at a point ten or fifteen miles below the mouth of the Tongue, and gave him instructions to return with his troops to the mouth of the Rosebud. Returning, I gave orders for the transfer of all troops and supplies from the stockade to a depot to be established at the mouth of the Powder, and thence proceeded to the camp of the column.

The next day Maj. M. A. Reno, Seventh Cavalry, with six companies of his regiment and one Gatling gun, was directed to reconnoiter the valley of the Powder as far as the forks of the river, then to cross to Mizpah Creek, to descend that creek to near its mouth, thence to cross to Tongue River and descend to its mouth. He was provided with rations for ten days, carried on pack-saddles. On the 11th the remainder of the column marched to the Yellowstone, where it remained until the 15th, in order to give time for Major Reno's movements. During this interval the troops at the stockade, and all the supplies which had been landed there, were brought up. On the morning of the 15th, Lieutenant-Colonel Custer, with six companies of his regiment, one Gatling gun, and a train of pack-mules, marched for Tongue River, all the wagons with their infantry-guard having been left at the depot. He reached the Tongue on the 16th. Here we waited for news from Major Reno until the evening of the 19th, when a dispatch was received from him, by which it appeared that he had crossed to the Rosebud and found a heavy Indian trail; and that after following it for some distance he had retraced his steps, had descended the stream to its mouth, and was then on his way to the Tongue. Orders were at once sent to him to halt and await the arrival of Lieutenant-Colonel Custer; and the latter was instructed to march the next morning for the mouth of the Rosebud. He arrived at this last-named point on the 21st. On the same day Colonel Gibbon's column was put in motion for a point on the north bank of the Yellowstone, opposite the mouth of the Big Horn; with it were sent the Gatling guns which had until this time accompanied the Seventh Cavalry.

At a conference which took place on the 21st between Colonel Gibbon, Lieutenant-Colonel Custer, and myself, I communicated to them the plan of operations which I had decided to adopt. It was that Colonel Gibbon's column should cross the Yellowstone near the mouth of the Little Big Horn, and thence up that stream, with the expectation that it would arrive at the last-named point by the 26th; that Lieutenant-Colonel Custer with the whole of the Seventh Cavalry should proceed up the Rosebud until he should ascertain the direction in which the trail discovered by Major Reno led; that if it led to the Little Big Horn it should not be followed; but that Lieutenant-Colonel Custer should keep still farther to the south before turning toward that river, in order to intercept the Indians should they attempt to pass around his left, and in order, by a longer march, to give time for Colonel Gibbon's column to come up.

This plan was founded on the belief that at some point on the Little Big Horn a body of hostile Sioux would be found; and that although it was impossible to make movements in perfect concert, as might have been done had there been a known fixed objective point to be reached, yet, by the judicious use of the excellent guides and scouts which we possessed, the two columns might be brought within co-operating distance of each other, so that either of them which should be first engaged might be a "waiting fight"—give time for the other to come up. At the same time it was thought that a double attack would very much diminish the chances of a successful retreat by the Sioux, should they be disinclined to fight. It was believed to be impracticable to join Colonel Gibbon's column to Lieutenant-Colonel Custer's force; for more than one-half of Colonel Gibbon's troops were infantry, who would be unable to keep up with cavalry in a rapid movement; while to detach Gibbon's mounted men and add them to the Seventh Cavalry would leave his force too small to act as an independent body.

The written instructions given to Lieutenant-Colonel Custer were as follows:

HEADQUARTERS DEPARTMENT OF DAKOTA, (IN THE FIELD,)
Camp at Mouth of Rosebud River, Montana, June 22, 1876.

COLONEL: The brigadier-general commanding directs that as soon as your regiment can be made ready for the march, you proceed up the Rosebud in pursuit of the Indians whose trail was discovered by Major Reno a few days since. It is, of course, impossible to give you any definite instructions in regard to this movement; and were it not impossible to do so, the department commander places too much confidence in your zeal, energy, and ability to wish to impose upon you precise orders, which might hamper your action when nearly in contact with the enemy. He will, however, indicate to you his own views of what your action should be, and he desires that you should conform to them unless you shall see sufficient reason for departing from them. He thinks that you should proceed up the Rosebud until you ascertain definitely the direction in which the trail above spoken of leads. Should it be found (as it appears to be almost certain that it will be found) to turn toward the Little Horn, he thinks that you should still proceed southward, perhaps as far as the headwaters of the Tongue, and then turn toward the Little Horn, feeling constantly, however, to your left, so as to preclude the possibility of the escape of the Indians to the south or southeast by passing around your left flank.

The column of Colonel Gibbon is now in motion for the mouth of the Big Horn. As soon as it reaches that point it will cross the Yellowstone and move up at least as far as the forks of the Little and Big Horns. Of course its future movements must be controlled by circumstances as they arise; but it is hoped that the Indians, if upon the Little Horn, may be so nearly inclosed by the two columns that their escape will be impossible. The department commander desires that on your way up the Rosebud you should thoroughly examine the upper part of Tullock's Creek; and that you should endeavor to send a scout through to Colonel Gibbon's column with information of the result of your examination. The lower part of this creek will be examined by a detachment from Colonel Gibbon's command.

The supply-steamer will be pushed up the Big Horn as far as the forks, if the river is found to be navigable for that distance; and the department commander (who will accompany the column of Colonel Gibbon) desires you to report to him there not later than the expiration of the time for which your troops are rationed, unless in the mean time you receive further orders.

Very respectfully, your obedient servant,

ED. W. SMITH.
Captain, Eighteenth Infantry, A. A. A. G.

Lieut. Col. G. A. CUSTER,
Seventh Cavalry.

The movements which followed have already been reported in telegraphic dispatches sent to the headquarters of the division from the field. These dispatches, however, were very imperfectly transmitted. I therefore repeat them here:

[Telegram.]

HEADQUARTERS DEPARTMENT OF DAKOTA,
Camp on Little Big Horn River, Montana, June 27, 1876.
To the Adjutant-General of the Military Division of the Missouri,
Chicago, Ill., via Fort Ellis:

It is my painful duty to report that day before yesterday, the 25th instant, a great disaster overtook General Custer and the troops under his command. At 12 o'clock of the 22d he started with his whole regiment and a strong detachment of scouts and guides from the mouth of the Rosebud Proceeding up that river about twenty miles, he struck a very heavy Indian trail which had previously been discovered, and, pursuing it, found that it led, as it was supposed that it would lead, to the Little Big Horn River. Here he found a village of almost unexampled extent, and at once attacked it with that portion of his force which was immediately at hand. Major Reno, with three companies, A, G, and M, of the regiment, was sent into the valley of the stream, at the point where the trail struck it. General Custer, with five companies, C, E, F, I, and L, attempted to enter it about 3 miles lower down. Reno forded the river, charged down its left bank, dismounted, and fought on foot until finally, completely overwhelmed by numbers, he was compelled to mount, recross the river, and seek a refuge on the high bluffs which overlook its right bank. Just as he recrossed, Captain Benteen, who, with three companies, D, H, and K, was some two miles to the left of Reno when the action commenced, but who had been ordered by General Custer to return, came to the river, and, rightly concluding that it was useless for his force to attempt to renew the fight in the valley, he joined Reno on the bluffs. Captain McDougall, with his company, B, was at first at some distance in the rear, with the train of pack-mules; he also came up to Reno. Soon this united force was nearly surrounded by Indians, many of whom, armed with rifles of long range, occupied positions which commanded the ground held by the cavalry—ground from which there was no escape. Rifle-pits were dug, and the fight was maintained, though with heavy loss, from about half past two o'clock of the 25th till 6 o'clock of the 26th, when the Indians withdrew from the valley, taking with them their village. Of the movements of General Custer and the five companies under his immediate command scarcely anything is known from those who witnessed them, for no officer or soldier who accompanied him has yet been found alive. His trail, from the point where Reno crossed the stream, passes along and in the rear of the crest of the bluffs on the right bank for nearly or quite three miles. Then it comes down the bank of the river, but at once diverges from it as if he had unsuccessfully attempted to cross; then turns upon itself, almost completes a circle, and ceases. It is marked by the remains of his officers and men and the bodies of his horses, some of them dotted along the path, others heaped in ravines and upon knolls, where halts appear to have been made. There is abundant evidence that a gallant resistance was offered by the troops, but that they were beset on all sides by overpowering numbers. The officers known to be killed are: General Custer, Captains Keogh, Yates, and Custer, Lieutenants Cook, Smith, McIntosh, Calhoun, Porter, Hodgson, Sturgis, and Riley, of the cavalry; Lieutenant Crittenden, of the Twentieth Infantry; and Acting Assistant Surgeon De Wolf, Lieutenant Harrington, of the cavalry, and Assistant Surgeon Lord are missing; Captain Benteen and Lieutenant Varnum, of the cavalry, are slightly wounded. Mr. Boston Custer, a brother, and Mr. Reed, a nephew, of General Custer, were with him and were killed. No other officers than those whom I have named are among the killed, wounded, and missing.

It is impossible as yet to obtain a nominal list of the enlisted men who were killed and wounded; but the number of killed, including officers, must reach 250; the number of wounded is 51. At the mouth of the Rosebud, I informed General Custer that I should take the supply-steamer Far West up the Yellowstone to ferry General Gibbon's column over the river; that I should personally accompany that column; and that it would, in all probability, reach the mouth of the Little Big Horn on the 26th instant. The steamer reached General Gibbon's troops, near the mouth of the Big Horn, early in the morning of the 24th, and at 4 o'clock in the afternoon all his men and animals were across the Yellowstone. At 5 o'clock, the column, consisting of five companies of the Seventh Infantry, four companies of the Second Cavalry, and a battery of three Gatling guns, marched out to and across Tullock's Creek. Starting soon after 5 o'clock in the morning of the 25th, the infantry made a march of twenty-two miles over the most difficult country which I have ever seen. In order that scouts might be sent into the valley of the Little Big Horn, the cavalry, with the battery, was then pushed on thirteen or fourteen miles farther, reaching camp at midnight. The scouts were sent out at half past 4 in the morning of the 26th. They soon discovered three Indians, who were at first supposed to be Sioux; but, when overtaken, they proved to be Crows, who had been with General Custer. They brought the first intelligence of the battle. Their story was not credited. It was supposed that some fighting, perhaps severe fighting, had taken place; but it was not believed that disaster could have overtaken so large a force as twelve companies of cavalry. The infantry, which had broken camp very early, soon came up, and the whole column entered and moved up the valley of the Little Big Horn. During the afternoon efforts were made to send scouts through to what was supposed to be General Custer's position, to obtain information of the condition of affairs; but those who were sent out were driven back by parties of Indians, who, in increasing numbers, were seen hovering in General Gibbon's front. At twenty minutes before 9 o'clock in the evening, the infantry had marched between twenty-nine and thirty miles. The men were very weary and daylight was fading.

The column was therefore halted for the night, at a point about eleven miles in a straight line above the mouth of the stream. This morning the movement was resumed, and, after a march of nine miles, Major Reno's intrenched position was reached. The withdrawal of the Indians from around Reno's command and from the valley was undoubtedly caused by the approach of General Gibbon's troops. Major Reno and Captain Benteen, both of whom are officers of great experience, accustomed to see large masses of mounted men, estimate the number of Indians engaged at not less than twenty-five hundred. Other officers think that the number was greater than this. The village in the valley was about three miles in length and about a mile in width. Besides the lodges proper, a great number of temporary brush-wood shelters was found in it, indicating that many men besides its proper inhabitants had gathered together there. Major Reno is very confident that there were a number of white men fighting with the Indians. It is believed that the loss of the Indians was large. I have as yet received no official reports in regard to the battle; but what is stated herein is gathered from the officers who were on the ground then and from those who have been over it since.

ALFRED H. TERRY,
Brigadier-General.

[Telegram.]

HEADQUARTERS DEPARTMENT OF DAKOTA,
Camp on Little Horn, June 28, 1876.

ASSISTANT ADJUTANT-GENERAL,
Military Division of the Missouri, Chicago, Ill.:

The wounded were brought down from the bluffs last night and made as comfortable as our means would permit. To-day horse and hand litters have been constructed, and this evening we shall commence moving the wounded toward the mouth of the Little Big Horn, to which point I hope that the steamer has been able to come. The removal will occupy three or four days, as the marches must be short. A reconnaissance was made to-day by Captain Ball, of the Second Cavalry, along the trail made by the Indians when they left the valley. He reports that they divided into two parties, one of which kept the valley of Long Fork, making, he thinks, for the Big Horn Mountains; the other turned more to the eastward. He also discovered a very heavy trail leading into the valley that is not more than five days old. This trail is entirely distinct from the one which Custer followed, and would seem to show that at least two large bands united here just before the battle. The dead were all buried to-day.

ALFRED H. TERRY,
Brigadier-General.

[Telegram.]

HEADQUARTERS DEPARTMENT OF DAKOTA,
Camp on Yellowstone, near Big Horn River, Montana, July 2, 1876.

Lieut. Gen. P. H. SHERIDAN, Chicago, Ill.:

In the evening of the 28th we commenced moving down the wounded, but were able to get on but four miles, as our hand-litters did not answer the purpose. The mule-litters did exceedingly well, but they were insufficient in number. The 29th, therefore, was spent in making a full supply of them. In the evening of the 29th we started again, and at 2 a. m. of the 30th the wounded were placed on a steamer at the mouth of the Little Big Horn. The afternoon of the 30th they were brought to the depot on the Yellowstone. I now send them by steamer to Fort Lincoln, and with them one of my aids, Capt. E. W. Smith, who will be able to answer any questions which you may desire to ask. I have brought down the troops to this point. They arrived to-night. They need refitting, particularly in the matter of transportation, before starting again. Although I had on the steamer a good supply of subsistence and forage, there are other things which we need, and I should hesitate to trust the boat again in the Big Horn.

Colonel Sheridan's dispatch informing me of the reported gathering of Indians on the Rosebud, reached me after I came down here. I hear nothing of General Crook's movements.

At least a hundred horses are needed to mount the cavalrymen now here.

ALFRED H. TERRY,
Brigadier-General.

90

For further details of the movements of Colonel Gibbon's column from the 21st to the 30th of June, I refer to his report.

For further details of the march of the Seventh Cavalry from the Rosebud to the Little Big Horn, and of the action of the 25th and 26th of June, I refer to the appended report of Major Reno, Seventh Cavalry.

When Colonel Gibbon's column left the Yellowstone the supply-steamer Far West, upon which was Company B of the Sixth Infantry, was directed to make the attempt to ascend the Big Horn as far as the mouth of the Little Horn, in order that supplies might be near at hand to replace the scanty amount of subsistence which Colonel Gibbon's pack-animals were able to carry. Thanks to the zeal and energy displayed by Capt. Grant Marsh, the master of the steamer, the mouth of the Little Horn was reached by her, and she was of inestimable service in bringing down our wounded. They were sent upon her to Fort Lincoln.

The whole command reached the Yellowstone and went into camp on the north bank of the river on the 2d of July. Immediately afterward attempts were made to communicate with General Crook, in order that concert of action might be established between his forces and my own. The first and second of these efforts failed, the third succeeded. Three private soldiers of the Seventh Infantry, whose names, James Bell, William Evans, and Benjamin H. Stewart, deserve honorable mention here, succeeded in carrying a dispatch from me to General Crook, and two of them brought me his reply, from which I learned his own position and the position of the Indians. On the 15th of July, I received a telegraphic dispatch from the Lieutenant-General commanding, informing me that large re-enforcements would be sent to me. I had previously sent for recruits and horses for the Seventh Cavalry, and for guns to replace the Gatlings; and in order to increase my force, I determined to break up the depot on Powder River and bring the train and stores further up the Yellowstone.

Three possible lines for future operations presented themselves. The first by the left bank of the Big Horn; the second up Tullock's Creek; the third up the Rosebud. The second was inadmissible, for it was not practicable for wagons, and the pack-train which we had the means of improvising could not carry supplies for more than fifteen days. The first would have permitted wagons to be used, but it would have left between my own force and that of General Crook an almost, if not quite, impassable stream, the Big Horn, and besides would, if chosen, have rendered it necessary to keep a steamboat at the mouth of that river, while the Yellowstone was falling rapidly, and was already scarcely navigable to that point. The third line was therefore adopted. The depot was moved to the north bank of the Yellowstone, opposite the mouth of the Rosebud, and the troops from both above and below were brought to it.

The first of the re-enforcements sent to me, six companies of the Twenty-second Infantry, under Lieut. Col. E. S. Otis, arrived on the 1st of August.

On the 2d of August six companies of the Fifth Infantry, under Col. N. A. Miles, arrived.

On the 3d the crossing of the river commenced. It was completed on the 7th, and on the 8th the march up the Rosebud began.

The column had been re-organized, and now consisted of a brigade of four battalions of infantry, under Colonel Gibbon.

The Seventh Cavalry, organized as eight companies, under Maj. M. A. Reno.

91

Four companies of the Second Cavalry, under Maj. J. S. Brisbin, and a battery of two ten-pound rifles and one twelve-pounder, under Lieut. W. H. Low, Twentieth Infantry.

Major Brisbin was appointed chief of cavalry, on the staff of the department commander, but still retained the immediate command of his battalion.

At the depot were left one company of the Seventeenth Infantry, the dismounted men of the Seventh Cavalry, and three Gatling guns, all under the command of Capt. L. H. Sanger, Seventeenth Infantry. The depot had been well intrenched, and was believed to be perfectly secure with the force assigned to its defense. The valley of the Lower Rosebud is very difficult, and our marches on the 8th and 9th were necessarily short. In the forenoon of the 10th, our advanced scouts brought information that a large body of Sioux were in our front, and preparations for an attack upon them were at once made; but just as these preparations were completed, one of General Crook's couriers rode into our lines and announced that it was General Crook's force that confronted us. The march was resumed, and in the afternoon the two columns were united.

I learned from General Crook that the Sioux, leaving their position at the base of the Big Horn Mountains and passing around his right, had descended the Rosebud to the point at which we then were, and had then turned to the eastward, making apparently toward Tongue River. Their trail was broad and distinct, indicating that a very large number of Indians had passed over it. As it was impossible to carry wagons across the ridge which separates the Rosebud from the Tongue, orders were given for the organization of a pack-train for my own force from the wagon-mules; and the train itself, after we had issued from it subsistence and forage to General Crook's troops, was ordered back to the depot.

Colonel Miles, with his six companies and the battery, was directed to return at once to the mouth of the Rosebud, to take the steamboat lying there, proceed down the Yellowstone, and place detachments on the north bank of that river to cover the fords near the mouths of the Tongue and the Powder. Colonel Miles marched with great rapidity, and speedily had his men well entrenched at the points named. Subsequently he placed a detachment opposite the mouth of Glendive Creek, and then employed the steamboat in patrolling the river.

On the 11th the two columns moved, with fifteen days' rations. During that day and the five following days the trail of the Sioux was followed. It led us from the Rosebud to the Tongue; thence down the Tongue to Pumpkin Creek; thence across the ridge between Pumpkin and Mizpah Creeks; then to the Powder; and thence down the Powder to a point about eighteen miles from the Yellowstone. Here it is turned to the east, as if leading to Beaver Creek and the Little Missouri. It was still several days old. Its further pursuit would take us almost directly away from our supplies, and it was thought to be imprudent to enter upon the country lying between the Powder and Missouri Rivers without the full amount of subsistence which our pack-mules could carry. Both General Crook's column and my own therefore moved on the 17th to the mouth of the Powder. To this point some supplies had already been sent; but of the subsistence sent, some had been consumed by General Miles's troops, and there was a deficiency of forage. Hitherto the animals of both General Crook's column and my own had been entirely dependent on grass. Many of them had become very weak, and a supply of grain for them had become a necessity. I therefore determined to remain at the mouth of the Powder until supplies could be brought by boat from the Rosebud depot. The boat arrived on the 23d. General Crook's troops were immediately supplied, and he commenced his march up the Powder on the 24th.

My own column, increased by four of Colonel Miles's companies, under himself, received supplies on the 24th, and marched on the 25th.

While at the mouth of the Powder I received repeated reports of the appearance of hostile Indians about Glendive Creek and on the Lower Yellowstone. No one of these reports taken by itself would have justified any departure from the plan that both General Crook's force and my own should continue to pursue the trail which we had hitherto followed, though the cumulative effect of them had been to make it doubtful whether it would not be better policy to throw my own column to the left bank of the Yellowstone.

At the close of our march on the 25th, however, I received dispatches giving further information of a similar character, which seemed to be sufficient to determine the question, and therefore the column, on the 26th, changed its direction, and marched for the mouth of O'Fallon's Creek.

It seemed that the retreat of the Sioux could not be indefinitely prolonged to the east. In that direction there was no refuge for them. They must, therefore, turn to the north or the south. If they turned to the south, unless they should succeed in eluding a pursuing force, they must be driven into the agencies. At the north they had a secure asylum beyond the Canadian line. It was known that a well-established and much-used trail leads from the fords of the Lower Yellowstone to the Dry Fork and to the Missouri at Fort Peck, and it was determined to push to the north until that trail should be reached.

Before parting with General Crook, it was arranged that supplies should be placed at the mouth of Glendive Creek, and should be at his disposal should the trail lead him in that direction, and that in any event he should communicate with me there.

On the 27th my own column crossed the Yellowstone and made a short march. Our line of march on the 27th, 28th, and 29th lay up Bad Route Creek. In the forenoon of the 29th the column was close to the base of the high and rugged ridge which divides the waters of the Missouri from the waters of the Yellowstone. From this point the battalion of the Second Cavalry, under Captain Ball, was sent forward with instructions to examine the country as far north as the sources of the stream flowing into the Missouri for the trail which we were seeking. The main column then turned eastward, skirting the base of the ridge for the purpose of finding water. In the forenoon of the 30th Captain Ball, with his battalion, returned. He had found the great trail, but there were no indications that it had been used since early in the summer. Before Captain Ball's return a detachment of Indian scouts was pushed on to Three Tree Creek to search for trails. It returned at evening, having found nothing. Early in the morning of the 31st Major Reno, with the whole of the Seventh Cavalry and a detachment of scouts, was directed to make a reconnoissance from our camp to the mouth of the Yellowstone. He was instructed to proceed with his regiment to a point on the river forty or fifty miles below Glendive, and to send his scouts thence to the Missouri. The main column then moved down Turtle Creek, and reached the Yellowstone at Glendive late in the day. On the 2d of September Major Reno reported that his scouts had pushed through to the mouth of the river, but had found no trail. He was thereupon ordered to rejoin the column. The movement to the left bank of the Yellowstone had therefore failed to produce the hoped-for results. It is now known, however, that the reasoning which led to its adoption was correct. The Sioux *had* crossed the river in considerable numbers, but they had divided into numerous small parties and had burned the country behind them, leaving no traces of their passage.

On the 26th of August I received from the Lieutenant-General a dispatch, informing me that it had been determined to hold the Yellowstone Valley during the coming winter, and for this purpose to put fifteen hundred men, including a regiment of cavalry, in cantonment, at or near the mouth of Tongue River.

In this dispatch I was directed to send the Fifth Infantry, under Colonel Miles, and the battalion of the Twenty-second Infantry, under Lieutenant-Colonel Otis, to Tongue River, as soon as they should return to the mouth of the Rosebud. This order could not be literally fulfilled, for, though the column had returned to the Yellowstone, it was not at the mouth of the Rosebud, and it manifestly was not the intention of the Lieutenant-General to withdraw the troops from the field so early in the season. After receiving this dispatch I went in person to Wolf Rapids, below the mouth of the Powder, and found there three steamers loaded with supplies, upon one of which were two additional companies of the Fifth Infantry, under Lieutenant-Colonel Whistler. I directed Colonel Whistler to proceed on his steamer (the Josephine) to Tongue River and commence building huts. The water was very low on the rapids, but the Josephine ascended them and proceeded on her voyage. The master of each of the other steamers refused to attempt the rapids, for the reason that there was not enough water upon them for his boat. I therefore directed that their freight should be unloaded, hauled around the rapids, and transferred to the Far West, which was still in the upper river.

When we arrived at Glendive, on the 31st of August, we found that the water in the river was much lower than when we crossed it at O'Fallon's Creek. The Far West had come out of the upper river and had gone to Fort Buford. One boat with supplies was at Glendive, but was unable to go farther.

On the 2d of September information was received that three boats, with supplies for the troops in the field and for the cantonment on the Tongue, were aground eighteen miles below Glendive, and must be partially unloaded before they could reach even the latter place.

It thus became evident that the Yellowstone could not be depended upon as a line of supply for the cantonment, and that more than ordinary activity would be required to get the needed stores up by land. The establishment of the cantonment, as directed by the Lieutenant-General, was manifestly of paramount importance. It promised results in the future of far greater importance than any which we could hope to obtain by continuing field-operations. It was more than questionable whether the troops then in the field could be fed, and at the same time a winter's supply of subsistence at Tongue River be accumulated.

On the 3d of September I received a dispatch from General Crook, dated Beaver Creek, opposite Sentinel Buttes, September 2d, informing me that he had followed the trail to that point, and that there it had divided; that the Sioux had broken into small parties, and had dispersed.

In view of all these facts and considerations, on the 5th of September it was determined to break up the column, send the troops to their posts, and devote all our land transportation to the task of supplying the cantonment. Colonel Miles, with that portion of his regiment which had been with the column, and two additional companies, which had reached him from Buford, had already, on the 3d, been sent to Tongue River, and orders were now given to Colonel Gibbon to return to Montana with the battalions of the Second Calvary and Seventh Infantry. The companies of the Twenty-second Infantry, under Lieutenant-Colonel Otis, were assigned to the duty of guarding the supplies which had arrived and were to arrive at Glendive, and of furnishing escorts for the trains going thence to the cantonment. The two companies of the Seventeenth Infantry, under Captain Sanger, were directed to remain at the depot at the mouth of the Powder until all the stores there should have been sent to the Tongue, and then to assist in escorting trains.

The Seventh Cavalry and Moore's battalion of the Sixth Infantry, all under Major Reno, were placed *en route* for Fort Buford; but, in view of the possibility that General Crook might yet push some of the Sioux toward the Yellowstone, Major Reno was directed to occupy temporarily the north bank of the river in such manner as to prevent any considerable body of Indians from crossing it. These dispositions having been made, I went in person to Fort Buford.

On the 9th, information was received at Buford that a considerable number of Sioux had crossed and were crossing the Missouri, at Wolf Point, about eighty-five miles by land above Buford.

Major Reno, in obedience to instructions sent to him, immediately collected his force and made a very rapid march to Wolf Point; but when he arrived there the Sioux had effected a crossing, and were so far on their way to the Canadian line, distant but sixty miles, that it was thought to be useless to pursue them. The Seventh Cavalry was therefore ordered to Fort Lincoln, and the companies of the Sixth Infantry were directed to proceed to their respective posts.

Early in October I received instructions from the Lieutenant-General to dismount and disarm the Indians at Standing Rock and at Cheyenne agency. In pursuance of these instructions, a force of nearly twelve hundred men was organized at Fort Lincoln under Col. S. D. Sturgis, Seventh Cavalry. It consisted of the Seventh Cavalry, three companies of infantry, and a section of artillery. It was divided into two parts, one of which, consisting of four companies of cavalry under Major Reno, marched by the right bank of the Missouri to Standing Rock, and reported to Lieutenant-Colonel Carlin, Seventeenth Infantry, the commanding officer of that post, who, with his own garrison and Reno's troops, dismounted the Indians on that bank of the river. The other portion, under Colonel Sturgis in person, moved on the left bank. It reached the camps on that bank at the same time that Major Reno arrived on the other side, and was equally successful in accomplishing the object of the movement. Not a shot was fired and no violence was used.

Colonel Sturgis's column then marched on Cheyenne agency, to which place three companies of infantry from the garrison of Fort Sully were also brought, reporting to Lieut. Col. George P. Buell, Eleventh Infantry, the commander of the post. This display of force was quite sufficient to effect our object, and the Indians quietly surrendered their arms and their animals. About nine hundred ponies from Cheyenne agency and about twelve hundred from Standing Rock are now on their way to this place, where they will be sold. Without doubt many more will be obtained from Indians who will come in to the agencies for food during the coming winter. The money produced by the sale of these ponies will be used to purchase cows and working-oxen for the Indians.

While preparations were making for dismounting and disarming the agency Indians, events of great importance were taking place on the Yellowstone. On the 10th of October, Capt. C. W. Miner, Twenty-second Infantry, with four companies of his regiment, escorting ninety-four wagons, started from Glendive Creek for the cantonment at Tongue River. He made during the day a march of fourteen miles.

At five o'clock in the evening he went into camp. At three o'clock in the morning of the 11th a party of Indians attacked the camp, and during the skirmish which ensued, forty-seven mules of the trains escaped and fell into the hands of the Indians.

At six o'clock in the morning of the 11th, Captain Miner again moved forward, but after a march of about eight miles, during which the Indians constantly skirmished with his rear-guard, he came to the conclusion that the safety of the valuable train in his charge required him to return to Glendive. He therefore retraced his steps, reaching the last-named place at eleven o'clock at night. Captain Miner's report of this affair is appended.

Lieut. Col. E. S. Otis, Twenty-second Infantry, the commanding officer at Glendive, immediately re-organized the train, increased its escort to five companies of infantry, counting one hundred and eighty-five rifles, took command of it in person, and on the 16th started for Tongue River. His formal report of the operations of his column has been delayed or lost in the mail, but from a verbal report made by him to the adjutant-general of the department it appears that he was successfully engaged with the Sioux for two days; that he punished them severely, so severely that they sued for peace, and promised that after going to Fort Peck to trade they would go to Tongue River and surrender themselves there. These terms were consented to by Colonel Otis, and the Indians withdrew. I shall forward Colonel Otis's report as soon as it is received.

At about the same time, though upon what day I am unable to say, for Colonel Miles has omitted all dates in his report, Colonel Miles, having received information that Sitting Bull was about to cross the Yellowstone and go to the Dry Fork of the Missouri for the purpose of hunting buffalo, moved from Tongue River with the Fifth Infantry with the design of intercepting or following him. When on Custer's Creek he received news of the attack on Captain Miner's train and of Colonel Otis's engagement. Moving in a northeasterly direction from Custer's Creek he was approaching the Sioux camp, when a flag of truce appeared and was received. Two conferences between Colonel Miles and Sitting Bull followed. The Indians were informed of the terms upon which alone they could surrender. These terms were not accepted, and an engagement followed; an engagement of which the result was the complete discomfiture of the Indians, nearly all of whom were driven across the Yellowstone, abandoning in their flight tons of dried meat, lodge-poles, travois, camp equipages, ponies, and broken-down cavalry horses. Sitting Bull, with about thirty lodges, escaped to the northward. Colonel Miles estimates the number of Indians engaged at one thousand.

On the 27th of October four principal chiefs and one head-warrior of the hostile bands surrendered themselves to Colonel Miles, and agreed to conduct their bands to Cheyenne agency and there remain at peace, subject to the orders of the Government.

It was understood also that they would, on arrival, give up their arms and horses. Five days were allowed the Indians to obtain meat, and thirty days to make the journey to the agency. The chiefs and head warrior above mentioned, who represent the Minneconjou and Sans Arc tribes, placed themselves in the hands of the military authorities as hostages for the faithful fulfillment of this agreement, and have been sent to Cheyenne agency under guard. Colonel Hazen, Sixth Infantry, commanding Fort Buford, acting upon information received by him of the movement of hostile Indians toward Fort Peck, proceeded to that point with four companies of his regiment, arriving November 1. A considerable body of Uncapapas, representing one hundred and eighteen lodges, had come to the agency for supplies, but on receipt of news of Hazen's approach had, on the day before his arrival, fled southward across the Missouri River. Some disabled horses and personal property belonging to the Seventh Cavalry, and captured in Lieutenant-Colonel Custer's fight, were left behind by the Indians.

The information obtained by Colonel Hazen goes to show that these Indians are in a state of extreme destitution. It is said that they went out last spring with one thousand good lodges, of which not one now remains in their possession; their ponies are so reduced in condition that it is doubtful if they can be wintered; they are without food or ammunition.

It would seem from this statement, which is fully corroborated by the observation of Colonel Miles, that Sitting Bull's following is in a helpless condition; and that a firm adherence to the policy adopted, of preventing them from getting ammunition, and requiring the surrender of arms and horses as the essential condition upon which they can receive supplies of food, will, during the coming winter, force them into subjection.

The reports of Colonels Hazen and Miles, relative to the matters last mentioned, are hereto appended.

Very respectfully, your obedient servant,
ALFRED H. TERRY,
Brigadier-General.

ADJUTANT GENERAL
Of the Military Division of the Missouri, Chicago, Ill.

---

3 A.—REPORT OF GENERAL GIBBON.

HEADQUARTERS DISTRICT OF MONTANA,
Fort Shaw, Montana, October 17, 1876.

SIR: I have the honor to submit the following report of the military operations o the troops under my command during the past spring and summer:

In accordance with telegraphic instruction from the brigadier-general commanding the department, five companies of the Seventh Infantry left Fort Shaw on the 17th of March, and proceeded toward Fort Ellis.

The ground was covered with a heavy snow and the roads a mass of mud and slush, but the command made good time and reached Fort Ellis on the 28th, a distance of 183 miles. In the mean time, one company of the Seventh (Clifford's) had been ordered to march from Camp Baker, and the snow being too deep on the direct road to Fort Ellis, Captain Clifford dug his way through snow-drifts to the Missouri River and reached Fort Ellis on the 22d of March. From that point he was instructed by telegraph to proceed as an escort to our supply-train as far as the new Crow agency.

The battalion of the Seventh Infantry from Fort Shaw, under command of Captain Freeman, left Fort Ellis on the 30th of March, and on the 1st of April the four companies of the Second Cavalry left the post under command of Captain Thompson. Major Brisbin, although on crutches from rheumatism, and unable to mount a horse, insisted so strongly upon accompanying the expedition that I consented to his going, although he was obliged to travel in an ambulance.

The road over the divide, between Fort Ellis and the Yellowstone River, was in an almost impassable condition, and to add to our difficulties a furious snow-storm set in on the 3d of April, and it was midnight on the 4th before our train succeeded in getting across and reaching Shields River, a distance of thirty miles. From there the cavalry and wagon-train was pushed down the river after the infantry, fording the

Yellowstone twice, and overtook Captain Freeman's command in camp on the river opposite the new agency on the 7th. On the 8th I proceeded to the agency, 18 miles, held a council with the Crows the next day, and the day after (10th) enlisted 25 of them as scouts. Lieutenant Jacobs having arrived with wagons, our supplies were loaded up to transfer them to the north bank of the Yellowstone.

Clifford's company having left the agency the day before, (9th,) on the 11th the train was started in a furious snow-storm which had raged all night, and, pulling for a part of the way through snow two feet deep, reached the point selected for our depot; the command in the mean time having marched there.

Having established the supply camp, and left "A" Company (Logan's) in charge of it, the command resumed the march down the river on the 13th. The ground, however, was very soft, and our heavily-loaded wagons made but slow progress, but after fording the Yellowstone four times we reached the vicinity of Fort Pease on the 20th. The next day I received a dispatch from the department commander to proceed no farther than the mouth of the Big Horn for the present, and placed the command alongside of Fort Pease. On the 23d, Captain Freeman's company was sent back with the wagon-train to bring up the supplies; and on the 24th Captain Ball, with two companies of the Second Cavalry, was started on a scout to old Fort C. F. Smith. He returned by the way of the Little Big Horn and Jallock's Fork on the 1st of May without having seen any signs of Indians. Captain Freeman, with Logan's company and our train, got back on the 8th of May, and on the 10th the march down the river was resumed with the consolidated command, and all our supplies in the train.

Up to the 3d of May we had seen no sign of Indians, but on the morning of that day the ponies of the Crow scouts, which had been carelessly permitted to roam at large, were found to be missing, together with two animals belonging to one of our guides, and the signs demonstrated the fact that a war party had been in our vicinity.

On the 14th we went into camp near the Little Porcupine, (Table Creek of Lewis and Clarke,) where we were visited by a terrific storm of hail and rain which rendered the prairies impassable for our wagons and detained us till the 20th. Scouts had been sent out constantly, not only on the north side toward the mouth of Tongue River, but on the south side of the Yellowstone. These reported seeing various war parties of Sioux, and finally the smoke of a camp on the Rosebud about thirty-five miles from us. With the design of striking this camp and surprising it by a night march, I attempted to cross the Yellowstone on the 17th, but that river had become a rapid torrent, and after drowning four of our horses in attempting to get them across, the effort was abandoned. On the 20th, our scouts having reported a large body of Indians moving toward the mouth of the Rosebud with an evident design of crossing the Yellowstone, I moved with the whole of the command, except Kirtland's company, hastily down the river and camped for the night below the mouth of the Rosebud, but saw no Indians, and the next day brought Captain Kirtland's company and the train down to the new position.

On the 23d Lieutenant English, with I Company, Seventh Infantry, and Lieutenant Roe's Company F, Second Cavalry, to accompany it a part of the way, was started back to meet and escort in a contract-train, bringing us supplies from Fort Ellis. The morning the escort left (23d) two soldiers and a citizen teamster, while hunting in the hills a few miles from camp, were murdered by Indians, who, however, rapidly disappeared before a scouting party of two companies, under Captain Ball, sent after them. On the 27th I started a dispatch for the department commander down the river in a small boat in charge of Privates Evans and Stewart, Company E, Seventh Infantry, and Scout Williamson, the two soldiers having volunteered for the service; and the next day I received the department commander's dispatch of the 15th instant, directing me to march at once for the stockade above Glendive Creek, cross the Yellowstone, and move out eastward to meet him. Captain Sanno, Seventh Infantry, with two companies—his own and Lieutenant Roe's, Second Cavalry—was at once started, with all our wagons under charge of Lieutenant Jacobs, regimental quartermaster Seventh Infantry, back to lighten the contract-train and hurry it forward; and on the 4th of June it reached camp after a rapid march in spite of a furious storm of snow and sleet, which raged all day on the 1st. The next day (5th) the march was resumed down the river, but we were delayed by steep hills and rugged country, and in four days made only 57 miles, which brought us about 17 miles below the mouth of Tongue River. That night (8th) I received by scouts the department commander's dispatch of that day from Powder River, and the next morning met him on the steamboat Far West a few miles below our camp. In accordance with his instructions the command was at once prepared to move up the river again, but a furious rain-storm that afternoon delayed the movement by converting the alkali flats surrounding us into impassable ground. The cavalry, however, got off on the afternoon of the 10th and the infantry the next day, and after a march of 50 miles was again concentrated in camp below the mouth of the Rosebud on the 14th. On the 18th Major Reno, with a force of cavalry, arrived opposite our camp after a scout on Powder, Tongue, and Rosebud Rivers, during which he reported he had seen no Indians, and the next day he proceeded down the river.

A cavalry scout up the river having reported the side streams almost impassable, by reason of floods from recent rains, I started Captain Freeman with three companies of infantry on the 21st, up the road to build bridges. General Terry reaching the camp by steamer shortly afterward, the whole command was started up the river. I, at his request, accompanied him on the Far West, for the purpose of conferring with Lieutenant-Colonel Custer, who reached a point on the opposite side of the river with the whole of the Seventh Cavalry that afternoon.

That evening the plan of operations was agreed upon. Lieutenant-Colonel Custer, with the Seventh Cavalry, was to proceed up the Rosebud till he struck an Indian trail, discovered during Major Reno's scout. As my scouts had recently reported smoke on the Little Big Horn, the presence of an Indian camp some distance up that stream was inferred.

Lieutenant-Colonel Custer was instructed to keep constantly feeling toward his left, well up toward the mountains, so as to prevent the Indians escaping in that direction, and to strike the Little Big Horn, if possible, *above* (south of) the supposed location of the camp, while my command was to march up the Yellowstone to the mouth of the Big Horn, there to be ferried across by the steamer, then to move up the Big Horn to the mouth of the Little Big Horn, and up that stream, with the hope of getting the camp between the two forces. As it would take my command three days to reach the mouth of the Big Horn, and probably a day to cross it over the Yellowstone, besides two more to reach the mouth of the Little Big Horn, and Lieutenant-Colonel Custer had the shorter line over which to operate, the department commander strongly impressed upon him the propriety of not pressing his march too rapidly. He got off with his regiment at 12 o'clock the next day, (22d,) three Gatling guns, under Lieutenant Low, Twentieth Infantry, being detached from his regiment and sent to join my command. The steamer got away at 4 o'clock that day, and reached Fort Pease early on the morning of the 24th. My command, except the train and Captain Kirtland's company, (B, Seventh Infantry,) being at once ferried across, was, that evening, moved out to the crossing of Tullock's Fork. I did not accompany it, and General Terry took command of the troops in person. The next day the steamer entered the mouth of the Big Horn and proceeded up that stream.

The next morning early, (26th,) I left the Far West and overtook the infantry portion of the command, General Terry having made a night-march with the cavalry and Gatling guns, and later in the day that portion of the command was overtaken on a high ridge overlooking the valley of the Little Big Horn near its mouth, where, by direction of General Terry, I resumed command of my troops. Shortly afterward our scouts brought in news that they had encountered some Indians, and, giving chase, had run them across the Big Horn. They had dropped articles in their flight which proved them to be Crows, assigned to duty with Lieutenant-Colonel Custer's command. They, having discovered that their pursuers belonged to their own tribe, refused to come back, and called across the river that Custer's command had been entirely destroyed by the Sioux, who were chasing the soldiers all over the country and killing them. We now pushed up the valley of the Little Big Horn as rapidly as the men could march, large fires being seen in the distance. Efforts were made to communicate with Lieutenant-Colonel Custer by scouts, but our Crow interpreter deserted and took the Crows with him, and two attempts made by white men to precede the command with dispatches failed, the scouts in both cases running into Indians. As we proceeded up the valley the fires increased in number and volume, giving rise to the impression that Custer had captured the camp and destroyed it. The Indians, who late in the afternoon remained in sight on the hills in front of us, rather militated against the supposition, however, and after marching until dark we halted and bivouaced on the prairie.

The next morning the march was resumed, and after proceeding about 3 miles we came in sight of a large deserted Indian camp, in which two teepies were still standing, and these were found to contain the dead bodies of Indians. Many lodge-poles were still standing, and the quantity of property scattered about testified to the hasty departure of the Indians. Our scouts reported only a few scattering horsemen in sight on the distant hills. We continued to move rapidly forward, still uncertain as to the fate of Custer's command, Captain Ball's company about a mile in advance. While passing through the Indian camp a report reached me from our scouts in the hills to the north of the river that a large number of bodies of white men had been discovered, and shortly afterward Lieutenant Bradley came in with the information that he had counted 194 bodies of dead soldiers. All doubt that a serious disaster had happened to Lieutenant-Colonel Custer's command now vanished, and the march was continued under the uncertainty as to whether we were going to rescue the survivors or to battle with the enemy who had annihilated him. At length we caught sight of a number of animals congregated upon the slope of a distant hill, and on a point nearer to us three horsemen were evidently watching us. After Captain Ball's company had passed them these cautiously approached us, our troops being in plain sight and marching in two columns abreast of each other. At length, being convinced we were friends, they came forward more rapidly and announced that the Seventh Cavalry had been cut to pieces and the remnant, under Major Reno, were intrenched in the bluffs close by. Communication was now soon opened with Major Reno. His command was found intrenched upon the tops of several small ridges, their dead and living horses lying about them, with some fifty wounded men lying on the hot, dusty hill-tops, where, until about 6 o'clock on the evening before, they had been unable to obtain any water except at the imminent risk of life. We were informed that in this spot they had been surrounded by overwhelming numbers of Indians from the close of Major Reno's charge on the 25th (about 2½ p. m.) until about 6 p. m. the next day, the Indians pouring upon them all that time a very close and almost continuous fire from the neighboring ridges, some of which commanded the position in reverse. The first inquiry made was if General Custer was with us, and the command appeared to know nothing of the fate of himself and that portion of his command immediately with him until we informed them of it. As described to us, the whole movement of the Indians when they abandoned their camp was visible from Major Reno's position, and the last portion disappeared in the hills to the south just at dusk on the 26th, when my command was 8¾ miles from Major Reno's position.

My command was at once placed in camp, and arrangements made to bring down and properly care for the suffering wounded. This was effected by night-fall. The next day, 28th, Captain Ball, Second Cavalry, was sent out with his company, and followed the main trail some ten or twelve miles. He found that it led directly south toward the Big Horn Mountains, and in returning to camp he discovered a large fresh trail leading down the Little Big Horn toward the scene of the battle. The day was occupied in burying the dead and in constructing litters for the wounded. In the performance of this latter duty Lieut. G. C. Doane, Second Cavalry, was detailed to devise mule-litters, and, with the very crudest material, (cottonwood poles, raw-hide, and ropes,) made some six or eight. But the mules, when attached to them, proved so intractable that the attempt was abandoned, and hand-litters of lodge-poles and canvas constructed. With these, and the men to carry them, the command left camp at sunset on that day. The movement, however, was exceedingly slow and tedious. The whole command, afterward assisted by two companies of the Seventh Cavalry, was used by relays, and it was long past midnight when camp was reached, at a distance of four and one-half miles.

The next day (29th) was occupied in destroying the large quantity of property abandoned by the Indians in their hasty flight. An immense number of lodge-poles, robes, and dressed skins, pots, kettles, cups, pans, axes, and shovels, were found scattered through the camp and along the trail followed by the Indians. Our progress with the hand-litters having proved so exceedingly slow and tedious Lieutenant Doane was called upon to continue the construction of the mule-litters, and by selecting from all the pack-mules in the command he succeeded in obtaining fifty gentle enough for the service, and in constructing a sufficient number of litters to carry all the wounded. With these a second start was made at 6 p. m., with the expectation of making a short march. But the litters worked so admirably as to call forth the most unbounded commendation in praise of the skill and energy displayed by Lieutenant Doane, and after proceeding a few miles information was received by courier that the Far West was waiting for us at the mouth of the Little Big Horn. The department commander therefore decided to continue the march with the view of placing the wounded in comfort and rest as soon as possible. The march was then resumed, but the night proved dark and stormy and the road down from the plateau to the steamer rough and obscure, so that it was two o'clock on the morning of the 30th before the wounded were safely housed on board the boat. This was done without a single accident of any moment, and I desire to invite special attention to the invaluable services of Lieutenant Doane in the construction of the requisite litters in so short a time out of the rude material of clumsy poles, horse raw-hide, and refractory mules. But for his energy, skill, and confidence our suffering wounded would probably have been several days longer on the road.

The Far West left that day for the mouth of the Big Horn, which point I reached with the command, after a two days' march, on the 2d of July. The whole command was then ferried across the Yellowstone River and placed in camp. Here it remained until the 27th, when, in obedience to the orders of General Terry, it was transferred down the river to the new depot at the mouth of the Rosebud, and on the 3d of August my portion of it was ferried across the Yellowstone, preparatory to the movement up the Rosebud.

The troops in the field were now re-organized, and I was assigned to the command of the four battalions of infantry belonging to the Fifth, Sixth, Seventh, and Twenty-second Infantry. On the 8th the command started up the Rosebud, but the road was difficult, required a great deal of work, and our progress was slow.

On the 10th we encountered General Crook's command coming down, and the next day the united commands started with pack-mules on the Indian trail which General Crook was following, the battalion of the Fifth Infantry being sent back to escort our supply-train and scout the river to prevent the Indians crossing to the north of it. In the midst of very heavy rain the command moved across to Tongue River, down that and across to Powder River, and down that to its mouth, which it reached on the 17th. On the 25th my command, further reduced by the detachment of the Sixth Infantry, started up Powder River again, but the following day, on information that the Indians were below us, on the Yellowstone, we retraced our steps, and marched across the country to a point on the river near O'Fallon's Creek, and the day following, 27th, were ferried across the Yellowstone by steamer. That night the whole command made a night-march to the north, entering upon an almost entirely unknown country without guides, where, for the next four days, our movements were hampered by the necessity for marching toward the water-pools, which had to be first sought for. Our general course, however, was northward, and scouting parties sent across the main divide and down the Yellowstone having demonstrated that no large bodies of Indians had made their way north, toward the Fort Peck agency, the command came in again to the Yellowstone, near Glendive Creek, on the 31st.

On the 5th of September I received orders for my command to return to its station in Montana.

Starting on the 6th, we reached our wagon-train a few miles above the mouth of Powder River, 81 miles, on the 9th, and placing our pack-mules in harness, resumed the march the next day. On the 12th we reached the mouth of Tongue River, and on the 17th passed Fort Pease. On our arrival at the month of Big Timber, on the 26th, the command was divided, the cavalry companies under Captain Ball marching to Fort Ellis, and the infantry to Camp Baker, via the forks of the Muscleshell. The cavalry reached Fort Ellis on the 29th of September, and the five companies of the Seventh Infantry arrived at Fort Shaw on the 6th instant, having left Company E (Clifford's) at Camp Baker on the 2d. I preceded the cavalry into Fort Ellis, and, having arranged for the muster-out and payment of the Crow scouts, returned to this post on the 4th instant.

It gives me great pleasure to testify to the cheerful manner in which the whole command performed the long marches and arduous duties of the campaign. Starting out in the depths of winter, with the expectation of an absence of two or three months, they submitted to the tedious delays, long marches, and exposures of an unprecedentedly wet and cold season during six months with a soldierly cheerfulness worthy of the highest praise.

In concluding this report I beg leave to submit the following suggestions:

It became evident during the campaign that we were attempting to carry on operations in an extensive region of something like four or five hundred miles square with inadequate means. Had we been called upon to operate against only the Indians known to be hostile, any one of the three columns sent against them would have been amply sufficient to cope with any force likely to be brought against it; but when the hostile body was largely re-enforced by accessions from the various agencies where the malcontents were doubtless in many cases driven to desperation by starvation and the heartless frauds perpetrated upon them, the problem became less simple, and when these various bands succeeded in finding a leader who possessed the tact, courage, and ability to concentrate and keep together so large a force, it was only a question of time as to when one or other of the exterior columns would meet with a check from the overwhelming numbers of the interior body. The first information we had of the force and strategy opposed to us was the check given to Custer's column, resulting in a disaster which might have been worse but for the timely arrival of General Terry's other column.

The inadequate means at the disposal of the troops became painfully apparent at an early day. Operating on one bank of a deep and rapid stream for a distance of several hundred miles, my column was entirely without the means of crossing to the other bank to strike exposed camps of the hostile bands.

Incumbered with heavily-loaded wagon-trains, our movements were necessarily slow, and when we did cut loose from these our only means of transporting supplies were the mules taken from the teams, and unbroken to packs, unsuitable pack-saddles, and inexperienced soldiers as packers. These latter soon learned to do their part tolerably well, but at the expense of the poor animals, whose festering sores after a few days' marching appealed not only to feelings of humanity, but demonstrated the false economy of the course pursued.

At the end of one scout with pack-mules most of our animals had to be replaced by others from the train, and at the end of the campaign many of them were in anything but a serviceable condition for either pack or draught purposes. The contrast between the mobility of our force and that of General Crook's was very marked, especially for rapid movements. General Crook's well-organized pack-train, with trained mules and its corps of competent packers, moved almost independently of the column of troops, and as fast as they could move. His ranks were not depleted by drafts to take charge of the packs and animals, for each mule faithfully followed the sound of the leader's bell and needed no other guide, and his pack-mules were neither worn out nor torn to pieces by bad saddles and worse packing.

In addition to our other wants, we were entirely devoid of any proper means for the transportation of sick or wounded. This, with a well-organized pack-train, was comparatively easy. As it was, a few wounded men were all-sufficient to cripple, for offensive operations, a large body of troops; for in savage warfare to leave one's wounded behind is out of the question.

Maps of the route passed over by the command will be forwarded as soon as they can be completed. The country visited by the troops is by no means the desert it has been frequently represented. There is, of course, a great deal of barren, worthless land, but there is also much land in the valleys susceptible of cultivation, and an immense region of good grazing country which will in time be available for stock-raising. Even where from the valleys the appearance of the so-called "bad lands" was most forbidding, we found on the plateau above excellent grass in the greatest abundance covering the country for great distances. This was particularly noticeable in the region north of Powder River, between the Yellowstone and Missouri Rivers, and along the Tongue and Rosebud and the country between the two. The country along the Little Big Horn is also a fine grass country, and along the Big Horn itself immense valleys of fine grass extend.

During the summer's operations the cavalry marched nearly 1,500 miles, and the infantry nearly 1,700, besides some 900 miles by portions of the cavalry and 500 miles by portions of the infantry in scouting and escort duty.

I am, sir, very respectfully, your obedient servant,

JOHN GIBBON,
Colonel Seventh Infantry, Commanding District.

Maj. GEO. D. RUGGLES,
Assistant Adjutant-General, Department of Dakota.

---

3 B.—REPORT OF MAJOR M. H. RENO.

HEADQUARTERS SEVENTH UNITED STATES CAVALRY,
Camp on Yellowstone River, July 5, 1876.

Capt. E. W. SMITH,
A. D. C. and A. A. A. Gen.:

The command of the regiment having devolved upon me as the senior surviving officer from the battle of the 25th and 26th of June, between the Seventh Cavalry and Sitting Bull's band of hostile Sioux, on the Little Big Horn River, I have the honor to submit the following report of its operations from the time of leaving the main column until the command was united in the vicinity of the Indian village:

The regiment left the camp at the mouth of the Rosebud River, after passing in review before the department commander, under command of Bvt. Maj. Gen. G. A. Custer, lieutenant-colonel, on the afternoon of the 22d of June, and marched up the Rosebud 12 miles and encamped; 23d, marched up the Rosebud, passing many old Indian camps, and following a very large pole-trail, but not fresh, making 33 miles; 24th, the march was continued up the Rosebud, the trail and signs freshening with every mile, until we had made 28 miles, and we then encamped and waited for information from the scouts. At 9.25 p. m. Custer called the officers together and informed us that beyond a doubt the village was in the valley of the Little Big Horn, and in order to reach it it was necessary to cross the divide between the Rosebud and the Little Big Horn, and it would be impossible to do so in the day-time without discovering our march to the Indians; that we would prepare to march at 11 p. m. This was done, the line of march turning from the Rosebud to the right up one of its branches which headed near the summit of the divide. About 2 a. m. on the 25th the scouts told him that he could not cross the divide before daylight. We then made coffee and rested for three hours, at the expiration of which time the march was resumed, the divide crossed, and about 8 a. m. the command was in the valley of one of the branches of the Little Big Horn. By this time Indians had been seen and it was certain we could not surprise them, and it was determined to move at once to the attack. Previous to this, no division of the regiment had been made since the order had been issued on the Yellowstone annulling wing and battalion organizations, but Custer informed me that he would assign commands on the march.

I was ordered by Lieut. W. W. Cook, adjutant, to assume command of Companies M, A, and G; Captain Benteen, of Companies H, D, and K. Custer retained C, E, F, I, and L under his immediate command, and Company B, Captain McDougall, in rear of the pack-train.

I assumed command of the companies assigned to me, and, without any definite orders, moved forward with the rest of the column, and well to its left.

I saw Benteen moving farther to the left, and, as they passed, he told me he had orders to move well to the left, and sweep everything before him. I did not see him again until about 2.30 p. m. The command moved down the creek toward the Little Big Horn Valley, Custer with five companies on the right bank, myself and three companies on the left bank, and Benteen farther to the left, and out of sight.

As we approached a deserted village, and in which was standing one tepee, about 11 a. m., Custer motioned me to cross to him, which I did, and moved nearer to his column until about 12.30 a. m., [p. m. ?] when Lieutenant Cook, adjutant, came to me and said the village was only two miles above, and running away; to move forward at as rapid a gait as prudent, and to charge afterward, and that the whole outfit would support me. I think those were his exact words. I at once took a fast trot, and moved down about two miles, when I came to a ford of the river. I crossed immediately, and halted about ten minutes or less to gather the battalion, sending word to Custer that I had everything in front of me, and that they were strong. I deployed, and, with the Ree scouts on my left, charged down the valley, driving the Indians with great ease for about two and a half miles. I, however, soon saw that I was being drawn into some trap, as they would certainly fight harder, and especially as we were nearing their village, which was still standing; besides, I could not see Custer or any other support, and at the same time the very earth seemed to grow Indians, and they were running toward me in swarms, and from all directions. I saw I must defend myself and give up the attack mounted. This I did. Taking possession of a front of woods, and which furnished, near its edge, a shelter for the horses, dismounted and fought them on foot, making headway through the woods. I soon found myself in the near vicinity of the village, saw that I was fighting odds of at least five to one, and that my only hope was to get out of the woods, where I would soon have been surrounded, and gain some high ground. I accomplished this by mounting and charging the Indians between me and the bluffs on the opposite side of the river. In this charge, First Lieut. Donald McIntosh, Second Lieut. Benjamin H. Hodgson, Seventh Cavalry, and Acting Assistant Surgeon J. M. De Wolf, were killed.

I succeeded in reaching the top of the bluff, with a loss of three officers and twenty-nine enlisted men killed and seven men wounded. Almost at the same time I reached the top, mounted men were seen to be coming toward us, and it proved to be Colonel Benteen's battalion, Companies H, D, and K. We joined forces, and in a short time the pack-train came up. As senior, my command was then A, B, D, G, H, K, and M, about three hundred and eighty men, and the following officers: Captains Benteen, Weir, French, and McDougall, First Lieutenants Godfrey, Mathey, and Gibson, and Second Lieutenants Edgerly, Wallace, Varnum, and Hare, and Acting Assistant Surgeon Porter.

First Lieutenant De Rudio was in the dismounted fight in the woods, but, having some trouble with his horse, did not join the command in the charge out, and, hiding himself in the woods, joined the command after night-fall on the 26th.

Still hearing nothing of Custer, and, with this re-enforcement, I moved down the river in the direction of the village, keeping on the bluffs.

We had heard firing in that direction and knew it could only be Custer. I moved to the summit of the highest bluff, but seeing and hearing nothing sent Captain Weir with his company to open communication with him. He soon sent back word by Lieutenant Hare that he could go no farther, and that the Indians were getting around him. At this time he was keeping up a heavy fire from his skirmish-line. I at once turned everything back to the first position I had taken on the bluffs, and which seemed to me the best. I dismounted the men and had the horses and mules of the pack-train driven together in a depression, put the men on the crests of the hills making the depression, and had hardly done so when I was furiously attacked. This was about 6 p. m. We held our ground, with a loss of eighteen enlisted men killed and forty-six wounded, until the attack ceased, about 9 p. m. As I knew by this time their overwhelming numbers, and had given up any support from that portion of the regiment with Custer, I had the men dig rifle-pits, barricade with dead horses and mules, and boxes of hard bread, the opening of the depression toward the Indians in which the animals were herded, and made every exertion to be ready for what I saw would be a terrific assault the next day. All this night the men were busy, and the Indians holding a scalp-dance underneath us in the bottom and in our hearing. On the morning of the 26th I felt confident that I could hold my own, and was ready, as far as I cou'd be, when at daylight, about 2.30 a. m., I heard the crack of two rifles. This was the signal for the beginning of a fire that I have never seen equaled. Every rifle was handled by an expert and skilled marksman, and with a range that exceeded our carbines, and it was simply impossible to show any part of the body before it was struck. We could see, as the day brightened, countless hordes of them pouring up the valley from the village and scampering over the high points toward the places designated for them by their chiefs, and which entirely surrounded our position. They had sufficient numbers to completely encircle us, and men were struck from opposite sides of the lines from where the shots were fired. I think we were fighting all the Sioux Nation, and also all the deperadoes, renegades, half-breeds, and squaw-men between the Missouri and

103

the Arkansas and east of the Rocky Mountains, and they must have numbered at least twenty-five hundred warriors.

The fire did not slacken until about 9 30 a. m., and then we found they were making a last desperate effort and which was directed against the lines held by Companies H and M. In this charge they came close enough t) use their bows and arrows, and one man lying dead within our lines was touched with the coup-stick of one of the foremost Indians. When I say the stick was only ten or twelve feet long, some idea of the desperate and reckless fighting of these people may be understood.

This charge of theirs was gallantly repulsed by the men on that line, led by Colonel Benteen. They also came close enough to send their arrows into the line held by Companies D and K, but were driven away by a like charge of the line, which I accompanied. We now had many wounded, and the question of water was vital, as from 6 p. m. the previous evening until now, 10 a. m., about sixteen hours, we had been without.

A skirmish-line was formed under Colonel Benteen to protect the descent of volunteers down the hill in front of his position to reach the water. We succeeded in getting some canteens, though many of the men were hit in doing so. The fury of the attack was now over, and to our astonishment the Indians were seen going in parties toward the village. But two solutions occurred to us for this movement: that they were going for something to eat, more ammunition, (as they had been throwing arrows,) or that Custer was coming. We took advantage of this lull to fill all vessels with water, and soon had it by camp-kettles full. But they continued to withdraw, and all firing ceased save occasional shots from sharp-shooters sent to annoy us about the water. About 2 p. m. the grass in the bottom was set on fire and followed up by Indians who encouraged its burning, and it was evident to me it was done for a purpose, and which purpose I discovered later on to be the creation of a dense cloud of smoke behind which they were packing and preparing to move their village. It was between 6 and 7 p. m. that the village came out from behind the dense clouds of smoke and dust. We had a close and good view of them as they filed away in the direction of Big Horn Mountains, moving in almost perfect military order. The length of the column was full equal to that of a large division of the cavalry corps of the Army of the Potomac as I have seen it in its march.

We now thought of Custer, of whom nothing had been seen and nothing heard since the firing in his direction about 6 p. m. on the eve of the 25th, and we concluded that the Indians had gotten between him and us and driven him toward the boat at the mouth of the Little Big Horn River. The awful fate that did befall him never occurred to any of us as within the limits of possibility.

During the night I changed my position in order to secure an unlimited supply of water, and was prepared for their return, feeling sure they would do so, as they were in such numbers; but early in the morning of the 27th, and while we were on the *qui vive* for Indians, I saw with my glass a dust some distance down the valley. There was no certainty for some time what they were, but finally I satisfied myself they were cavalry, and, if so, could only be Custer, as it was ahead of the time that I understood that General Terry could be expected. Before this time, however, I had written a communication to General Terry, and three volunteers were to try and reach him. (I had no confidence in the Indians with me, and could not get them to do anything.) If this dust were Indians it was possible they would not expect any one to leave. The men started, and were told to go as near as it was safe to determine whether the approaching column was white men, and to return at once in case they found it so, but if they were Indians to push on to General Terry. In a short time we saw them returning over the high bluffs already alluded to. They were accompanied by a scout, who had a note from Terry to Custer saying Crow scouts had come to camp saying he had been whipped, but that it was not believed. I think it was about 10.30 a. m. when General Terry rode into my lines, and the fate of Custer and his brave men was soon determined by Captain Benteen proceeding with his company to his battle-ground, and where was recognized the following officers, who were surrounded by the dead bodies of many of their men: Gen. G. A. Custer, Col. W. W. Cook, adjutant; Capts. M. W. Keogh, G. W. Yates, and T. W. Custer; First Lieuts. A. E. Smith, James Calhoun; Second Lieuts. W. V. Reily, of the Seventh Calvary and J. J. Crittenden, of the Twentieth Infantry, temporarily attached to this regiment. The bodies of Lieut. J. E. Porter and Second Lieuts. H. M. Harrington and J. G. Sturgis, Seventh Cavalry, and Asst. Surg. G. W. Lord, U. S. A., were not recognized; but there is every reasonable probability they were killed. It was now certain that the column of five companies with Custer had been killed.

The wounded in my lines were, during the afternoon and evening of the 27th, moved to the camp of General Terry, and at 5 a. m. of the 28th I proceeded with the regiment to the battle-ground of Custer, and buried 204 bodies, including the following-named citizens: Mr. Boston Custer, Mr. Reed, (a young nephew of General Custer,) and Mr. Kellogg, (a correspondent for the New York Herald.) The following-named citizens and Indians who were with my command were also killed: Charles Reynolds, guide and hunter; Isaiah Dorman, (colored,) interpreter; Bloody Knife, who fell from immediately by my side; Bobtail Bull, and Stab, of the Indian scouts.

After traveling over his trail, it was evident to me that Custer intended to support me by moving farther down the stream and attacking the village in flank; that he found the distance greater to the ford than he anticipated; that he did charge, but his march had taken so long, although his trail shows that he had moved rapidly, that they were ready for him; that Companies C and I, and perhaps part of E, crossed to the village, or attempted it; at the charge were met by a staggering fire, and that they fell back to find a position from which to defend themselves, but they were followed too closely by the Indians to permit time to form any kind of a line.

I think had the regiment gone in as a body, and from the woods from which I fought advanced upon the village, its destruction was certain. But he was fully confident they were running away, or he would not have turned from me. I think (after the great number of Indians that were in the village,) that the following reasons obtain for the misfortune: His rapid marching for two days and one night before the fight; attacking in the day-time at 12 m., and when they were on the *qui vive*, instead of early in the morning; and lastly, his unfortunate division of the regiment into three commands.

During my fight with the Indians I had the heartiest support from officers and men, but the conspicuous services of Bvt. Col. F. W. Benteen I desire to call attention to especially, for if ever a soldier deserved recognition by his Government for distinguished services he certainly does. I inclose herewith his report of the operations of his battalion from the time of leaving the regiment until we joined commands on the hill. I also inclose an accurate list of casualties, as far as it can be made at the present time, separating them into two lists: A, those killed in General Custer's command; B, those killed and wounded in the command I had.

The number of Indians killed can only be approximated until we hear through the agencies. I saw the bodies of eighteen, and Captain Ball, Second Cavalry, who made a scout of thirteen miles over their trail, says that their graves were many along their line of march. It is simply impossible that numbers of them should not be hit in the several charges they made so close to my lines. They made their approaches through the deep gulches that led from the hill-top to the river, and, when the jealous care with which the Indian guards the bodies of killed and wounded is considered, it is not astonishing that their bodies were not found. It is probable that the stores left by them and destroyed the next two days was to make room for many of these on their travois. The harrowing sight of the dead bodies crowning the height on which Custer fell, and which will remain vividly in my memory until death, is too recent for me not to ask the good people of this country whether a policy that sets opposing parties in the field armed, clothed, and equipped by one and the same Government should not be abolished.

All of which is respectfully submitted.

M. A. RENO,
Major Seventh Cavalry, Commanding Regiment.

----

3 Bb.—REPORT OF CAPT. F. W. BENTEEN.

CAMP SEVENTH CAVALRY, *July* 4, 1876.

SIR: In obedience to verbal instructions received from you, I have the honor to report the operations of my battalion, consisting of Companies D, H, and K, on the 25th ultimo.

The directions I received from Lieutenant-Colonel Custer were, to move with my command to the left, to send well-mounted officers with about six men who should ride rapidly to a line of bluffs about five miles to our left and front, with instructions to report at once to me if anything of Indians could be seen from that point. I was to follow the movement of this detachment as rapidly as possible. Lieutenant Gibson was the officer selected, and I followed closely with the battalion, at times getting in advance of the detachment. The bluffs designated were gained, but nothing seen but other bluffs quite as large and precipitous as were before me. I kept on to those and the country was the same, there being no valley of any kind that I could see on any side. I had then gone about fully ten miles; the ground was terribly hard on horses, so I determined to carry out the other instructions, which were, that if in my judgment there was nothing to be seen of Indians, valleys, &c., in the direction I was going, to return with the battalion to the trail the command was following. I accordingly did so, reaching the trail just in advance of the pack-train. I pushed rapidly on, soon getting out of sight of the advance of the train, until reaching a morass, I halted to water the animals, who had been without water since about 8 p. m. of the day before. This watering did not occasion the loss of fifteen minutes, and when I was moving out the advance of the train commenced watering from that morass. I went at a slow trot until I came to a burning lodge with the dead body of an Indian in it on a scaffold. We did not halt. About a mile farther on I met a sergeant of the regiment with orders from Lieutenant-Colonel Custer to the officer in charge of the rear-guard and train to bring it to the front with as great rapidity as was possible. Another mile on I met Trumpeter Morton, of my own company, with a written order from First Lieut. W. W. Cook to me, which read:

"Benteen, come on. Big village. Be quick. Bring packs.

"W. W. COOK.

"P. Bring pac's."

I could then see no movement of any kind in any direction; a horse on the hill, riderless, being the only living thing I could see in my front. I inquired of the trumpeter what had been done, and he informed [me] that the Indians had "skedaddled," abandoning the village. Another mile and a half brought me in sight of the stream and plain in which were some of our dismounted men fighting, and Indians charging and recharging them in great numbers. The plain seemed to be alive with them. I then noticed our men in large numbers running for the bluffs on right bank of stream. I concluded at once that those had been repulsed, and was of the opinion that if I crossed the ford with my battalion, that I should have had it treated in like manner; for, from long experience with cavalry, I judge there were 900 veteran Indians right there at that time, against which the large element of recruits in my battalion would stand no earthly chance as mounted men. I then moved up to the bluffs and reported my command to Maj. M. A. Reno. I did not return for the pack-train because I deemed it perfectly safe where it was, and we could defend it, had it been threatened, from our position on the bluff; and another thing, it savored too much of coffee-cooling to return when I was sure a fight was progressing in the front, and deeming the train as safe without me.

Very respectfully,

F. W. BENTEEN,
Captain Seventh Cavalry.

Lieut. GEO. D. WALLACE,
Adjutant Seventh Cavalry.

---

3 C.—REPORT OF MAJ. ORLANDO H. MOORE.

IN THE FIELD, CAMP NEAR MOUTH OF ROSEBUD, MONT.,
August 4, 1876.

DEAR GENERAL: I have the honor to submit the following report of my operations, executed in compliance with instructions from the department commander to take the steamer Far West, (Capt. Grant Marsh, master,) and such force as was thought proper, and proceed down the Yellowstone to Powder River, rescue the forage stored at that place, and attack any hostile Indians that might be encountered.

I left the mouth of the Rosebud August 1, 1876, at 3 p. m., on board the steamer Far West. My force consisted of Companies D, Captain Murdock, and I, Lieut. George B. Walker, Sixth Infantry; Company C, Captain McArthur and Lieutenant Garretty, Seventeenth Infantry; three scouts—Messrs. Brockmeyer, Morgan, and Smith; one Napoleon and one Gatling gun, commanded by Lieut. C. A. Woodruff, Seventh Infantry.

I reached Powder River early on the morning of August 2d, and passed on down the Yellowstone around the bend to Wolf Rapids, in order to better discover and attack Indians. None could be seen, although numerous fires indicated their presence in the vicinity. I then moved to the landing where the forage had been stored, and a large quantity of oats was found with nearly all the sacks removed by the Indians, and at once made preparations to take the grain on board. The ground near the landing, on account of a circular ridge, made a strong military position, which I at once occupied. In a few minutes, some of the Indians made their appearance. I at once made a disposition of my forces for a fight, leaving ten men on board to guard the steamer.

The larger portion of my command was carefully concealed from the view of the Indians, in the hope that they would advance to an attack upon the infantry. This, however, they declined to do. I then concluded to treat them with something new, and accordingly placed Lieutenant Woodruff's artillery in position, and opened fire upon a party on our right—toward Powder River—with spherical-case shell from our 12-pounder Napoleon gun, which spread consternation among them, and they were driven all along from the ravines and fled to the bluffs, as the shells went on their exploring expeditions, bearing more to the left each successive shot, until the whole ground in the bend between Powder River and Wolf Rapids on our left was commanded by our artillery. We then went to work loading the oats.

At about 11 o'clock more Indians made their appearance on the flank near Wolf

Rapids, and were repulsed by the artillery. About 1 o'clock Mr. Campbell, pilot on the boat, and the scouts Brockmeyer and Morgan rode out down the river and near the bluffs, when skirmishers reported that Indians were attempting to cut them off. I discovered about twenty Indians maneuvering for this purpose, who were concealed from the view of the scouts. At this moment a well-directed shot from the Napoleon gun apprised the scouts of their danger, and defeated the movements of all but a small party of Indians, who were in advance, and who opened fire on the scouts, in which Brockmeyer and his horse fell. The scout, mortally wounded, was cared for on the spot by the gallant Dr. Porter.

The Indian who shot Brockmeyer fell under the fire of the other scout; and the remainder of the Indians fled to the hills under the continued fire of the artillery, while Lieutenant Garretty was promptly hastening on to aid the scouts with a detachment ordered from the left flank of the line of infantry.

While this was going on some Indians were seen at Powder River Bluffs on our right.

After this diversion, near dark, we completed loading the grain, which was estimated at about seventy-five tons. Nothing more being seen of the Indians, I returned with the command to the Rosebud.

The entire command deserve commendation for their energy and concord in the discharge of every duty at Powder River, including the officers of the steamer Far West.

I am, general, very respectfully, your obedient servant,

ORLANDO H. MOORE,
Major Sixth Infantry.

The ASSISTANT ADJUTANT-GENERAL,
Headquarters Department of Dakota, in the field.

---

3 D.—REPORT OF GENERAL W. B. HAZEN.

HEADQUARTERS BATTALION SIXTH INFANTRY,
Fort Peck, Mont., November 2, 1876.

SIR: I arrived here yesterday and discharged the steamboat at once. I have just received a note from General Miles upon the subject of supplies here, and the inclosed is my reply. I believe this matter, so far as it relates to Sitting Bull's people, can be closed this winter, with a little activity. Some cavalry with the infantry is very important. They have no lodges, nor in fact anything else but their horses, thin as shadows. The people here say they are on the last verge of destitution. There were a dozen Seventh Cavalry horses left here on their flight, and so poor as to be barely able to winter.

The ammunition question is now all-important, and I will see that they get none in this quarter. A paymaster's check for $127, given to Captain Yates, indorsed in favor of Lieutenant Cook, taken in the Custer fight, has been turned over to the agent here and awaits a claimant.

I arrived here none too soon, as a large number of the Un-ca-pa-pas—they claim 118 lodges, although they have no lodges—were already settled here for the purpose of getting supplies.

Very respectfully, your obedient servant,

W. B. HAZEN,
Colonel Sixth Infantry, Bvt. Maj. Gen., Commanding.

THE ASSISTANT ADJUTANT-GENERAL,
Department of Dakota, Saint Paul, Minn.

[Inclosure.]

HEADQUARTERS BATTALION SIXTH INFANTRY,
Fort Peck, Mont., 10 a. m., November 2, 1876.

General N. A. MILES:

Your dispatch of October 27 and 28 reached me here this moment. I arrived here yesterday with thirty days' rations for 500 men, and 20,000 pounds grain, and 140 men. We will be compelled to use some of this, but if necessary it can be supplemented here from Indian supplies.

Sitting Bull, two days ago, with 30 lodges, was on the Dry Fork, twenty miles south. About a hundred lodges Un-ca-pa-pas, under Iron Dog and Sitting Bull's brother-in-law, were here encamped with the agency Indians, on my approach, but getting messengers from Wolf Point, left instanter, and have recrossed the Missouri River, which is no longer an impediment to them, and are now probably with Sitting Bull. Long Dog is still here with the Yanctonnais. They have left, in flight, about a dozen of the Seventh Cavalry horses, but they are so poor as to hardly be able to winter.

Their own animals are also racks of bones. The Indians are entirely destitute, and of the 1,000 good lodges the hostile party had in the spring they have not one left. I don't think they can stand the winter if kept stirred up. The need of some cavalry is all-important. For fear of freezing up I discharged the steamboat on arrival. The Indians have formerly got ammunition at all the places you mention, but for the past three months have not been getting it here, at Jounox or Carroll; but to make sure I will seize it all. There is none at Jounox, and but very little in the half-breed camp.

Very respectfully, your obedient servant,

W. B. HAZEN,
Colonel Sixth Infantry, Bvt. Maj. Gen., Commanding.

HEADQUARTERS FORT BUFORD, DAK.,
November 9, 1876.

SIR: I have the honor to report my return from Fort Peck, where for the present I have left one officer and thirty men. I have also received your two telegrams upon the subject of Indians there, one embracing the directions of the Lieutenant-General.

Sitting Bull did not think it prudent to cross the river, but, with thirty lodges, remained on the Dry Fork, twenty miles away.

The agent had issued rations to one hundred and eighteen lodges that had joined the agency Indians the day before my arrival. He had received no instructions upon the subject, and is glad to receive them definitely, and will gladly co-operate in their execution. He had offered them peace by coming to the agency, settling there, and turning over the United States property in their possession.

In their hasty departure they left many horses, and of those belonging to the United States I could only find ten that seemed able to travel to Fort Buford. These will be taken up by the quartermaster.

I deem it of the utmost importance that an officer be sent from Benton to seize and carry out of the country the fixed cartridges from Forts Belknap and Clagget. The honest intentions of citizens at those points to obey the order regarding its use or sale are not sufficient. They in good faith furnish it to their employés and others for hunting, as they suppose, which finally finds its way to the Indians. I found this to be the case at Peck, and in place of 1,500 rounds, as I had been repeatedly assured was the total quantity there, I found about 6,000 rounds, while servants and others were trading them to Indians without the knowledge of their employers. There were also 1,000 pounds of other ammunition there. I will leave only 60 rounds to each white man for purposes of defense, and the same amount at Wolf Point, and send an officer to Carroll for the same purpose. Belknap is beyond my reach.

I am, sir, very respectfully, your obedient servant,

W. B. HAZEN,
Colonel Sixth Infantry, Brevet Major-General, U. S. A., Commanding.

The ASSISTANT ADJUTANT-GENERAL,
Headquarters Department of Dakota, Saint Paul, Minn.

---

3 E.—REPORT OF GENERAL NELSON A. MILES.

CAMP OPPOSITE CABIN CREEK,
On the Yellowstone River, Montana, October 25, 1876.

SIR: I have the honor to report that, having received information of the movement of hostile Indians from the south toward the Yellowstone, also of the design of Sitting Bull to go north to the Big Dry for buffalo, I moved with the Fifth Infantry to intercept or follow his movement. On Custer Creek I learned that he had attacked and turned back one train from Glendive, and made a second unsuccessful attack upon an escort and train under command of Colonel Otis. Moving northeast and approaching their trail and camp, they appeared in considerable numbers and presented a flag of truce and desired to communicate.

I met Sitting Bull between the lines. He expressed a desire to "make a peace." He desired to hunt buffalo, to trade, (particularly for ammunition,) and agreed that the Indians would not fire upon soldiers if they were not disturbed. He desired to know why the soldiers did not go into winter-quarters, and in other words he desired an old-fashioned peace for the winter. He was informed of the terms of the Government, and on what grounds he could obtain peace, and that he must bring his tribe in near our camp. The interview ended near sundown with no definite result, they retiring to their camp and my command moving and camping on Cedar Creek, in position to more easily intercept their movement north. Sitting Bull was told to come in next day. As the command was moving north between their camp and the Big Dry, they again appeared and desired to talk. A council followed between the lines with Sitting Bull,

Pretty Bear, (chief in council,) Bull Eagle, John Sans Arco, Standing Bear, Gall, (big war-chief,) White Bull, and others of their head-men present. Sitting Bull was anxious for peace, provided he could have his own terms, yet to surrender to the Government would be a loss of prestige to him as a great war-chief. His taste and great strength is as a warrior, and I should judge that influence would have great weight with him as against wiser councils. Several of his head-men and people, I believe, desire peace. The demands of the Government were fully explained to him, and the only terms required of him were that he should camp his tribe at some point on the Yellowstone near the troops, or go into some Government agency and place his people under subjection to the Government. He said he would come in to trade for ammunition, but wanted no rations or annuities, and desired to live as an Indian; gave no assurance of good faith, and as the council ended was told that a non-acceptance of the liberal terms of the Government would be considered an act of hostility. An engagement immediately followed. They took position on a line of hills and broken ground, occupying every mound and ravine. They were driven from every part of the field, through their camp-ground, and down Bad-Route Creek, and finally across the Yellowstone at the ford they had crossed about a week before. In their camp and on the line of their retreat they abandoned tons of dried meat, lodge-poles, travoys, camp-equipage, ponies, and broken-down cavalry horses, &c. They fought principally dismounted, and were driven forty-two miles to the south side of the Yellowstone. During the fight, as we passed rapidly over the field, five dead warriors were reported to me as left on the field, besides those they were seen to carry away. I intend to continue the pursuit. They are in great want of food, their stock is nearly worn down, and they cannot have a large amount of ammunition. What they have has been taken from citizens in the Black Hills, from troops in the Custer massacre, or from friendly Indians. Several of the Indians who had just come out from the Standing Rock agency were seen to have a fresh supply of 50-caliber ammunition. Long Dog, one of Sitting Bull's chiefs, and one of the worst men in the tribe, is now at Peck getting ammunition.

I have the honor to recommend that all communication between the hostile and agency Indians, except through military channels, be discontinued, when I believe the trouble can be settled during the winter. I believe that Fort Peck should be occupied and all ammunition in that vicinity seized by the Government. Since the engagement, I believe they will be more inclined to make peace. Their force was estimated at upward of 400 lodges and nearly 1,000 men.

If they do not accept the terms of the Government within one month, I am satisfied they will go to the Big Horn country for grass and game. If any supplies have been placed in that vicinity, I would be glad to be apprised of it, as the command may move in that direction.

I am, sir, very respectfully, your obedient servant,

NELSON A. MILES,
Colonel Fifth Infantry, Brevet Major General, U. S. A., Commanding.

The ASSISTANT ADJUTANT-GENERAL,
Department of Dakota, Saint Paul, Minn.

CAMP OPPOSITE CABIN CREEK,
On Yellowstone River, Montana, October 26, 1876.

SIR: Since my report of the 25th instant I learn from Bull Eagle, principal chief of the hostiles now south of the Yellowstone, that in their retreat the bands divided; Sitting Bull and thirty lodges broke off to the left for Fort Peck, and the main body heading for the Cheyenne agency. His small trail was seen, but it was considered of more importance to follow the main body south of the Yellowstone. These are more anxious for peace now than ever, and when they are started in the right direction we will turn our attention to those near Peck and the Little Horn. I will endeavor to keep them divided, and take them in detail.

I am, sir, very respectfully, your obedient servant,

NELSON A. MILES,
Colonel Fifth Infantry, Brevet Major-General, U. S. A., Commanding.

The ASSISTANT ADJUTANT-GENERAL,
Department of Dakota, Saint Paul, Minn.

HEADQUARTERS YELLOWSTONE COMMAND, CAMP OPPOSITE CABIN CREEK,
On Yellowstone River, Montana, October 27, 1876.

SIR: I have the honor to report that four principal chiefs and one head-warrior surrendered themselves to-day as hostages that their tribes, the Minneconjous and Sans-Arcs, will continue their retreat to the Cheyenne agency, and there remain at peace, subject to the orders of the Government. I consider this the beginning of the end. In sending them this way I avoid escorting them three hundred miles, and it enables me to turn north for the remainder of Sitting Bull's band. They represent upward of four hundred lodges of hostile Sioux Indians, and if their tribes are not in within the stated time their people, and they, understand the position they occupy as hostages, the chiefs Bull Eagle, Small Bear, and Bull take the tribes to the agency. I gave them five days to obtain meat, and thirty days to make the journey, and gave them a statement showing the terms of their surrender, (copy inclosed.) Having driven them out of the buffalo range they are nearly starving for food, and I recommend that, as they give themselves up, if they cannot be fed by the Interior Department, they be fed as prisoners of war.

I am, sir, very respectfully, your obedient servant,

NELSON A. MILES,
Colonel Fifth Infantry, Brevet Major-General, U. S. A., Commanding.

The ASSISTANT ADJUTANT-GENERAL,
Department of Dakota, Saint Paul, Minn.

CAMP OPPOSITE CABIN CREEK,
On the Yellowstone River, Montana, October 27, 1876.

This is to certify that since the recent engagement (October 21) and pursuit of this body of hostile Sioux they have surrendered five of their principal chiefs and head-men as hostages that their tribes will continue their retreat to the Cheyenne agency, Dakota, and there remain at peace, and submit to the orders of the Government. Bull Eagle's, Small Bear's, and Bull's tribes are given permission to delay five days in their present camp to enable them to obtain sufficient meat, and thirty days to make the journey. The faith of the Government is pledged to their protection so long as they are faithfully complying with the terms of their surrender, and any United States officer in command of troops is respectfully requested to honor this communication. Should they be found away from their line of march, or absent after December 2, then this protection becomes void.

NELSON A. MILES,
Colonel Fifth Infantry, Brevet Major-General, U. S. A., Commanding.

Official:

FRANK D. BALDWIN,
First Lieutenant Fifth Infantry, Acting Assistant Adjutant-General.

CAMP OPPOSITE CABIN CREEK,
On Yellowstone River, Montana, October 27, 1876.

DEAR GENERAL: I send you in to-day five principal chiefs and head-men of the Sioux as hostages that their tribes will go in and surrender at the Cheyenne agency. Lieutenant Forbes will explain to you the condition of their surrender, and I hope that you will see that they are fairly treated, especially Bull Eagle, whom I think a magnificent young Indian, and one who is disposed to be friendly. While we have fought and routed these people, and driven them away from their ancient homes, I cannot but feel regret that they are compelled to submit to starvation, for I fear they will be reduced to that condition as were the southern tribes in 1874. It is in view of these considerations that I send these head-men to you, for in your hands they will be not only under your protection but at your mercy. The result of the last few weeks cannot but reflect credit upon your department.

Yours, very truly,

NELSON A. MILES,
Colonel and Brevet Major-Genral U. S. A., Commanding.

General A. H. TERRY,
Commanding Department of the Dakota, Saint Paul, Minn.

HEADQUARTERS YELLOWSTONE COMMAND,
Camp on Bar-Route Creek, Montana, October 28, 1876.

GENERAL: Fearing that you may not fully understand just the condition upon which these chiefs surrendered, I write you again. Red Skirt is principal chief of the Minneconjous, and related to Bull Eagle, who takes his tribe of about 60 lodges to the agency. White Bull is father of Small Bear, who takes in his band of about 50 lodges. Black Eagle and Sunrise are chiefs, and Foolish Thunder head-warrior, of the Sans-Arcs. I cannot say the exact number that they will take in; although Red Skirt claims to be chief of 1,300 lodges. I presume this includes some now at the agencies. I think they should take in 200, and possibly 500 lodges. I believe the work, as far as this command is concerned, has been well done, and what is to be accomplished will depend upon the manner in which these chiefs are treated, and the reception their people receive on their arrival. Bull Eagle was told, and I believe fully understood, that on his arrival there he should turn in his arms, particularly the Springfield carbines, and such horses as the Government should require. I would recommend that what property is taken from them be sold at some good market and the proceeds returned to the owners in domestic stock, for there is no doubt but what they will be poor enough in a short time. If they can be encouraged to become a pastoral people, they should in that way soon become self-sustaining. They are very suspicious, and of course afraid that some terrible punishment will be inflicted upon them. Bull Eagle tells me that the interpreter at the Cheyenne, agency informs them that "the whites are going to do something terrible with them." This, of course, does no good, and frightens his people. If any change is made in their condition, I think that it would be well that it be made late in the winter, and after they are all in. If we can keep them divided and destroy Sitting Bull's influence, I think we can end this trouble in time. Sitting Bull's band is the wildest on the continent, and, strange as it may seem, there were people in his tribe who had never seen the face of a white man before October 21, and when one of my soldiers went with the interpreter to his band, he was looked upon as a strange and curious being. I believe Sitting Bull would be glad to make a peace, at least for a time, but he is afraid he has committed an unpardonable offense. The Cheyennes reported as having gone to the Little Horn country, I believe have crossed or will cross near its mouth, and will be found on the Big Dry. I presume they, with Sitting Bull's band, will number near five hundred lodges.

I am, general, with great respect, your obedient servant,

NELSON A. MILES,
Colonel Fifth Infantry, Brevet Major-General, U. S. A., Commanding.
General A. H. TERRY,
Commanding Department of Dakota, Saint Paul, Minn.

P. S.—Since sending these warriors in I have apprised General Hazen of my intention of moving immediately north from Tongue River, in order to move upon any Indians that may be on the Big Dry, and also to follow those gone to Peck, and have requested him to place supplies at the latter point.

N. A. MILES,
U. S. A.

---

3 F.—REPORT OF LIEUT. COL. E. S. OTIS.

HEADQUARTERS BATTALION TWENTY-SECOND INFANTRY,
Glendive Creek, Mont., October 13, 1876.

SIR: I have the honor to inform you that a loaded train started from this station for Tongue River on the 10th instant, under the command of Capt. C. W. Miner, Twenty-second Infantry, and returned the next day, the reasons for which are fully set forth in the accompanying report of Captain Miner.

I have caused the train to be re-organized, and will start with it myself to-morrow morning, with Companies C and G, Seventeenth Infantry, G, H, and K, Twenty-second Infantry, which force will have one hundred and eighty rifles. I will also take a section of Gatling guns, caliber 50. I have so few serviceable horses here that I cannot have more than three or four mounted men. I am satisfied, from all the information I can gather, that there is a large force of Indians in the country, who seem to be bold and defiant; they have been hovering around this camp, on both sides of the river, for the past two days, and no doubt it is their plan to attempt to break up the communication between this place and Tongue River, but I think we can pass through the country with the force I am taking.

I leave this camp under the command of Captain Clarke, Twenty-second Infantry; with his company, (I,) and with the men attached, he will have eighty rifles and one Gatling gun, caliber 45.

Very respectfully, your obedient servant,

E. S. OTIS,
Lieutenant-Colonel Twenty-second Infantry, Commanding.
ASSISTANT ADJUTANT-GENERAL DEPARTMENT OF DAKOTA,
Saint Paul, Minn.

CAMP MOUTH GLENDIVE CREEK,
October 12, 1876.

POST-ADJUTANT:

SIR: In compliance with the verbal orders of the commanding officer, I have the honor to report that on the morning of the 10th instant I started for Tongue River with a train of ninety-four wagons and one ambulance, escorted by four companies of infantry, strength as follows:

Company C, Seventeenth United States Infantry.. 39
Company H, Twenty-second United States Infantry ....
Company G, Twenty-second United States Infantry ....
Company K, Twenty-second United States Infantry ....

That I moved from camp, at the mouth of Glendive Creek, at half past 10 in the morning. So soon as the head of my train appeared on the hills on the west side of the camp I saw a signal-fire spring up on the opposite bank of the Yellowstone River, some ten miles above, and opposite the camp I intended to make that evening. I arrived in camp, what is called Fourteen-mile Camp, about 5 in the evening. The camp is in the bed of a creek, and commanded by hills at short range on all sides but the south, where it is open toward the Yellowstone River. There is a good deal of brush, and some timber along the banks of the creek. The corrals were made as compactly as possible for the night, and secured with ropes; the companies were camped close to them, two on each side; thirty-six men and four non-commissioned officers were detailed for guard; two reserves were formed and placed on the flanks not protected by the companies. At 3 o'clock a. m. of the 11th the Indians made an attack on camp, accompanied by yells and a hot fire, from a ravine about two hundred yards away. The fire was entirely directed on the corral, and they had the range exactly. This fire excited the mules, so that they broke the ropes of the corrals and stampeded, falling into the hands of the Indians—forty-one from the Government train, and six from the

Ⓡ; one mule was shot through. The firing continued for about half an hour, when the Indians moved off; not only the party who had done the firing, but another party on the other side of camp, who had not fired, but who were heard to move off. At 6 I prepared to move forward. The road here for about three miles runs up the bed of the creek camped on, and there are a number of cross-ravines. After the train started, but before the rear guard had left camp, they were fired on from the timber skirting the creek, and a large body of Indians, estimated at from two to three hundred, came over the foot-hills between the camp and the Yellowstone River on the east side of camp. These Indians engaged the rear-guard, commanded by Captain McArthur, Seventeenth Infantry, at long range, and kept up a continual skirmish, firing out of all the depressions in the ground and from behind the crests of hills. This forced me to move at a snail's pace so as to keep the train closed up and that the rear-guard should not be left too far behind. As soon as I reached the high prairie I could see large numbers of Indians on my left coming up apparently from the Yellowstone River, and passing to my front. These were entirely distinct and in addition to those in my rear. My impression was that they intended to attack me at the next water, Clear Creek, 8 miles from my camp of the night of the 10th instant. Clear Creek is in a deep ravine, very bad to get down to and hard to pull up out of. It is so narrow that the hills on either side will command its entire width. At half-past 11 a. m., I had gotten within about half a mile of Clear Creek. My rear was still fired on, and Indians could be seen on all sides. I sent my wagon-master ahead to examine Clear Creek, if possible. He came back and reported that he saw twelve in the ravine through which we would be obliged to descend, and that he heard firing on the creek itself, and believed they were in force there. I at once decided that in the crippled condition of the train it would be best to return to the camp at the mouth of Glendive creek My reasons were these: So far, the Indians had shown a force, as near as I could estimate, of from 400 to 600; their signal-fires were springing up in all directions. I was satisfied that if I took the train into the bed of Clear Creek it would be attacked and be so much further crippled as to necessitate the abandonment of some of the wagons. That the same performance would take place at the next creek, and in all probability in much larger force, if I were not compelled to corral away from both wood and water. That with the force I had I could not cover the herd in its necessary grazing. That in going forward I should lose the major part of the train; and, finally, if I turned at once I could take the train back to the supply-camp in safety. I at once turned back up Clear Creek to reach the upper trail and reached it in about two miles. This trail is on high open ground and there are no intersecting ravines, so that it gave me all the advantage in moving. So soon as I reached the new trail the attack on my rear ceased, although the Indians followed me at some distance and could be seen in small parties till late in the afternoon. I had no further trouble with them and reached camp at 9 p. m.. after a hard march of twenty-nine miles. In closing I wish to state that it is my belief that a much larger force than four companies of about forty men each will be required to force the train through; that it should be supplied with a force of at least twenty-four good mounted men, plenty of water-kegs kept constantly filled and not used from except in case of real necessity, and at least one gun—two would be better. In reply to the signal-fires I saw a dense smoke arise apparently in the Little Missouri country about the head of Beaver, and believe that one of their main camps with their families is in that section of country, and that there is a camp somewhere about O'Fallon Creek for the purpose of annoying trains.

The men and officers did all of them exceedingly well, and it is due to them that the train came off as well as it did. The wagon-masters were the only men that I had available as scouts, and were invaluable to me in that capacity in looking over the country in my front.

Very respectfully, your obedient servant,

CHARLES W. MINER,
Captain Twenty-second Infantry.

Crowskin Necklace and Case

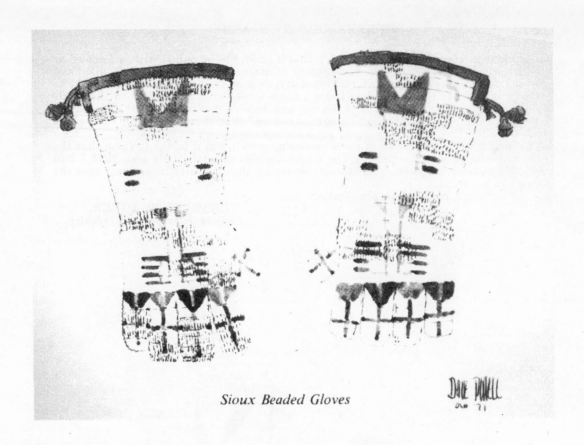

Sioux Beaded Gloves

No. 6.—REPORT OF GENERAL CROOK.

HEADQUARTERS DEPARTMENT OF THE PLATTE,
Omaha, Nebr., September 25, 1876.

SIR: At the date of my annual report for 1875, September 15, the settlers along the line of the Pacific Railroad and in Wyoming, Nebraska, and Colorado, were very much excited and exasperated by the repeated incursions made upon them by Indians coming from the north, and although many of the trails of stolen stock ran directly upon the Sioux reservation, the agency Indians always asserted that the depredations were committed by certain hostile bands under Crazy Horse, Sitting Bull, and other outlaw chiefs.

These bands roamed over a vast extent of country, making the agencies their base of supplies, their recruiting and ordnance depots, and were so closely connected by intermarriage, interest, and common cause with the agency Indians that it was difficult to determine where the line of the peaceably-disposed ceased and the hostile commenced.

In fact it was well known that the treaty of 1868 had been regarded by the Indians as an instrument binding on us but not binding on them.

On the part of the Government, notwithstanding the utter disregard by the Sioux of the terms of the treaty, stringent orders, enforced by military power, had been issued prohibiting settlers from trespassing upon the country known as the Black Hills.

The people of the country, against whom the provisions of the treaty were so rigidly enforced, naturally complained that if they were required to observe this treaty some effort should be made to compel the Indians to observe it likewise.

114

Although, in the treaty of 1868, the Indians expressly agree—

*　　　　*　　　　*　　　　*　　　　*　　　　*

"3d. That they will not attack any persons at home, or traveling, nor molest or disturb any wagon-trains, coaches, mules, or cattle belonging to the people of the United States, or to persons friendly therewith.

"4th. That they will never capture or carry off from the settlements white women or children.

"5th. That they will never kill or scalp white men, nor attempt to do them harm."

It is notorious that, from the date of the treaty to the present, there has been no time that the settlers were free from the very offenses laid down in the sentences quoted.

Indians have, without interruption, attacked persons at home, murdered and scalped them, stolen their stock; in fact, violated every leading feature in the treaty.

Indeed, so great were their depredations on the stock belonging to the settlers that at certain times they have not had sufficient horses to do their ordinary farming-work, all the horses being concentrated on the Sioux reservation, or among the bands which owe allegiance to what is called the Sioux Nation.

In the winter months these renegade bands dwindle down to a comparatively small number, while in summer they are recruited by restless spirits from the different reservations, attracted by the opportunity to plunder the frontiersmen, so that by midsummer they become augmented from small bands of one hundred to thousands.

Sitting Bull's band has been regarded by the white people and Indians as renegades, and when it was decided by the Interior Department that they should no longer be permitted to roam at large, but be required to come in and settle down upon the reservation set apart for them, messengers were dispatched to them setting forth these facts, and that from and after a certain time, unless they came in upon the reservation, they would be regarded and treated as hostile.

The time having expired, and the Indians failing to embrace the terms offered by the Government, by direction of the Lieutenant-General commanding I commenced preparations for a campaign against these bands.

I believe that the most successful campaign, though of course involving the most hardship, would be that prosecuted in winter, or, at least, in the early spring months. So, in the latter end of February, 1876, I took the field, with Fort Fetterman as the base.

Of the movements which transpired during this campaign, the surprise and destruction of the village of Crazy Horse on Powder River, and the subsequent failure of the command to fully profit by the success thus far obtained, reference may be had to my report of May 7, 1876, copy herewith, marked "A."

My second expedition was organized in May, and marched from Fort Fetterman on May 29.

Of the movements which transpired during this campaign, up to and including the fight on the Rosebud, reference may be had to my report of June 20, herewith inclosed, marked " B."

Knowing as I do, from personal knowledge, the large numbers of Indians in other localities who require the restraining influence of troops, I have carefully refrained from embarrassing the division commander by calls for re-enforcements. I have rather left that matter entirely to him, satisfied that he understood the necessities of the case, and would send me troops as fast and as early as he could get them. I mention this simply from the fact that there has been much of an unpleasant nature said in regard to the matter. I repeat that I did not ask for re-enforcements because I felt that we were abundantly able to take care of ourselves until they came, and that when they could be sent they would be; and they were.

The troops assigned to my command having reached me, the second movement of this expedition commenced on the morning of August 5, from our camp on Tongue River, Wyoming Territory.

For the details of this movement, reference may be had to my expedition report, copy inclosed, and marked "C."

The expedition reached the mining-camp of Deadwood, Dakota, on the 16th instant, where our temporary necessities were supplied by purchase.

The march from the head of Heart River to this point was one of unusual hardship, and tested the endurance of the command to its fullest extent.

During the campaign, from May 29 to this date, our losses, embracing those in the engagements on Tongue River, Rosebud, and Slim Buttes, have been but twelve killed, thirty-two wounded, (most of whom have since been returned to duty,) one death by accident, and one by disease.

Of the difficulties with which we have had to contend, it may be well to remark that when the Sioux Indian was armed with a bow and arrow he was more formidable, fighting as he does most of the time on horseback, than when he got the old-fashioned muzzle-loading rifle. But when he came into possession of the breech-loader and metallic cartridge, which allows him to load and fire from his horse with perfect ease, he became at once ten thousand times more formidable.

With the improved arms, I have seen our friendly Indians, riding at full speed, shoot and kill a wolf, also on the run, while it is a rare thing that our troops can hit an Indian on horseback, though the soldier may be on his feet at the time. The Sioux is a cavalry soldier from the time he has intelligence enough to ride a horse or fire a gun. If he wishes to dismount, his hardy pony, educated by long usage, will graze around near where he has been left, ready when his master wants to mount either to move forward or escape.

Even with their lodges and families, they can move at the rate of fifty miles per day. They are perfectly familiar with the country; have their spies and hunting-parties out all the time at distances of from twenty to fifty miles each way from their villages; know the number and movements of all the troops that may be operating against them, just about what they can probably do, and hence can choose their own times and places of conflict, or avoid it altogether.

At the fight on the Rosebud, June 17, the number of our troops was less than one thousand, and within eight days after that the same Indians we there fought met and defeated a column of troops of nearly the same size as ours, killing and wounding over three hundred, including the gallant commander, General Custer himself.

I invite attention to the fact that in this engagement my troops beat these Indians on a field of their own choosing, and drove them in utter rout from it, as far as the proper care of my wounded and prudence would justify. Subsequent events proved beyond dispute what would have been the fate of the command had the pursuit been continued beyond what judgment dictated.

The occupation by settlers of the Black Hills country had nothing to do with the hostilities which have been in progress. In fact, by the continuous violations by these Indians of the treaty referred to, the settlers were furnished with at least a reasonable excuse for such occupation, in that a treaty so long and persistently violated by the Indians themselves should not be quoted as a valid instrument for the preventing of such occupation. Since the occupation of the Black Hills there has not been any greater number of depredations committed by the Indians than previous to such occupation; in truth, the people who have gone to the Hills have not suffered any more and probably not as much from Indians as they would had they remained at their homes along the border.

The Sioux Nation numbers many thousands of warriors, and they have been encouraged in their insolent, overbearing conduct by the fact that those who participated in the wholesale massacre of the innocent people in Minnesota during the brief period that preceded their removal to their present location, never received adequate punishment therefor.

Following hard upon and as the apparent result of that horrible affair, the massacre of over eighty officers and men of the Army at Fort Phil Kearney, the Government abandoned three of its military posts and made a treaty of unparalleled liberality with the perpetrators of these crimes, against whom any other nation would have prosecuted a vigorous war. Since that time the reservations, instead of being the abode of loyal Indians, holding the terms of their agreement sacred, have been nothing but nests of disloyalty to their treaties and the Government, and scourges to the people whose misfortune it has been to be within the reach of the endurance of their ponies.

And in this connection, I regret to say, they have been materially aided by subagents who have disgraced a bureau established for the propagation of peace and good-will to man.

What is the loyal condition of mind of a lot of savages who will not allow the folds of the flag of the country to float over the very sugar, coffee, and beef they are kind enough to accept at the hands of the nation to which they have thus far dictated their own terms?

Such has been the condition of things at the Red Cloud agency.

The agents have informed us that the hoisting of a flag over the agency or a persistence in the determination to find by actual count the number of warriors out on the war-path would result in their massacring all the people there. When, therefore, the present campaign was inaugurated against the hostile bands it was impossible to find out what force we should probably meet. It has transpired that they could and did re enforce the hostiles by thousands of warriors. If, therefore, by the placing of these agencies under control of the military, and insisting upon the points not heretofore required, any portion of those ostensibly peaceable Indians go out, I submit that it will be better than a doubtful loyalty, as we shall know something about what we have to encounter.

The nature of the duties of the department commander have required me to be absent from headquarters much of the time, and the duties of Col. R. Williams, assistant adjutant general, Maj. J. P. Hawkins, chief commissary of subsistence, and Maj. M. I. Ludington, chief quartermaster, have been complicated not only by this absence but by the changing phases of the campaign from time to time.

It gives me pleasure to be able to say that they have discharged their duties in the most able and satisfactory manner, and I am under obligations to them therefor.

Capt. J. V. Furey, assistant quartermaster, who has been field-quartermaster for me this summer and fall, has had a multitude of duties not properly belonging to him devolving upon him, while at the same time he has been performing the onerous duties pertaining to his department. He has at times been thrown upon his own responsibility in situations not only involving the safety of his trains and our supplies, but the fu-

117

ture of the entire command itself. He has performed all these duties with ability and a zeal that merits the highest commendation.

I am also under obligations to the other staff-officers on duty at department headquarters, to the officers of my personal staff, and the officers on duty with my headquarters in the field. For details of the affairs of the several staff departments, I refer to copies of their several reports, inclosed, and marked, respectively, D, E, F, G, H, I, and K.

I have the honor to be, very respectfully, your obedient servant,

GEORGE CROOK,
Brigadier-General, U. S. A., Commanding.

ASSISTANT ADJUTANT-GENERAL,
Military Division of the Missouri, Chicago, Ill.

---

6 A.—SUBREPORT OF GENERAL CROOK.

HEADQUARTERS DEPARTMENT OF THE PLATTE,
Omaha, Nebr., May 7, 1876.

SIR: For a long time it has been the opinion of well-informed men that the principal source of all the depredations committed by Indians along the line of the Union Pacific Railroad has been in the camps of certain hostile bands of renegade Sioux, Cheyenne, and other tribes, who have roamed over the section known as the Powder, Big Horn, and Yellowstone country.

Having the run and many of the privileges of all the reservations, where those of these tribes who are supposed to be at peace are located, and enjoying immunity from any restraint upon their movements, they have been able to procure arms and ammunition, and when any important raid was contemplated, re-enforcements from the restless young warriors on these reservations, thus inflicting incalculable damage to the settlements upon which their raids have fallen.

To correct this and remove the principal cause, the Interior Department caused these hostile bands to be notified that they must come in upon the reservations set apart for them by a certain date, January 31, current year, or thereafter be considered and treated as hostile.

The date up to which they were allowed to accomplish this movement having arrived, and the bands notified having treated the summons with the utmost contempt, acting under the instructions of the Lieutenant-General commanding, I commenced operations against them in March with a detachment of troops known as the Big Horn expedition.

The object of this expedition was to move, during the inclement season, by forced marches, carrying by pack-animals the most meager supplies, secretly and expeditiously surprise the hostile bands, and, if possible, chastise them before spring fairly opened, and they could receive, as they always do in summer, re-enforcements from the reservations; the number of hostiles being largely augmented in summer, while in winter the number is comparatively small.

The campaign was, up to the moment our troops entered the large camp on the Powder River, on the 17th of March, a perfect success; the Indians were surprised, the troops had their camp and about 800 ponies before the Indians were aware of their presence, or even proximity.

Of the mismanagement, if not worse, that characterized the actions of portions of the command during the skirmish that followed, and its movements for the following twenty-four hours, it is unnecessary to speak, as they have been made the subject of serious charges against several officers, notably the immediate commander of the troops, Col. J. J. Reynolds, Third Cavalry.

The failures, however, may be summed up thus:

1st. A failure on the part of portions of the command to properly support the first attack.

2d. A failure to make a vigorous and persistent attack with the whole command.

3d. A failure to secure the provisions that were captured for the use of the troops, instead of destroying them.

4th. And most disastrous of all, a failure to properly secure and take care of the horses and ponies captured, nearly all of which again fell into the hands of the Indians the following morning.

The successes may be summed up thus:

1st. A complete surprise of the Indians.

2d. The entire destruction of their village, with their camp equipage, and large quantities of ammunition.

The undersigned accompanied the expedition, not as its immediate commander, but in his capacity of department commander, for several reasons, chief of which may be mentioned that it had been impressed upon him, and he had almost come to believe, that operations against these Indians were impossible in the rigors of the climate during the winter and early spring, and he wished to demonstrate by personal experience whether this was so or not.

When the attacking column was sent to surprise the village, the department commander, having given the immediate commander ample instructions as to his wishes, did not accompany it, but remained with the train-guard, to the end that the command might not be embarrassed by any division or appearance of such on the field, and the commander himself might feel free from all embarrassment that he might otherwise feel if the department commander were present; my intention being to take the horses and ponies, which I was certain we should capture, and from them remount my command, and with the supplies we captured push on and find whatever other force there might be.

The failure, therefore, to properly secure the captured horses rendered a further prosecution of the campaign, at this time, abortive, and the expedition returned, reaching Fort Fetterman on the 26th of March.

Attention is respectfully invited to copies of the report of Colonel Reynolds, commanding the expedition, with subreports and accompanying papers, delays in receipt of which have caused my delay in forwarding this.

I am, sir, very respectfully, your obedient servant,

GEORGE CROOK,
Brigadier-General, Commanding.

The ASSISTANT ADJUTANT-GENERAL, U. S. A.,
Headquarters Military Division of the Missouri, Chicago, Ill.

HEADQUARTERS DEPARTMENT OF THE PLATTE,
ASSISTANT ADJUTANT-GENERAL'S OFFICE,
Omaha, Nebr., September 28, 1876.

Official copy.

R. WILLIAMS,
Assistant Adjutant-General.

6 B.—SUBREPORT OF GENERAL CROOK.

HEADQUARTERS BIG HORN AND YELLOWSTONE
EXPEDITION, CAMP CLOUD PEAK,
Base Big Horn Mountains, W. T., June 20, 1876.

SIR: I have the honor to report that the detachments of Crow and Shoshone Indian scouts I had been negotiating for, reached me on the night of the 14th instant. I immediately parked my trains, pack-animals, &c., in a secure place, so arranged that the civilian employés left with them could, if necessary, defend them till our return, and marched on the morning of the 16th with every available fighting man and four days' rations, carried by each officer and man on his person or saddle.

I allowed no led-horses, each officer and man being equipped alike, with one blanket only, and every man who went, whether citizen, servant, or soldier, armed and with some organization for fighting purposes only.

The Crow Indians were under the impression that the hostile village was located on Tongue River or some of its smaller tributaries, and were quite positive that we would be able to surprise it. While I hardly believed this to be possible, as the Indians had hunting-parties out, who must necessarily become aware of the presence of the command, I considered it would be worth while to make the attempt. The Indians, (ours,) of course, being experts in this matter, I regulated my movements entirely by their efforts to secure this end.

Marching from our camp on the South Fork of Tongue River, or Goose Creek, as sometimes called, towards the Yellowstone, on the evening of the first day's march we came to a small stream near the divide that separates the waters of the Tongue and Rosebud. We discovered that a small party of hunters had seen us. We crossed the divide that evening and camped on the headwaters of a small stream, laid down on the maps as Rosebud Creek, and about 35 or 40 miles from our camp on Tongue River.

Pushing on next morning down the Rosebud, with my Indian scouts in front, when about 5 miles down the stream, near the mouth of a deep cañon, the scouts came in, reported that they had seen something and wished me to go into camp where we were, lying close till they could investigate, and very soon after others came in, reporting the Sioux in the vicinity, and within a very few minutes we were attacked by them in force.

The country was very rough and broken; the attack made in greater or less force on all sides, and, in advancing to meet it, the command necessarily soon became much separated. Under the circumstances I did not believe that any fight we could have would be decisive in its results unless we secured their village, supposed to be in close proximity. I therefore made every effort to close the command and march on their village. I had great difficulty in getting the battalions together, each command being pressed by the Indians, as the effort to concentrate them was made; the roughness of the ground facilitating this, the Indians apparently being aware of the reason for the movement, and assembling on the bluffs overlooking the cañon through which the command would have to pass.

While the engagement was in progress I succeeded, however, in throwing a portion of the command into and down the cañon for several miles, but was obliged to use it elsewhere, and, before the entire command was concentrated, it was believed that the cañon was well covered, our Indians refusing to go into it, saying it would be certain death. The bluffs on the side of the cañon being covered with timber, they could fire upon the command at short range, while a return-fire would be of no effect.

The troops having repulsed the attacks, and, in connection with the Indian scouts, driven the Sioux several miles, and our Indians refusing to go down the cañon to the supposed location of the village, it remained to follow the retreating Sioux, without rations, dragging our wounded with us on rough mule-litters or return to our train, where they could be cared for. The latter being the course adopted, we camped that night on the field, and marched next morning, reaching camp yesterday evening, having been absent, as intended when we started, four days.

Our casualties during the action were ten killed, including one Indian scout, and twenty-one wounded, including Capt. Guy V. Henry, Third Cavalry, severely wounded in the face. It is impossible to correctly estimate the loss of the enemy, as the field extended over several miles of rough country, including rocks and ravines not examined by us after the fight; thirteen of their dead bodies being left in close proximity to our lines.

I respectfully call attention to the inclosed reports of Lieutenant-Colonel Royall, Third Cavalry, and Major Chambers, Fourth Infantry, commanding the cavalry and infantry battalions respectively, and commend the gallantry and efficiency of the officers and men of the expedition as worthy of every praise.

Lieutenant-Colonel Royall and Major Chambers have given me great strength by the able manner in which they have commanded their respective columns. I am particularly grateful to them for their efficiency during the trip and engagement.

I am, sir, very respectfully, your obedient servant,

GEORGE CROOK,
Brigadier-General, Commanding.

The ASSISTANT ADJUTANT-GENERAL, U. S. A.,
Headquarters Military Division of the Missouri, Chicago, Ill.

---

6 Ba.—TELEGRAM FROM GENERAL CROOK.

[Telegram.]

BIG HORN AND YELLOWSTONE EXPEDITION,
Camp at head of Heart River, Dak. Ty., September 5, 1876.

Lieutenant-General SHERIDAN, *Chicago, Ill.:*

On 26th of August I left Powder River on the trail of the Indians that we had followed down from the Rosebud, General Terry going north of the Yellowstone to intercept the trail of any Indians taking that direction. My column followed this trail down Beaver Creek to a point opposite Sentinel Buttes, where the Indians scattered, and the deluging rains to which we have been exposed during the past week have so obliterated their trails as to make it very difficult and laborious to work up the case, but undoubtedly a very large majority of the trails led over toward the Little Missouri, going in the direction of the Black Hills, the separation taking place apparently about twelve days ago.

I have every reason to believe that all the hostile Indians left the Big Horn, Tongue, and Powder River country in the village the trail of which we followed.

This village was very compact, and arranged in regular order of seven circles of lodges, covering an area of at least two thousand acres. With the exception of a few lodges that had stolen off toward the agencies, there was no change in the size or arrangement of the village until it disintegrated. All indications show the hostile Indians were much straitened for food, and that they are now traveling in small bands, scouring the country for small game.

I feel satisfied that if they can be prevented from getting ammunition or supplies from the agencies, a large majority of them will surrender soon.

I have with me only about two days' provisions, but I shall push out for the Black Hills, to try to reach there in advance of the hostiles or as soon as they do, scouting the country on the march as thoroughly as the circumstances will admit. We have traveled over four hundred miles since leaving our wagon-train; our animals are now much jaded, and many of them have given out, while our men begin to manifest symptoms of scorbutic affections. As things look now, Custer City will probably be the base to operate from. I would like to have 200,000 pounds of grain sent there at once, together with twenty days' full rations of vegetables for the men. I would also like to have two companies of cavalry sent across the country from Red Cloud, via Pumpkin Buttes, by forced marches, to escort my wagon-train from the Dry Fork of Powder River, by the miner's road, to Deadwood City in the Black Hills, so as to get it there with all possible dispatch.

I make these requests of you, as I have not heard anything reliable from the outside world since your telegram of July 26, and do not know what changes may have transpired to modify the disposition of troops in my department.

GEORGE CROOK,
Brigadier-General.

---

6 Bb.—TELEGRAM FROM GENERAL CROOK.

[Telegram.]

HEADQUARTERS DEPARTMENT OF THE PLATTE,
BIG HORN AND YELLOWSTONE EXPEDITION,
Camp on Owl River, Dakota, September 10, 176.8

General SHERIDAN, *Chicago :*

Marched from Heart River, passing a great many trails of Indians going down all the different streams we crossed between Heart River and this point, apparently working their way in toward the different agencies.

Although some of the trails seemed fresh, our animals were not in condition to pursue them.

From the North Fork of Grand River, I sent Captain Mills, of the Third Cavalry, with 150 men, mounted on our strongest horses, to go in advance to Deadwood and procure supplies of provisions.

On the evening of the 8th, he discovered, near the Slim Buttes, a village of thirty-odd lodges, and lay by there that night and attacked them by surprise yesterday morning, capturing the village, some prisoners, and a number of ponies, and killing some of the Indians. Among the Indians was the chief American Horse, who died from his wounds, after surrendering to us. Our own casualties were slight, but among them was Lieutenant Von Leuttwitz, of the Third Cavalry, wounded seriously n knee, and leg since amputated.

In the village were found, besides great quantities of dried meat and ammunition, an army guidon, portions of officers' and non-commissioned officers' uniforms, and other indications that the Indians of this village had participated in the Custer massacre.

Our main column got up about noon that day, and was shortly after attacked by a considerable body of Indians, who, the prisoners said, belonged to the village of Crazy Horse, who was camped somewhere between their own village and the Little Missouri River. This attack was undoubtedly made under the supposition that Captain Mills's command had received no re-enforcements.

The prisoners further stated that most of the hostile Indians were now going into the agencies, with the exception of Crazy Horse and Sitting Bull with their immediate followers. Crazy Horse intended to remain near the headwaters of the Little Missouri; and about one-half of Sitting Bull's band, numbering from sixty to one hundred lodges, had gone north of the Yellowstone, while the remainder of that band, with some Sans-Arcs, Minneconjous, and Uncapapas, had gone in the vicinity of Antelope Buttes, there to fatten their ponies and to trade with the Rees and others.

I place great reliance in these statements, from other corroboratory evidence which I have.

Those Indians with Sitting Bull will amount probably to three hundred or four hundred lodges, and in my judgment can very easily be struck by General Terry's column, provided it go in light marching order and keep under cover.

Our prisoners in their conversation also fully confirmed in every particular my opinions as already telegraphed you.

We had a very severe march here from Heart River eighty for consecutive miles. We did not have a particle of wood; nothing but a little dry grass, which was insufficient even to cook coffee for the men. During the greater portion of the time we were drenched by cold rains, which made traveling very heavy. A great many of the animals gave out and had to be abandoned. The others are now in such weak condition that the greater number of them will not be able to resume the campaign until after a reasonable rest.

I should like to have about five hundred horses, preferably the half-breed horses raised on the Laramie plains or in the vicinity of Denver and already acclimated to this country.

I intend to carry out the programme mentioned in my last dispatch via Fort Lincoln, and shall remain in the vicinity of Deadwood until the arrival of my wagon-train.

GEORGE CROOK,
Brigadier-General.

---

6 C.—SUBREPORT OF GENERAL CROOK.

HEADQUARTERS BIG HORN AND YELLOWSTONE EXPEDITION,
Fort Laramie, Wyo., September 25, 1876.

SIR: Having been advised by the Lieutenant-General that ten companies of the Fifth Cavalry would re-enforce me, I waited with my command in the vicinity of the Big Horn Mountains till they arrived August 3d, and the expedition moved out on the morning of the 5th of August.

In view of the fact that I had been somewhat embarrassed by the care of our wounded, in the movement we made on the Rosebud in June, our organization was made with a view to the possible contingencies

123

that constantly arise in conflict with a savage foe. In war with a civilized foe it has been considered that the wounding of the enemy was better than to kill him, inasmuch as the force is not only deprived of the services of the wounded man but of those required to take care of him.

Hence it sometimes happens that a hospital falling into the hands of an enemy is a decided advantage to the army losing it. In such case the wounded would be tenderly cared for.

But in this war the case is different. The falling into the hands of our savage foe of our wounded would be a calamity not necessary to expatiate upon to be appreciated.

In starting on this second movement I first stripped the command of everything in excess of the absolute necessities of the officers and men, and after selecting the best position available for it, left my wagon-train in charge of Captain Furey, assistant quartermaster, with only the men belonging to it to guard it, with the sick and hospital attendants.

My pack-trains were in five detachments, each led by a bell-animal and so well drilled that the train would go wherever the troops were required to, leaving absolutely nothing to guard or embarrass us, and in case of an engagement it was impossible to separate the mules from the bell-animals.

Material for travaux for our wounded was transported on the pack-train and the entire command was in the most perfect fighting condition, ready to move in any direction and over any country with celerity, and to attack with power.

The wounded needed no guard, as they, with the pack-animals, were kept up with the troops all the time. Three days' march from our camp, and on Rosebud Creek, we found the trail of the hostile force going down that stream toward the Yellowstone.

Their camps were made in seven distinct circles, and were compact encampments covering an area of at least two thousand acres.

These camps and the trail showed that there was no material scattering or diminution of their force until they separated on Beaver Creek.

We followed this trail down the Rosebud to within thirty miles of where it empties into the Yellowstone, when we met General Terry's column, in conjunction with which we followed it across to Powder River, and down that stream to within twenty miles of its mouth. Here the trail left Powder River and ran in an easterly direction, while our command marched down to the Yellowstone River to replenish our rations. Here we were detained seven days by the difficulties the steamer carrying supplies experienced in navigating that stream.

Both columns then marched back up Powder River to renew pursuit on the trail, when we received information that the Indians had attacked the intrenched camp at the mouth of Glendive Creek, and fired on the steamer on the Yellowstone.

This was evidently for the purpose of covering some movement embracing a possible breaking into smaller bands and a crossing of the Yellowstone by some portion of them.

General Terry then returned to and crossed the Yellowstone to the north side to intercept any movement in that direction, while I moved with my column south on the trail to a point on Beaver Creek opposite Sentinel Buttes, where it broke up into small parties, the majority going toward the agencies and the Black Hills.

As the whole frontier of my department was thus exposed, and the people in the Black Hills in imminent danger, I marched via the head of Heart River toward their camps in the hills.

This march of ten days was made on a little over two days' rations, eighty-odd miles being over a country that had no wood, shrubbery, or even weeds with which to make fires for cooking coffee; ten days being in a deluging rain, the men not having during that time a dry blanket; the deep sticky mud making a toilsome march, which for severity and hardship has but few parallels in the history of our Army.

Notwithstanding this, when we reached 'Belle Fourche, there was but two and one-tenth per cent. of the command sick, and this included fifteen wounded in the engagement near Slim Buttes.

On the march down, our advance, under Capt. Anson Mills, Third Cavalry, attacked and destroyed a village of thirty-seven lodges, containing a large quantity of robes and property of value to the hostiles.

A report of this engagement is inclosed, and marked C.

The trains of supplies sent to meet us are now with the command, which is comfortably camped in the vicinity of Custer City, waiting future movements.

I cannot close my report without expressing my deep sense of gratitude for the courtesy with which I was treated by Brigadier-General Terry during the time our expeditions acted in conjunction. He not only did not assume command of my column, as he might have done, but shared everything he had with us.

I have the honor to be, very respectfully, your obedient servant,

GEORGE CROOK,
Brigadier-General U. S. Army, Commanding.

ASSISTANT ADJUTANT-GENERAL,
Military Division of the Missouri, Chicago, Ill.

---

6 D.—REPORT OF CAPTAIN MILLS.

HEADQUARTERS DETACHMENT THIRD CAVALRY,
In Bivouac on Rabbitt Creek, Dakota, September 9, 1876.

Lieut. GEORGE F. CHASE,
Adjutant Battalion Third Cavalry:

SIR: I have the honor to submit the following report of the engagement of this date between my command and a village of thirty-seven lodges, under Brulé Sioux chiefs American Horse and Roman Nose, at Slim Buttes, Dakota Territory.

My command consisted of four officers and 150 enlisted men, all from the Third Cavalry, save Lieutenant Bubb, Fourth Infantry, acting commissary subsistence and acting quartermaster to the general commanding the expedition, being fifteen men from each of the ten companies of the regiment serving with the expedition, selected with reference to both men and horses; one chief packer, Thomas Moore; fifteen packers, and sixty-one pack-mules.

Lieut. Emmet Crawford commanded the detachment of 75 men from Second Battalion, and Lieut. A. H. Von Luettwitz commanded the detachment of same strength from the First Battalion.

The detachment separated from the expedition on the night of the 7th, at camp on a branch of the North Fork of Grand River, with orders to proceed as rapidly as possible to Deadwood City, in the Black Hills, for rations, the expedition being then in almost a destitute condition.

Lieut. Frederick Schwatka was appointed adjutant to the detachment. The command marched south at 7 p. m., under the guidance of Mr. Frank Gruard, chief to the guide, assisted by Captain Jack, 18 miles, and camped because of the utter darkness. Marched at daylight on the 8th through heavy rain and mud, when, at 3 p. m., the guide discovered, on the slope of Slim Buttes, some forty ponies grazing, about three miles distant. As the commanding general had instructed me to lose no opportunity to strike a village, the command was rapidly put out of sight, when I, with the guides, proceeded to ascertain, if possible, if there was a village, and its location. The approaches were so difficult, that it was impossible for us to learn anything without being discovered until dark, when I decided to move back about a mile and put the command in a deep gorge, wait there until 2 o'clock a. m., and attack at daylight. The night was one of the ugliest I ever passed—dark, cold, rainy, and muddy in the extreme. At 2 a. m. we moved to within a mile of the village, where I left the pack-train, one hundred and twenty-five horses, with twenty-five men to hold them, under the command of Lieutenant Bubb, and marched on. Crawford and Von Luettwitz, each with fifty men dismounted, and Schwatka with twenty-five men mounted, the plan being, if possible, for Crawford to close on one side of the village and Von Luettwitz on the other, when Schwatka was to charge through at the bugle's sound, drive off all the stock, when the dismounted men would close on them; but when we were within a hundred yards of the lower end of the village, which was situated on either side of a small creek called Rabbit Creek, a small herd of loose ponies stampeded and ran through the village. Gruard informed me that all chance for a total surprise was lost, when I ordered the charge sounded, and right gallantly did Schwatka with his twenty-five men execute it.

Immediately, the dismounted detachments closed on the south side and commenced firing on the Indians, who, finding themselves laced in their lodges, the leather drawn tight as a drum by the rain, had quickly cut themselves out with their knives and re-turned our fire, the squaws carrying the dead, wounded, and children up the opposite bluffs, leaving everything but their limited night-clothes in our possession, Schwatka having rounded up the principal part of the herd.

All this occurred about day-break. Lieutenant Von Luettwitz, while gallently cheering his men, was severely wounded at almost the first volley, grasping my arm as he fell.

I then turned my attention to getting up the pack-train and led horses, which was quite a difficult task; and Gruard informing me from trails, the action of the Indians, and other indications that he was satisfied there were other villages near, I sent two couriers to General Crook, advising what I was doing, and requesting him to hurry forward as rapidly as possible.

The Indians, as soon as they had their squaws and children in security, returned to the contest, and soon completely encompassed us with a skirmish-line, and as my command was almost entirely engaged with the wounded, the held horses, and the skirmish-line, I determined to leave the collection of the property and provisions, with which the village was rich, to the main command on its arrival.

American Horse and his family, with some wounded, had taken refuge in a deep gorge in the village, and their dislodgment was also, from its difficulty, left to the coming re-enforcements.

The Indians were constantly creeping to points near enough to annoy our wounded, and Lieutenants Bubb and Crawford rendered themselves conspicuous in driving them each with their small mounted detachments.

The head of General Crook's column arrived at 11.30 a. m. and American Horse, mortally wounded, his family of some twelve persons, two warriors, a niece of Red Cloud, and four dead bodies were taken from the gorge; not, however, without loss.

About 5 p. m. the Indians resumed the contest with more than double their force, but were handsomely repulsed by our then strong command.

I learn from the prisoners that Crazy Horse, with the Cheyennes, a village of some three hundred lodges, was within eight or ten miles, and that the strength of the village taken consisted of about two hundred souls, one hundred of whom were warriors.

My loss was:

Killed.—Private John Winzel, Company A, Third Cavalry.

Wounded.—First Lieut. A. H. Von Luettwitz, severely; Sergeant John A. Kirkwood, Company M, Third Cavalry; Sergeant Edward Glass, Company E, Third Cavalry; Private Edward Kiernan, Company E, Third Cavalry; Private William B. DuBois, Company C, Third Cavalry; Private August Doran, Company D, Third Cavalry; Private Charles Foster, Company B, Third Cavalry.

It is impossible to estimate the enemy's loss, as they were principally carried away, although several were left on the field.

We captured a vast amount of provisions and property, over 5,500 pounds dried meat, large quantities of dried fruit, robes, ammunition, and arms, and clothing, and 175 ponies, all of which, not appropriated to the use of the command, was utterly destroyed. Among the trophies was a guidon of the Seventh Cavalry, a pair of gloves marked Colonel Keogh, 3 Seventh Cavalry horses, and many other articles recognized to have belonged to General Custer's command.

It is usual for commanding officers to call special attention to acts of distinguished courage, and I trust the extraordinary circumstances of calling on 125 men to attack, in the darkness, and in the wilderness, and on the heels of the late appalling disasters to their comrades, a village of unknown strength, and in the gallant manner in which they executed everything required of them to my entire satisfaction, will warrant me in recommending for brevet Lieutenants Bubb, Crawford, Von Luettwitz, and Schwatka; and for medals the following enlisted men, who also appeared to excel: Sergeant Galob Bigalski, Co. A, Third Cavalry; Sergeant Peter Forster, Co. I, Third Cavalry; Sergeant Edward Glass, Co. E, Third Cavalry; Sergeant W. H. Conklin, Co. G, Third Cavalry; Sergeant John A. Kirkwood, Co. M, Third Cavalry; Corporal Frank Askwell, Co. I, Third Cavalry; Corporal John Cohen, Co. F, Third Cavalry; Corporal

John D. Sanders, Co. D, Third Cavalry; Private John Hale, Co. C, Third Cavalry; Private Edward McKiernan, Company E, Third Cavalry; Private William B. DuBois, Co. C, Third Cavalry; Private Robert Smith, Co. M, Third Cavalry; also Mr. Thomas Moore, chief packer.

I am, sir, very respectfully, your obedient servant,

ANSON MILLS,
Captain Third Cavalry, Commanding Detachment.

[First indorsement.]

CAMP ON WHITEWOOD CREEK, DAKOTA, *September* 15, 1876.
Respectfully forwarded.

A. W. EVANS,
Major Third Cavalry.

[Second indorsement.]

HEADQUARTERS BATTALIONS SECOND AND THIRD CAVALRY,
CAMP ON WHITEWOOD CREEK, DAKOTA,
September 15, 1876.

Respectfully forwarded. Captain Mills's report is supplemented as follows : My command, composed of two battalions of the Third Cavalry and one of the Second, arrived at the site of the Indian village after the engagement, but Private John M. Stevenson, Co. I, Second Cavalry, having responded when a call for volunteers was made to dislodge wounded Indians from a ravine, he was severely wounded in the left foot. Lieutenant Von Luettwitz subsequently lost his right leg by amputation. During the afternoon an attack upon the camp was made by Indians in increased force, and a skirmish-line established, which successfully resisted for several hours and repulsed the same. On the morning of the 10th instant, a desultory firing was maintained by the Sioux until after my command, under the instructions of the chief of cavalry, had left camp in charge of the pack-train. To cover this movement, Company I, Second Cavalry, commanded by Lieut. F. W. Kingsbury, was, for a short time, detached.

W. B. ROYALL,
Lieutenant-Colonel Third Cavalry, Commanding Battalions Second and Third Cavalry.

––––––

6 E.—REPORT OF LIEUT. COL. E. A. CARR.

OPERATIONS OF FIFTH CAVALRY NEAR SLIM BUTTES, DAKOTA.

HEADQUARTERS FIFTH CAVALRY,
Camp on Whitewood Creek, Dakota, September 15, 1876.

SIR: I have the honor to submit the following report of the operations of this regiment on the 9th and 10th instants.

On the morning of the 9th instant, soon after leaving camp, I was directed to drop out of the regiment all the men with horses not able to go rapidly for seventeen miles, placing them in charge of an officer, and with the remainder proceed with the brevet major-general commanding the cavalry to the scene of Mills's engagement.

I marched with about 250 men and 17 officers, and we arrived at the village near Slim Buttes at 11.30 a. m., finding it in possession of our troops, and the command was bivouaced, this regiment in the right front as we marched. But there was still a number of Indians intrenched in a rifle-pit, and in the attempts to get them out we lost one private and one scout killed.

About 4 p. m., after the whole regiment had arrived, the pickets gave the alarm of "Indians!" when I sounded "To arms!" and "Forward!" and the companies formed and marched out beyond the horses very promptly and handsomely.

The horses of Company B stampeded and went outside the line, followed by parts of others, but were skilfully brought round by the herders, under the lead of Corporal J. S. Clanton, Company B, Fifth Cavalry. The companies remained in their positions firing at the Indians, who were circling round and crawling behind ridges and firing at us, till the infantry advanced on the left flank, driving them around to the right, when the battalion commanders advanced their battalions to the right, and the Indians were driven up and over the pass at the head of the valley and out of sight.

Next morning (10th) the Indians again appeared. The companies were sent out and engaged them, and when the time for marching arrived, by direction of General Merritt, they saddled by detachments, still holding the hills on the right of the infantry. I was ordered to place one battalion on the right, relieving the infantry skirmishers, and one in rear of the village, and for the regiment to form the rear guard on the day's march.

Upham's battalion was placed on the ridge in rear of camp, and Mason's on the right.

In this operation it was necessary to withdraw Upham's battalion under fire and replace it with part of Mason's, as well as to relieve the infantry skirmishers also under fire.

I was also ordered by General Merritt to release, upon leaving the site of the village, the squaws and children in our hands, and to see that all property was effectually destroyed, both of which orders were carried out.

After the column was well under way, I directed the battalion commanders to withdraw and follow, which was done slowly from ridge to ridge, the Indians following and pressing quite boldly till we were about two miles from camp.

Our loss in the two engagements was as follows:

Killed—1. Private J. W. Kennedy, Company C, Fifth Cavalry; 2. Scout Jonathan White.

Wounded—1. Sergeant Lucifer Schreiber, Company K; 2 Trumpeter Michael Donnelly, Company F; 3. Private Daniel Ford, Company F; 4. Private George Clotier, Company D; 5. Private William Madden, Company M.

The horses which made the rapid march were much jaded, the ground being very soft and slippery, and we lost about fifteen horses, unable to travel.

The officers and soldiers behaved with their usual courage and coolness.

The officers present, besides the colonel, Bvt. Maj. Gen. Wesley Merritt, commanding all the calvary, were:

Battalion commanders.—Maj. J. J. Upham, Fifth Cavalry; Capt. J. W. Mason, Fifth Cavalry.

Company officers.—1. Capt. Edward Leib, Company M; 2. Capt. Samuel S. Sumner, Company D; 3. Capt. Emil Adam, Company C; 4. Capt. Robert N. Montgomery, Company B; 5. Capt Sanford C. Kellogg, Company I; 6. Capt. George F. Price, Company E; 7. Capt. Edward M. Hayes, Company G; 8. Capt. J. Scott Payne, Company F; 9. Capt. Albert E. Woodson, Company K; 10. Capt. Calbraith P. Rodgers, Company A.

1. Lieut. Alfred B. Bache, sick in hospital in camp, under fire; 2. Lieut. Bernard Reilly, jr.; 3. Lieut. W. C. Forbush, Acting Assistant Adjutant-General, cavalry command, present, under fire; 4. Lieut. Charles King, acting regimental adjutant; 5. Lieut. William P. Hall, acting assistant quartermaster cavalry command, present, under fire; 6. Lieut Charles D. Parkhurst, battalion adjutant, Second Battalion; 7. Lieut. Edward L. Keyes; 8. Lieut. Robert London; 9. Lieut. Noel S. Bishop, battalion adjutant, First Battalion; 10. Lieut S. C. Plummer, Fourth Infantry, attached to Company I, and Acting Assistant Surgeon J. L. Powell, of Richmond, Va.

Private Patrick Nihil, Company F, shot an Indian from his saddle and got his pony.

According to the best and most reliable accounts we killed and wounded as many as seven or eight Indians.

I would add to this report, that on the 12th instant Major Upham was ordered, with 150 of the best mounted men of the regiment, to follow a trail leading down Avol Creek. He returned on the 14th, p. m., not having found a village. His men had no rations whatever, except about two ounces of dried buffalo-meat and one-fourth ounce of coffee per man, and what horse-meat the men had saved from the night before starting. It rained most of the time, making them constantly wet, and the ground very heavy and sticky, and they were without wood for two nights. Upon their return they were the worst tired men I ever saw. One of his men, Private Cyrus B Milner, Company A, while out hunting from camp on Belle Fourche, was killed by two Indians, who approached him stealthily. The whole of his scalp was taken off, his throat cut from ear to ear, and his breast gashed. His horse was killed.

Very respectfully, your obedient servant,

E. A. CARR,
Lieutenant-Colonel Fifth Cavalry, Commanding Regiment.

ACTING ASSISTANT ADJUTANT-GENERAL,
Headquarters Cavalry Command,
Big Horn and Yellowstone Expedition,
Camp on Whitewood Creek, Dakota.

HEADQUARTERS CAVALRY,
BIG HORN AND YELLOWSTONE EXPEDITION,
Camp on Whitewood Creek, September 15, 1876.

Respectfully forwarded, approved. This report and that of Colonel Royall, Third Cavalry, cover so completely the ground of the day's operations, that there is nothing to add by the commanding officer of the cavalry.

W. MERRITT,
Colonel Fifth Cavalry, Bvt. Major-General, United States Army.

[Second indorsement.]

HEADQUARTERS DEPARTMENT OF THE PLATTE,
ASSISTANT ADJUTANT-GENERAL'S OFFICE,
Omaha, Nebr., October 5, 1876.

Official copy respectfully forwarded to the assistant adjutant-general, Headquarters Military Division of the Missouri, Chicago, Illinois, with the request that this report be filed with inclosure marked C, to annual report of the department commander, dated September 25, 1876.

By command and in absence of Brigadier-General Crook,

R. WILLIAMS,
Assistant Adjutant-General.

---

6 F.—REPORT OF MAJOR CHAMBERS.

HEADQUARTERS PRINCIPAL DEPOT GENERAL RECRUITING SERVICE,
FORT COLUMBUS, NEW YORK HARBOR,
November, 1876.

SIR: I have the honor to make the following report of the disposition of the troops of the infantry battalion on the afternoon of the 9th and morning of the 10th of September, 1876, at Slim Buttes, on Rabbit Creek, Dakota Territory.

Four companies—F, Capt. G. L. Luhn; D, First Lieut. Henry Seton, Fourth; H, Ninth, Second Lieut. Charles M. Rockefeller, and C, Fourteenth Infantry, Capt. D. W. Burke—under command of Capt. A. S. Burt, Ninth Infantry, took the commanding hills and bluffs to the south and southwest of the camp, driving away the Indians who were annoying the camp by a desultory fire at long range. This movement was made without causalty, with the exception of private Robert Fitz Henry, Company H, Ninth Infantry, slightly wounded.

Companies B, Capt. J. Kennington; F, Capt. Thomas F. Tobey, and I, First Lieut. Frank Taylor, Fourteenth Infantry, were posted on the south side of camp, concealed by bluffs, ready in case an attack should be made from that direction.

Companies C, Capt. Samuel Munson, and G, First Lieut. William L. Carpenter, Ninth Infantry, took a range of bluffs on north side of camp, driving away the Indians.

Company G, Fourth Infantry, Capt. William H. Powell, reported to General Crook to perform the duty of a complete destruction of the village.

These companies having performed the duties assigned them, were withdrawn after dark, and strong pickets posted.

Before daylight on the morning of the 10th, Capt. William H. Powell, with Company G, Fourth, and B, F, and I, Fourteenth Infantry, under their respective commanders, were moved to and occupied a strong position on the bluffs south and southwest of camp, skirmishing with Indians after daylight till the whole command was under march, when they joined the infantry battalion.

The report is made at this late day, owing to subreports having been lost and but recently found.

The officers and men of the command performed their duties in their usual gallant manner.

Attention is called to the inclosed subreports.

I am, sir, very respectfully, your obedient servant,

ALEX. CHAMBERS,
Major Fourth Infantry, Commanding Infantry Battalion.

The ASSISTANT ADJUTANT-GENERAL,
Big Horn and Yellowstone Expedition, Omaha, Nebr.

[1st indorsement.]

HEADQUARTERS DEPARTMENT OF THE PLATTE,
ASSISTANT ADJUTANT-GENERAL'S OFFICE,
Omaha, Nebr., Nov. 22, 1876.

Official copy respectfully forwarded to the assistant adjutant-general, U. S. A., Headquarters Military Division of the Missouri, Chicago, Ill., with request that these papers may be forwarded for file with inclosure A to inclosure C of the annual report of the department commander, dated September 25, 1876.

In absence of Brigadier-General Crook,

R. WILLIAMS,
Assistant Adjutant-General.

3 G.—REPORT OF LIEUT. COL. E. S. OTIS.

[NOTE.—This report is not printed in its proper place in General Sheridan's report for the reason that it was not received in time.]

HEADQUARTERS BATTALION TWENTY-SECOND INFANTRY,
STATION NEAR GLENDIVE CREEK, MONT.,
October 27, 1876.

SIR: I have the honor to report that, as communicated in my letter of the 13th instant to the headquarters of the department, I commenced the trip to Tongue River with the supply-train upon the morning of the 14th instant. Forty-one of the citizen teamsters having become too greatly demoralized to continue service upon the road, were discharged, and the necessary places filled with enlisted men. The train consisted of 86 wagons, and the escort of Companies C and G, Seventeenth Infantry, and G, H, and K, Twenty-second Infantry. Details were made from these companies and left behind, with Captain Clarke, commanding Company I, Twenty-second Infantry, who was directed to remain at Glendive, and his command, thus re-enforced, consisted of 4 officers and 97 enlisted men. The train-escort consisted of 11 commissioned officers, (myself included,) and 185 enlisted men. We proceeded the first day twelve miles and encamped upon the broad bottom of the Yellowstone River without discovering a sign of the presence of Indians. During the night a small thieving party was fired upon by the picket, but the party escaped, leaving behind a single pony, with its trappings, which was killed.

At dawn of day upon the 15th, the train pulled out in two strings and proceeded quietly to Spring Creek, distant from camp about three miles. Then I directed two mounted men (Scout Robert Jackson and Sergeant Kelly, F Company, Twenty-second Infantry) to station themselves upon a hill beyond the creek and watch carefully the surrounding country until the train should pass through the defile. The men advanced at swift pace in the proper direction, and when within fifty yards of the designated spot they received a volley from a number of concealed Indians, when suddenly men and Indians came leaping down the bluff. The men escaped without injury to person, although their clothing was riddled with bullets. I quickly advanced a thin skirmish-line to the bluffs, which drove out forty or fifty Indians, and making a similar movement on the opposite flank, the train passed through the gorge and gained the high table-land. Here three or four scouts, sent out by Colonel Miles from Tongue River, joined us. They had been driven into the timber upon the previous evening, there corraled; had lost their horses and one of their number, and escaped to the bluffs under the cover of the darkness. The dead scout was found and buried. The train proceeded quietly along the level prairie, surrounded by the skirmish-line, and the Indians were coming thick and fast from the direction of Cabin Creek. But few shots were exchanged, and both parties were preparing for the struggle, which it was evident would take place at the deep and broken ravine of Clear Creek, through which the train must pass. We cautiously entered the ravine, and from one hundred and fifty to two hundred Indians had gained the surrounding bluffs to our left. Signal-fires were lighted for miles around, and extended far away on the opposite side of the Yellowstone. The prairies to our front were fired, and sent up vast clouds of smoke. We had no artillery, and nothing remained to do except to charge the bluffs. G Company, Seventeenth, and H Company of the Twenty-second Infantry were thrown forward upon the run, and gallantly scaled the bluffs, answering the Indian yell with one equally as barbarous, and driving back the enemy to another ridge of hills. We then watered all the stock at the creek, took on water for the men, and the train slowly ascended the bluffs. The country now surrounding us was much broken; the Indians continued to increase in numbers, surrounded the train, and the entire escort became engaged. The train was drawn up in four strings, and the entire escort enveloped it by a thin skirmish-line. In that formation we advanced, the Indians pressing every point, especially the rear, which was only enabled to follow by charging the enemy and then retreating rapidly toward the train, taking advantage of all the knolls and ridges in its course.

The flanks were advanced about a thousand yards, and the road was opened in the front by repeated charges. In this manner we advanced several miles and then halted for the night upon a depression of the high prairie, the escort holding the surrounding ridge. The Indians had now attempted every artifice. They had pressed every point of the line; had run their fires through the train, which we were compelled to cross with great rapidity; had endeavored to approach under the cover of the smoke, when they found themselves overmatched by the officers and men, who, taking advantage of the cover, moved forward and took them at close range. They had met with considerable loss. A good number of their saddles were emptied and several ponies wounded. Their firing was wild in the extreme, and I should consider them the poorest of marksmen. For several hours they kept up a brisk fire and wounded but three of our men; two but slightly; and one, Private Donahoe, of Company G, Twenty-second Infantry, whom I was compelled to leave at Tongue River, but who will ultimately recover.

Upon the morning of the 16th the train pulled out in four strings, and we took up the advance, formed as upon the previous day. Many Indians occupied the surrounding hills, and soon a runner approached and left a communication upon a distant hill. It was brought in by the scout, Jackson, and read as follows:

YELLOWSTONE.

I want to know what you are doing traveling on this road. You scare all the buffalo away. I want to hunt on the place. I want you to turn back from here. If you don't I will fight you again. I want you to leave what you have got here, and turn back from here.

I am your friend,

SITTING BULL.

I mean all the rations you have got and some powder. Wish you would write as soon as you can.

I directed the scout, Jackson, to inform the Indians that I had nothing to say in reply, except that we intended to take the train through to Tongue River, and that we should be pleased to accommodate them at any time with a fight.

The train continued to proceed, and about 8 o'clock the Indians again began to gather for battle. We passed through the long narrow gorge near Bad Route Creek, exchanging but few shots, and soon reached the creek, where we again watered the stock and took on wood and water, consuming in this labor about an hour's time. When we had pulled up the gentle ascent the Indians had again surrounded us, but the lesson of the previous day taught them to keep at long range, and there was but little firing by either party. I counted 150 Indians in our rear, and from their movements and positions I judged their numbers to be between three and five hundred. After proceeding a short distance a flag of truce appeared on the left flank, borne by two Indians, whom I directed to be allowed to enter the lines. They proved to be Indian scouts from Standing Rock agency, bearing dispatches from Lieutenant-Colonel Carlin, of the Seventeenth Infantry, stating that they had been sent out to find Sitting Bull, and to endeavor to influence him to proceed to some military post and treat for peace. These scouts informed me that they had that morning reached the camp of Sitting Bull and Man-afraid-of-his-horses, near the mouth of Cabin Creek; that they had talked with Sitting Bull, who wished to see me outside the lines. I declined the invitation, but professed a willingness to see Sitting Bull within my own lines. The scouts left me and soon returned with three of the principal soldiers of Sitting Bull, the last-named individual being unwilling to trust his person within our reach. The chiefs said that their people were very angry because our trains were driving away the buffalo from their hunting-grounds; that they were hungry and without ammunition, and that they especially wished to obtain the latter; that they were tired of the war, and desired to conclude a peace. I informed them that I could not give them ammunition; that had they saved the amount already wasted upon the train it would have sufficed them for hunting purposes for a long time; that I had no authority to treat with them upon any terms whatever, but that they were at liberty to visit Tongue River, and there make known conditions. They wished to know what assurance I could give them of their safety should they visit that place, and I replied that I could give them nothing but the word of an officer. They then wished rations for their people, promising to proceed to Fort Peck immediately, and from there to Tongue River. I declined to give them the rations, but finally offered them as a present one hundred and fifty pounds of hard bread and two sides of bacon, which they gladly accepted. The train moved on, and the Indians fell to the rear. Upon the following day I saw a number of them from Cedar Creek, far away to the right, and after that time they disappeared entirely. Upon the evening of the 18th I met Colonel Miles, encamped with his entire regiment on Custer Creek. Alarmed for the safety of the train, he had set out from Tongue River upon the previous day. I told him of the situation of affairs, and informed him that he would find the Indian camp either about the mouth of Cabin Creek or far away on his left, traveling in the direction of Fort Peck. He concluded to go on to Cherry Creek and there await my return from Tongue River; but having reached that point, he found the Indians engaged in hunting the large bands of buffalo which were roaming between that and Cedar Creek. His future operations, I believe, he has fully reported, and forwarded his dispatches by carriers.

I returned to this station with the train yesterday, the 26th instant, having consumed thirteen days in making the journey. The train was returned richer by two mules and two horses than when it started out, and suffered no loss.

In concluding this report, I cannot speak too highly of the conduct of both officers and men. The officers obeyed instructions with alacrity, and executed their orders with great efficiency. They fought the enemy twelve hours, and fired during that time upward of seven thousand rounds of ammunition. They defeated a strong enemy, estimated by many at from seven to eight hundred, which had defiantly placed himself across our trail with the deliberate purpose of capturing the train,

EXTRACT FROM THE ANNUAL REPORT OF THE SECRETARY OF THE INTERIOR, COMMISSIONER OF INDIAN AFFAIRS REPORT FOR 1877

A Guidon Bearer

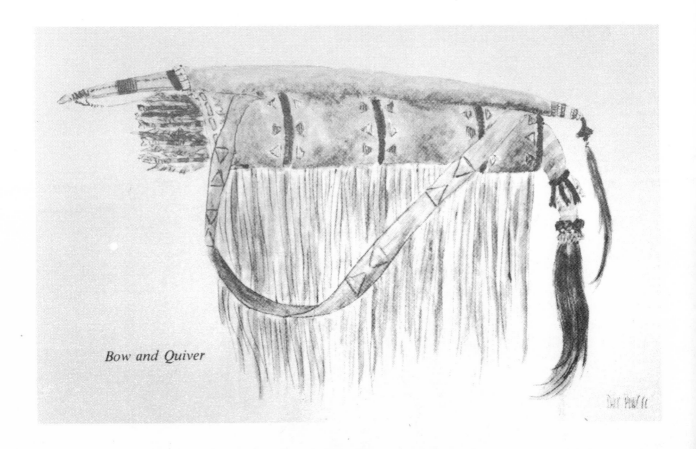

Bow and Quiver

REPORT OF THE SECRETARY OF WAR.

and gave him a lesson which he will heed and never forget. I was ably assisted by Lieut. O. M. Smith, my only staff-officer. All other officers were serving with the companies, and furnished to their men examples of fearless exposure and great endurance.

Very respectfully, your obedient servant,

E. S. OTIS,
Lieutenant-Colonel Twenty-second Infantry, Commanding.

ASSISTANT ADJUTANT-GENERAL,
Headquarters Department of Dakota, Saint Paul, Minn.

[First indorsement.]

HEADQUARTERS DEPARTMENT OF DAKOTA,
Saint Paul, Minn., December 5, 1876.

Respectfully forwarded to the adjutant-general, Military Division of the Missouri, as an appendix to my annual report.

ALFRED H. TERRY,
Brigadier-General, Commanding.

[Second indorsement.]

HEADQUARTERS MILITARY DIVISION OF THE MISSOURI,
Chicago, December 13, 1876.

Respectfully forwarded to the Adjutant-General of the Army.

P. H. SHERIDAN,
Lieutenant-General, Commanding.

133

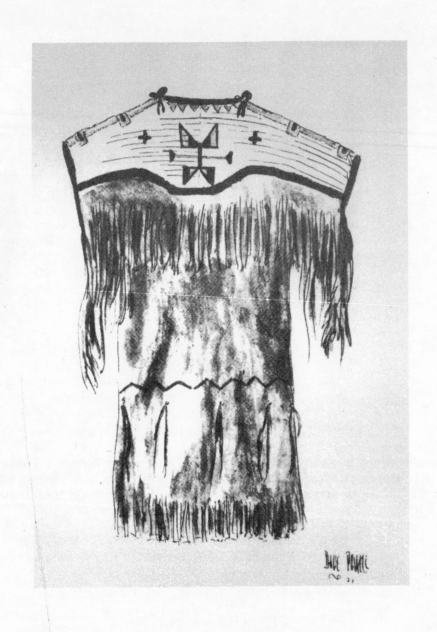

Plains Indian Squaw Dress

134

THE SIOUX WAR.

The causes which led in February, 1876, to a military campaign against that portion of the Sioux Nation, known as the non-treaty Sioux, or followers of Sitting Bull, were fully detailed in the last annual report of this office,* as also the fact that after the opening of hostilities they received large accessions to their number from the agency Sioux. This report showed that such desertions were largely due to the uneasiness which the Indians had long felt on account of the infraction of treaty stipulations by the white invasion of the Black Hills, seriously aggravated at the most critical period by irregular and insufficient issues of rations, necessitated by inadequate and delayed appropriations.

Of this campaign a full and detailed account will of course be found in the reports of the honorable Secretary of War. It has, however, seemed to me proper to present herewith a brief outline of its principal events, in order that the records of the Indian Department may contain, at least, a summary of the most important Indian war of recent date, and one which 'has involved every interest of the largest tribe with which this office has to deal. The campaign was carried on for the most part in the region south of the Yellowstone, between the Big Horn and Powder Rivers, in Montana and Wyoming. It opened with an attack made upon an Indian camp on the Powder River, March 17th, 1876, by forces under General Crook, who had approached from the north by way of Forts Reno and Phil Kearney. After this attack the troops returned to Fort Fetterman, March 26th, and remained there until the last of May, when they again started out, pursuing the same route as before, and on June 17th engaged in an all-day fight with the hostiles near the head of the Rosebud, after which they went into camp, and General Crook sent for reinforcements, which arrived August 4th.

About the middle of May a force of about one thousand men under General Terry left Fort Abraham Lincoln and ascended the Yellowstone to the mouth of the Rosebud. There the Seventh Cavalry, numbering 600 men, commanded by General Custer, left General Terry with orders to proceed up the Rosebud and across to the Little Big Horn. General Terry then proceeded to the mouth of the Big Horn, where he was met by a body of 450 men under General Gibbon, which had marched from Fort Ellis down the Yellowstone. The combined forces ascended the Big Horn to the mouth of the Little Big Horn, which latter stream they also ascended, and arrived June 27th at a point about forty miles above its mouth. Here they found that two days previous the forces under General Custer had had an engagement on this ground with the hostiles, which had resulted in the entire destruction of five companies under General Custer's immediate command; and that by their arrival the remaining seven companies, under Major Reno, had narrowly escaped sharing the same fate. The troops then returned to the mouth of the Big Horn, leaving behind 259 dead and carrying with them 53 wounded.

A month later, July 26th, at the request of Lieutenant-General Sheridan, the Interior Department conceded to the military the supervision of the Lower Brulé, Cheyenne River, and Standing Rock agencies; and military officers were made acting agents at the Red Cloud and Spotted Tail agencies.

About the same time, General Terry, who had meanwhile received reenforcements, descended the Yellowstone to the Rosebud, and ascended the Rosebud 36 miles, where, August 10th, he joined General Crook. The

---

* A still further account of the same is contained in Senate Ex. Doc. No. 52, 1st sess. 44th Congress.

Indians, however, took this opportunity to escape in the direction of Tongue River. The trail was followed down the Tongue, across to the Powder River, and down the Powder to its mouth. At this point, on August 25th, the two forces separated, General Terry going north of the Yellowstone to prevent escape in that direction. General Crook followed the trail southeast toward the Black Hills until it became so scattered as to be indistinguishable. During this pursuit, on September 14th, General Crook's advanced column surprised and attacked a village of thirty lodges near Slim Buttes, 180 miles from the Cheyenne River agency. This was followed up by an attack on his main column by the band of Crazy Horse. The troops then came into the vicinity of the Black Hills, and soon after assisted in disarming the agency Indians of Red Cloud and Spotted Tail. General Terry likewise disarmed and dismounted the Indians at Cheyenne River and Standing Rock.

The main body of the hostiles under Crazy Horse went in small companies toward the Yellowstone, near the Powder River, then up the Yellowstone to the Tongue River, and down that river to a point near Suicide Creek, where a winter camp was made in the heart of the buffalo country. This constituted the headquarters of the hostiles under Crazy Horse until March, 1877, when the camp removed to the Powder River. Another portion, under Sitting Bull, took a more northerly course toward the Yellowstone and Glendive Creek. The winter camp of this chief was about two hundred miles north of the Tongue River toward the Dry Fork of the Missouri. He seems to have made frequent trips between the camps for consultation and to distribute ammunition, which he obtained by trade with the Red River half-breeds near the British boundary.

On the 18th of October a large force under Sitting Bull attacked a supply-train near Glendive Creek, ran off sixty mules, and retreated across the Yellowstone in the direction of Fort Peck. This movement was anticipated by Colonel Miles, who, with troops belonging to the just-completed cantonment at the mouth of Tongue River, started to intercept them, and came upon their camp October 21. Under a flag of truce presented by the Indians, two councils were held with Sitting Bull and other leading men, at which the latter reiterated their old desire to be independent of the United States, their indifference to any government aid in the way of supplies and annuities, and their wish to be connected with agencies only to the extent of trading in ammunition; nor would they give any pledges of good faith. The second day's council was immediately followed by an engagement, in which the Indians were driven from their position and fled, closely pursued by the troops, a distance of 42 miles, until in the vicinity of Bad Route Creek, on the other side of the Yellowstone, the main body consisting of Minneconjoux and Sans Arcs, sued for peace on the terms which five days before they had rejected—unconditional surrender—and delivered up five of their number as hostages, viz, Red Skirt, White Bull, Black Eagle, Sun Rise, and Foolish Thunder. During the flight Sitting Bull, with his immediate followers, succeeded in breaking away to the left, and escaped in the direction of Fort Peck. The hostages were taken to the Cheyenne River agency, and their people, estimated at from four hundred to six hundred lodges, were placed, under the direction of Bull Eagle, Small Bear, and Bull, and ordered to reach the Cheyenne River agency not later than December 2, five days being allowed them to provide a supply of buffalo-meat, and thirty to make the march. This arrangement seems to have been made in good faith by some of the leading men taking part in it; but their influence over the others was

138

not great enough to prevent any but the immediate relatives of the hostages from again joining the hostile camp.

On the 15th of November a new expedition, under General Crook, started from Fort Fetterman to again follow up Crazy Horse. On the 25th of that month a detached camp of Cheyennes was struck by a portion of his troops under General Mackenzie, on the west fork of the Powder River, which resulted in the complete destruction of the village, and the loss to the Indians of all their ponies and camp equipage. The expedition then went down the Belle Fourche, and about the 1st of January returned to the cantonment, near Old Fort Reno.

On the 16th of December, five Sioux chiefs from the hostile camp on Tongue River, followed at a distance by twenty or thirty other Indians, approached the Tongue River post bearing the white flag; but while passing the camp of Crow scouts the five leaders were surrounded by twelve of their old enemies and instantly killed, whereupon their companions fled. The Crows were forthwith disarmed, and twelve of their horses, with other gifts, were immediately dispatched to the friends and relatives of those who had been killed. These presents were accompanied by assurances that no white man had taken part in the outrage. The Indians, though at first inclined to doubt the genuineness of these protestations, have since expressed their full belief that the troops were in no way responsible for the affair, and report their errand to have been to return some stolen horses.

After the surrender of October 27, Colonel Miles continued his operations against Sitting Bull. By sending three companies north of the Missouri and three others south, between the Muscle Shell and the Dry Fork of the Missouri, and four more to operate on the Dry Fork, he succeeded on the 18th of December in striking the hostile camp near the head of the Red Water, Sitting Bull having crossed the Missouri near Wolf Point. The Indians were driven south across the Yellowstone, and escaped with the loss of all their ponies and camp equipage.

The next move was made by Colonel Miles on the camp of six hundred lodges, under Crazy Horse, in the valley of the Tongue River. They were found below Suicide or Hanging Woman's Creek, and after skirmishes on the 1st, 3d, and 7th of January, 1877, and a five-hours' engagement on the 8th, were driven from their position, but, owing to worn-out army trains, could not be followed. On the 7th of May, Colonel Miles surprised and attacked a village of fifty lodges, under Lame Deer, near the mouth of the Rosebud. The village was well supplied with ponies, camp equipage, and dried meat; all of which were captured. In July following, raids were made by members of Lame Deer's band on settlers, surveying parties, and wagon trains in the vicinity of the Belle Fourche and the boundary-line of Wyoming.

On the 11th January, 1877, information was received from Inspector Walsh, commanding the detachment of mounted police at Cypress Hills, Canada, that one hundred and nine lodges of American Sioux had crossed the Canadian boundary near Wood Mountain, and were camped on the British side, and that they declared themselves to be desirous of peace and to have no intention of returning to the United States to carry on war. Later the number was reported to have been increased to over two hundred lodges, and they had been joined by Sitting Bull. On the 20th of June, 1877, the honorable Privy Council of Canada, with the approval of the governor-general, officially notified the United States Government of the presence of these Indians within the British Possessions, stating that owing to their destitute condition permits for the purchase of limited quantities of ammunition had been granted them, but that their presence was a source of grave apprehension and anxiety on the part of both the Indian and white population of that part of Canada, and requesting the United States Government, without delay, to "take such steps as will induce these Indians, and any others who may similarly cross the boundary-line, to return to their reserves in the United States territory."

In accordance with this request a commission, consisting of General A. H. Terry and A. J. Lawrence, esq., was appointed by the President in September last to proceed to Fort Walsh and negotiate with Sitting Bull for his peaceful return to the United States and settlement at some agency. At the council held on the 17th of October, Sitting Bull and his chiefs declined all proposals made by the commission, and announced their desire and intention always to remain within the British Possessions. After the close of the council, the Canadian authorities conferred with the Indians, warning them that after the extinction of the buffalo no help whatever beyond protection could be expected from the British Government, and that a crossing of the line by any of their young men with hostile intent would be considered an act of hostility by both governments. With this full understanding the Indians adhered to their former decision, and the commission returned, and Sitting Bull and his adherents are no longer considered wards of this government.

During the progress of the Sioux campaign, in the fall of 1876, small parties began to deliver themselves up at the different agencies, laying down their arms, with the declaration that they were "tired of war." Other parties who surrendered in the following spring so generally represented that sentiment to be shared by the main body of hostiles that the chief Spotted Tail agreed to visit in person the hostile camp, accompanied by 250 subchiefs and headmen, and urge the return of his people to their agency and allegiance. His return in April with a following of 1,100 attested the remarkable success of his mission; and for this eminent service, which virtually ended the Sioux war, and his unswerving loyalty throughout the whole campaign, some suitable testimonial should be tendered him.

In the following month most of the Cheyennes and 899 Indians under Crazy Horse surrendered at Red Cloud agency. Others found their way into the cantonment on Tongue River, and finally, in September last, Lame Deer's band of 500 gave up the contest.

THE SIOUX COMMISSION.

In the months of September and October, 1876, the various Sioux agencies were visited by a commission, appointed under act of August 15 of that year, to negotiate with the Sioux an agreement to surrender that portion of the Sioux reservation which included the Black Hills and certain hunting privileges outside that reserve guaranteed by the treaty of 1868; to grant a right of way across their reserve; and to provide for the removal of the Red Cloud and Spotted Tail agencies from Northwestern Nebraska to the Missouri River. The commission was also authorized to take steps to gain the consent of the Sioux to their removal to the Indian Territory.

From their report, which was published as an appendix to the last annual report of this office, it will be seen that the commission were successful in all the negotiations with which they were charged; and that the Indians made every concession that was desired by the government, although we were engaged at that very time in fighting their relatives and friends. On behalf of the United States, the agreement thus entered into provided for subsisting the Sioux on a stated ration until they should become self-supporting, for furnishing schools, and all necessary aid and instruction in agriculture and the mechanical arts, and for the allotment of lands in severalty. The agreement was ratified by Congress February 28, 1877.

Representatives from the Red Cloud and Spotted Tail agencies with two of the commissioners visited the Indian Territory as a preliminary to a practical consideration of the subject of removal thither. Whether it is probable that by following up the matter on the return of the delegation, any portion of the Indians of those agencies could have been induced to adopt as a home the country which they visited, I am unable to say. Any effort in that direction was promptly forestalled by a provision in the act of February 28, by which Congress explicitly prohibited "the removal of any portion of the Sioux Indians to the Indian Territory, until the same shall be authorized by an act of Congress hereafter enacted."

REMOVALS.

REMOVAL OF RED CLOUD AND SPOTTED TAIL AGENCIES.

In May last D. H. Jerome, of the Board of Indian Commissioners, Lieutenant-Colonel P. Lugenbeel, First Infantry, U. S. A., and J. H. Hammond, superintendent of Indian affairs for Dakota, were appointed a commission to select locations on the Missouri River for the new Red Cloud and Spotted Tail agencies. For the former, the site chosen is the junction of Yellow Medicine and Missouri Rivers, and at that point agency buildings have just been erected. For the latter, the old Ponca reserve was decided upon, where the agency dwellings, storehouses, one hundred and fifty Indian houses, and five hundred acres of cultivated fields, left vacant by the Poncas, offer special advantages for present quarters.

Notwithstanding their consent given to the commission, to hereafter receive supplies on the Missouri River, the Spotted Tail and Red Cloud Indians persisted in making strenuous objection to such removal, in which they were seconded by the surrendered "hostiles," who were not parties to the agreement. Their earnest desire to talk with the President in regard to the matter was finally gratified, and a delegation of twenty-three chiefs and leading men of the Sioux and Northern Arapahoes visited this city for that purpose, in the latter part of September last. The interview failed of results satisfactory to the Sioux, since by law and treaty no concession could be made by the President or the department beyond a promise to examine, next spring, the country lying along the Cheyenne and White Rivers, and to endeavor to find on them suitable locations for farming purposes.

The removal of fourteen thousand Sioux Indians at this season of the year, a distance of three hundred miles from their old agencies in Nebraska to their new quarters near the Missouri River, is not a pleasant matter to contemplate. Neither the present Secretary of the Interior, nor the present Commissioner of Indian Affairs is responsible for the movement, but they have carried out the law faithfully, though reluctantly. The removal is being made in accordance with the act of August 15, 1876. (Stat. 19, p. 191.) It is proper to say here, that I cannot but look on the necessity thus imposed by law on the executive branch of the government as an unfortunate one, and the consequences ought to be remedied as speedily as possible.

Let us for a moment consider that the Spotted Tail agency was in 1871 on the west bank of the Missouri River, where the whites became exceedingly troublesome, and the river afforded abundant facilities for the introduction of intoxicating liquors. In 1874 the Red Cloud and Spotted Tail agencies were removed to, what a subsequent survey proved to be, the State of Nebraska, the former agency 165 miles from Cheyenne and the latter 108 miles from Sidney, the nearest points on the Union Pacific Railroad. Here the usual ill fortune attending the removal of these Indians was again exemplified, in placing the agencies on absolutely barren land, where there was no possibility of cultivating the soil, no hope of their being enabled to become self-supporting, and where they have of necessity been kept in the hopeless condition of paupers.

In the hope of placing these Indians upon arable land, where they might become civilized and self-supporting, the determination was hastily taken to remove them back to the Missouri River. This step was undertaken without a proper examination of other points on the reservation, where it is stated, on good authority, that a sufficient quantity of excellent wheat-lands can be found on either bank of the White River running eastward into the Missouri, and where, also, there is timber sufficient in quantity and quality for all practical purposes. This, however, should be fully determined before another movement of these Indians is attempted.

The Indian chiefs, in their interview with the President in September last, begged that they might not be sent to the Missouri River, as whisky-drinking, and other demoralization, would be the consequence. This was the best judgment of the best men of the tribe, but the necessity was one that the President could not control. The provisions and supplies for the ensuing winter had been placed according to law on the Missouri, and, owing to the lateness of the season, it was impossible to remove them to the old agencies. Accordingly the necessities of the case compelled the removal of these Indians in the midst of the snows and storms of early winter, which have already set in.

REMOVAL OF THE NORTHERN CHEYENNES AND ARAPAHOES.

These Indians for several years past have been reported as receiving rations with the Sioux, at Red Cloud agency, but as "belonging" with their southern brethren in the Indian Territory, whom they could not be induced to join by any persuasion or command unsupported by force.

The same difference between the disposition of the two tribes has been shown during the Sioux war that was manifested in the Cheyenne and Arapahoe war of 1874 and 1875 in the Indian Territory. The whole body of the Cheyennes took prompt and active part in hostilities, while the Arapahoes, almost without exception, remained loyal to the government. After the surrender of the main portion of this tribe, the Cheyennes were suddenly seized by a desire to remove to the Indian Territory. This unexpected announcement was followed by prompt action, and on the 28th of May last, 937 Cheyennes left Red Cloud agency under military escort, and after 70 days' journey reported at Fort Reno, and were turned over to the Cheyenne and Arapaho agent.

In accordance with their earnest request made to the President during the recent visit of the delegation in this city, permission was given the Northern Arapahoes to join the Shoshones on the Wind River reserve in Wyoming. In a formal council held last month by Agent

Irwin with the Shoshones, their consent to the arrangement desired by the Arapahoes was obtained, and the removal of the latter is now in progress.

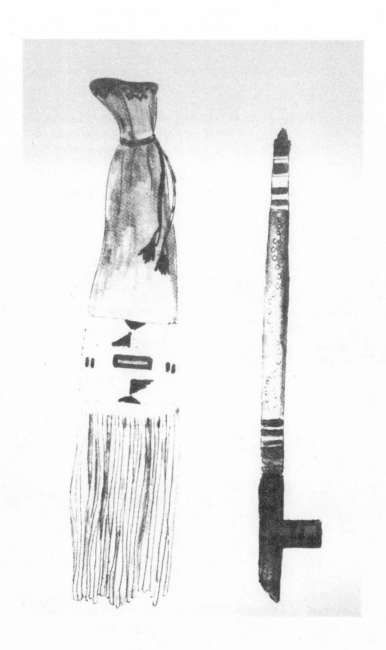

Pipe and Bag

ANNUAL REPORT
OF THE SECRETARY OF THE INTERIOR, COMMISSIONER OF INDIAN AFFAIRS, REPORT FOR 1877: THE SITTING BULL COMMISSION

Sitting Bull—Preparing Medicine

REPORT

OF

THE COMMISSION APPOINTED BY DIRECTION OF THE PRESIDENT OF THE UNITED STATES, UNDER INSTRUCTIONS OF THE HONORABLES THE SECRETARY OF WAR AND THE SECRETARY OF THE INTERIOR, TO MEET THE SIOUX INDIAN CHIEF, SITTING BULL, WITH A VIEW TO AVERT HOSTILE INCURSIONS INTO THE TERRITORY OF THE UNITED STATES FROM THE DOMINION OF CANADA.

To the honorable Secretaries of War and of the Interior:

GENTLEMEN: The undersigned have the honor to report that they were directed by the President through the War and Interior Departments to form a commission to act according to the following instructions:

DEPARTMENT OF THE INTERIOR,
Washington City, September 6, 1877.

GENTLEMEN: The President desires you to proceed at your earliest convenience to Fort Benton, and thence to a point on our northern frontier, from which the present encampment of the Sioux chief, Sitting Bull on British territory, is most easily accessible. At the frontier you will be met by a detachment of mounted Canadian police, detailed by the Government of the Dominion of Canada for your protection.

It is the object of your mission, undertaken at the suggestion of the Government of the Dominion, to ascertain what danger there may be of hostile incursions on the part of Sitting Bull and the bands under his command upon the territory of the United States, and, if possible, to effect such arrangements, not unacceptable to the Government of the Dominion, as may be the best calculated to avert that danger. To this end you will put yourself in communication with Sitting Bull in such manner as, under existing circumstances, may seem to you most judicious.

In doing so you will keep the following facts in view:

In the month of February last, Sitting Bull and his bands engaged in armed hostilities against the United States, and pursued by our military forces, crossed the boundary line of the British possessions, for the purpose of escaping from that pursuit. At that time the fugitive Indians appeared to be well armed, but their ammunition was so nearly exhausted that they were no longer able to continue the struggle. Under such circumstances they took refuge on British soil, where the troops of the United States could not follow them without violating the territory of a friendly power. It is reported, and there is good reason for believing, that these hostile Indians have availed themselves of the protection and security thus enjoyed to replenish their stock of ammunition, and thus to enable themselves to resume their hostilities against the United States as soon as they may find it convenient to do so.

According to all recognized principles of international law, every government is bound to protect the territory of a neighboring friendly state against acts of armed hostility on the part of the refugees who, for their protection from pursuit, have crossed the frontier. While the Government of Great Britain will be most mindful of this obligation, the President recognizes the difficulties which, in dealing with a savage population, may attend to its fulfillment, and he is, therefore, willing to do all in his power to prevent any interruption of the relations of good neighborhood, and to avert a disturbance of the peace of the border, even to the extent of entering into communication with an Indian chief who occupies the position of a fugitive enemy and criminal.

You are, therefore, instructed, in the name of the President, to inform Sitting Bull and the other chiefs of the bands of Indians recently escaped into the British possessions, that they will be permitted peaceably to return to the United States and occupy such reservations as may be assigned to them, and that they will be treated in as friendly a spirit as were other hostile Indians who, after having been engaged with Sitting Bull and his followers in hostilities against the United States, surrendered to our military forces. This treatment, however, can be accorded only on condition that Sitting

147

Bull and all the members of the Indian bands who take advantage of this offer of pardon and protection, when crossing the line from British territory to that of the United States, surrender to our military forces stationed at the frontier all their fire-arms and ammunition, as well as all their horses and ponies, the military commander permitting them the temporary use of such animals as may be necessary for the trans-portation of the aged and infirm among the Indians who may be unable to march on foot to the reservations. You will insist upon this condition to its full extent, and not make any promises beyond that of a pardon for the act of hostility committed as stated above.

Should Sitting Bull and the other chiefs with him express their willingness to return to the United States on these terms you will notify the commander of the United States forces at ———— of that fact, and instructions will be given for the reception of the Indians at the frontier. In case the Indians refuse to return to the United States upon such terms, you will then break off all communication with them, and the Government of Great Britain will, no doubt, take such measures as may be necessary to protect the territory of the United States against hostile invasion.

A copy of these instructions has been forwarded to General A. H. Terry, United States Army, who will act as the head of the commission.

Very respectfully, your obedient servant,

GEO. W. McCRARY,
Secretary of War.
C. SCHURZ,
Secretary of the Interior.

To Brig. Gen. ALFRED H. TERRY, *U. S. Army,*
To General A. G. LAWRENCE, *Washington.*

The commission met and organized at Saint Paul, on the 11th of September, 1877.

There were present: Brig. Gen. Alfred H. Terry, United States Army; Hon. A. G. Lawrence, Rhode Island; H. C. Corbin, brevet lieutenant-colonel, United States Army, secretary.

It was decided that the commission should leave the city on the 14th instant for Fort Benton, Mont., via Omaha, Nebr., and Helena, Mont., this route having been determined the most expeditious as to time. The chairman notified the Hon. Secretary of War of the action of the commission.

[Copy of telegram.]

HEADQUARTERS DEPARTMENT OF DAKOTA,
Saint Paul, Minn., September 11, 1877.

To the honorable Secretary of War, Washington, D. C.:

The commission to meet Sitting Bull organized here to-day. It has determined, in order to save time, to go to Fort Benton via the Union Pacific road and the Montana stage-line. I am directed to request that the Dominion authorities be notified that the commission desire to meet the escort which they will furnish at the point where the usually traveled road from Fort Benton to Fort Walsh crosses the boundary. I am also directed to suggest that the Canadian authorities should be asked to induce Sitting Bull and his chiefs and headmen to come to Fort Walsh to meet the commission. The object of this last suggestion is to save time. It has been recently reported that the Indians are one hundred and twenty miles beyond Fort Walsh. If this be true, to reach their present camp would involve six hundred miles travel, going from and re-turning to Fort Benton, a march which would consume nearly twenty-five days. If the Indians should accept the terms offered them, it would be extremely desirable, on many accounts, to bring them in as early as possible. We shall expect to reach the boundary on the 29th or 30th.

ALFRED H. TERRY,
Brigadier-General, Chairman.

A true copy.
H. C. CORBIN,
Captain Twenty-fourth Infantry, Secretary.

SAINT PAUL, MINN., *September 12, 1877.*

The commission met. It was then determined to ask a modification of so much of the instructions to the commission as required that the Indians be dismounted at the boundary.

SITTING BULL INDIAN COMMISSION.

[Copy of telegram.]

HEADQUARTERS DEPARTMENT OF DAKOTA,
Saint Paul, Minn., September 12, 1877.

To honorable G. W. McCRARY,
Secretary of War, Dayton, Ohio:

After examining their instructions, the commission think that it would be desirable to modify them in one particular. They require that all arms and all horses, except such as may be needed for the use of the infirm and sick, shall be surrendered at the boundary. The arms most certainly should be surrendered there; but we think that it would be very embarrassing to both the troops and the Indians if they should be dismounted before reaching their reservation. Deprived of their arms there would be no danger of their attempting to escape from their escort, even if they should have horses. We suppose that under the term, " as kind treatment as any of the hostiles have received," we may say to them that the horses will be sold for their benefit, as has been done in the case of other Indians.

An answer to this a week hence sent to Helena, Mont., will be in time.

ALFRED H. TERRY,
Brigadier-General and Chairman of Commission.

A true copy.
H. C. CORBIN,
Captain Twenty-fourth Infantry, Secretary.

A copy of the answer thereto, as furnished by the telegraph operator at Ross Forks, Idaho.

Govt.   CINCINNATI, OHIO, *September 16.*

General A. H. TERRY, *Helena, Mont.:*

The President directs me to say that the instructions of the commission are modified, as suggested in your dispatch of the twelfth.

GEO. W. McCRARY,
Secretary of War.

(Copy furnished at Ross Fork at request of General Terry.)

The commission decided to authorize the employment of a phonographic reporter and Indian interpreter, and Mr. Jay Stone, of Saint Paul, was appointed.

On the same day the following telegrams were received and answered:

WASHINGTON, D. C., *September 12, 1877.*

General A. H. TERRY, *Saint Paul:*

The request has been received through Department of State that you will telegraph to governor-general Dominion Canada, at Ottawa, before starting, the point on boundary where mounted escort to be furnished by that government should meet the commission.

E. D. TOWNSEND,
Adjutant-General.

HEADQUARTERS DEPARTMENT OF DAKOTA,
Saint Paul, Minn., September 12, 1877.

To his excellency the governor-general of the Dominion of Canada, Ottawa, Canada:

By direction of the War Department of the United States, I have the honor to inform your excellency that the commission appointed to meet Sitting Bull will proceed from Fort Benton, Montana Territory, to the point where the usually traveled road from that place to Fort Walsh crosses the boundary. The commission would be glad to meet at that point the escort which it understands is to be furnished to it by the Dominion Government. The commission will arrive at the point designated about the 29th instant.

ALFRED H. TERRY,
Brigadier-General, U. S. A., and Chairman of Commission.

A true copy.
H. C. CORBIN,
Captain Twenty-fourth Infantry, Secretary.

After making provision for very cold weather, the commission started from Saint Paul by rail on the evening of the 14th of September, and proceeded *via* Omaha, Ogden, Franklin, and Helena, arriving at Fort Shaw in advance of the mail on the 25th of September.

Before leaving Saint Paul, the commander of the Department of Dakota had directed General Miles, at Tongue River, to send three companies of the Second Cavalry to Fort Benton, to serve as an escort to the commission. It being foreseen, however, that these troops would be needed by General Miles in his pursuit of the Nes Percés, General Gibbon, at Fort Shaw, had taken measures to provide another escort, by calling up a company of the Seventh Cavalry from Fort Ellis. Awaiting the arrival of these last-named troops, the commission remained at Shaw until the 4th of October. On that day it started for Fort Benton, with one company of the Seventh Infantry and one of the Seventh Cavalry. It reached Fort Benton about noon of the 6th. At midnight of the same day news was received of the battle at Bear's Paw Mountain, accompanied by a call from General Miles for rations and forage. It was thereupon determined to remain at Benton and send forward supplies in such wagons as could be obtained, including the wagons provided for the commission, under the guard of its escort. On the night of the 8th, further dispatches were received from General Miles, announcing the final surrender of the Nes Percés, and informing the commission that the troops originally destined to be its escort would now be available for that purpose, and would in a day or two be put in march to meet it. The commission, therefore, moved out from Fort Benton on the 10th, met its escort on the evening of the 12th, and on the 13th again started for Fort Walsh. The boundary was reached in the afternoon of the 15th, when the commission was met by Lieut. Col. J. F. McLeod, commissioner of the Northwest Territory and commander of the Northwest Mounted Police, with a detachment of his command. Under this escort the commission proceeded to Fort Walsh, reaching it at 6 p. m. on the 16th.

FORT WALSH, *October* 17, 1877.

The commission met at 10 a. m., and the address to the Indians was determined upon.

Before being presented to them, Baptiste Shane, the interpreter of the commission, together with the official interpreter at Fort Walsh, also an interpreter, brought by Sitting Bull, were assembled, and the address read and its meaning fully explained, in order that they might be better able to make a proper and full interpretation.

FORT WALSH, *October* 17, 1877.

The commission assembled at 3 o'clock p. m. in Major Walsh's quarters. Present: General Terry, General Lawrence, Capt. H. C. Corbin, and Mr. Jay Stone, a stenographer.

Lieutenant-Colonel McLeod, Major Walsh, and other officers of the mounted police were also present.

The Indian chiefs were then brought in and their names announced, as follows: Bear's Head, head chief of the Uncapapas; Sitting Bull, The Spotted Eagle, The Flying Bird, The Whirlwind Bear, The Medicine-turns-around, The Iron Dog, The-man-that-scatters-the-Bear, Little Knife, The Crow, and Yellow Dog.

The Indians were informed that Baptiste Shane was to interpret, and that Mr. Provost and Joe Lanaval were to listen and see that it was correctly done. General Terry then read to them the propositions.

150

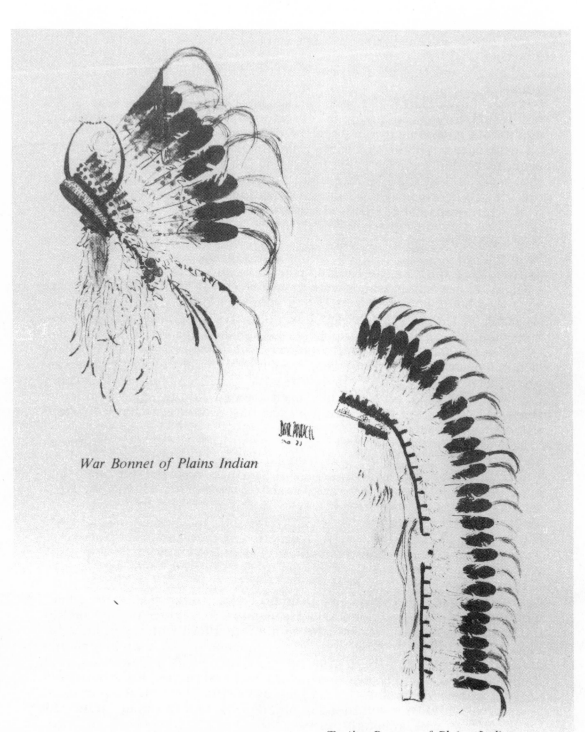

War Bonnet of Plains Indian

Trailer Bonnet of Plains Indian

151

We are sent a commission by the President of the United States, at the request of the Government of the Dominion of Canada, to meet you.

The President has instructed us to say to you that he desires to make a lasting peace with you and your people; he desires that all hostilities shall cease, and that all the people of the United States shall live together in harmony. He wishes this not for the sake of the whites alone, but for your sake as well; and he has instructed us to say that if you will return to your country, and hereafter refrain from acts of hostility against its government and people, a full pardon will be given to you for all acts committed in the past; that no matter what those acts have been, no attempt will be made to punish you or any man among you; that what is past shall be forgotten, and that you shall be received in the friendly spirit in which the other Indians who have been engaged in hostilities against the United States and have surrendered to its military forces have been received.

We will now explain to you what the President intends to say when he promises that, in case you accept these terms, you will be treated in as friendly a spirit as the Indians who have surrendered.

Of all those bands which were at war with the United States a year ago, this band of yours, which has sought refuge in the British possessions, is the only one which has not surrendered; every other one has come into some of the agencies established for the Sioux nation. Of these bands, no single man has ever been punished for his hostile or criminal acts. Every man, every woman, and every child has been received as a friend. Every one has received sufficient food and clothing for his support. Every one has been treated in the same manner as those of your nation who, during all the past troubles, remained peaceably at their agencies.

It is true that these Indians have been required to give up their horses and arms, but these horses and arms have been partially sold, and all will be sold, and whatever has been or may be received for them has been or will be applied for the benefit of those from whom they were taken. One of us has already caused to be purchased and sent to the agencies on the Missouri River 650 cows for the use of the Indians there. This has been done in the belief that the best hope for the future welfare of your people and their children is in the abandonment of your present mode of life and the adoption of the occupation of breeders of cattle. These same terms are now offered to you. The President cannot and will not consent that you should return to your country armed, mounted, and prepared for war. He cannot consent that you should return prepared to inflict injuries similar to those which you have inflicted in the past, but he invites you to come to the boundary of his and your country, and there give up your arms and ammunition, and thence to go to the agencies to which he will assign you, and there give up your horses, excepting those which are required for peace purposes. Your arms and horses will then be sold, and with all the money obtained for them cows will be bought and sent to you.

From these cows you will be able to raise herds, which will support you and your children; which will support you and them long after the game upon which you now depend for subsistence shall have disappeared. And in the mean time you will receive the clothing and food which the other bands of your nation are now receiving.

We have come many hundred miles to bring you this message from the President, who, as we have told you before, desires to live in peace with all his people. Too much white and Indian blood has already been shed. It is time that bloodshed should cease. Of one thing, however, it is our duty to assure you, you cannot return to your country and your friends unless you accept these propositions. Should you attempt to return with arms in your hands, you must be treated as enemies of the United States.

We ask you to take these propositions into consideration; to take time, consult together, and to weigh them carefully. When you have done so, we shall be glad to meet you and receive your answer.

Sitting Bull then said: For 64 years you have kept me and my people and treated us bad. What have we done that you should want us to stop? We have done nothing. It is all the people on your side that have started us to do all these depredations. We could not go anywhere else, and so we took refuge in this country. It was on this side of the country we learned to shoot, and that is the reason why I came back to it again. I would like to know why you came here. In the first place, I did not give you the country, but you followed me from one place to another, so I had to leave and come over to this country. I was born and raised in this country with the Red River Half-Breeds, and I intend to stop with them. I was raised hand in hand with the Red River Half-Breeds, and we are going over to that part of the country, and that is the reason why I have come over here. (Shaking hands with the British officers.) That is the way I was raised, in the hands of these people here, and that is the way I intend to be with them. You have got ears, and you have got eyes to see with them, and you see how I live with these people. You see me? Here I am! If you think I am a fool you are a bigger fool than I am. This house is a medicine-house. You come here to tell us lies, but we don't want to hear them. I don't wish any such language used to me; that is, to tell me such lies in my Great Mother's house. Don't you say two more words. Go back home where you came from. This country is mine, and I intend to stay here, and to raise this country full of grown people. See these people here. We were raised with them. (Again shaking hands with the British officers.) That is enough; so no more. You see me shaking hands with these people.

The part of the country you gave me you ran me out of. I have now come here to stay with these people, and I intend to stay here. I wish you to go back, and to "take it easy" going back. (Taking a Santee Indian by the hand.) These Santees—I was born and raised with them. He is going to tell you something about them.

"The-one-that-runs-the-Ree," a Santee Indian, said: Look at me. I was born and raised in this country. These people away north here, I was raised with my hands in their own. I have lived in peace with them. For the last 64 years we were over in your country, and you treated us badly. We have come over here now, and you want to try and get us back there again. You didn't treat us well, and I don't like you at all. (Shaking hands with the English officers.) I have been up and down these roads. We have been running up and down this country. I have been up and down there as often as these people have. I will be at peace with these people as long as I live. You come over here to tell us lies. I will shake hands with men here, and I have been in peace with them. I have come this far into this country. These are the people that learned me how to shoot the first time. This country is ours. We did not give it to you. You stole it away from us. You have come over here to our country to tell us lies, and I don't propose to talk much, and that is all I have to say. I want you to take it easy going back home. Don't go in a rush.

"Nine," a Yankton Indian, who joined the Santee band that left Minnesota some years ago during the massacre, said, after shaking hands all around : I have shaken hands with everybody in the house. I don't wear the same clothes that these people do. You come over here to tell lies on one another. I want to tell you a few, but you have got more lies than I can say. Sixty-four years ago you got our country and you promised to take good care of us and keep us. You ran from one place to another killing us and fighting us, and I was born and raised with these people over here. I have come here to see the council and to shake hands with you all. I wanted to tell you what I think of this. There are seven different tribes of us. They live all over the country. You kept part of us over there, and part of us you kept on this side. You did not treat us right over there, so we came back over here. These people sitting around here, you promised to take good care of them when you had them over there, but you did not fulfill your promises. They have come over here to this side again, and here we are all together. I come in to these people here and they give me permission to trade with the traders; that is the way I make my living. Everything I get I buy from the traders. I don't steal anything. For fourteen years I have not fought with your people, and that is what I have lost by waiting in this country. I have come over here to these people, and these people, if they had a piece of tobacco, they gave me half; and that is why I live over here. I have a little powder in my powder-horn, and I gave you a little fourteen years ago. Since then I have been over in this country. (Shaking hands all around and continuing.) We came over to this country, and I am going to live with these people here. This country over here is mine. The bullets I have over here I intend to kill something to eat with; not to kill anybody with them. That is what these people told me; to kill nothing but what I wanted to eat with the ammunition they gave me. I will do so.

A squaw named "The-one-that-speaks-once," wife of " The-man-that-scatters-the-Bear," said, I was over to your country; I wanted to raise my children over there, but you did not give me any time. I came over to this country to raise my children and have a little peace. (Shaking hands with the English officers.) That is all I have to say to you. I want you to go back where you came from. These are the people that I am going to stay with, and raise my children with.

The Flying Bird : These people here, God Almighty raised us together. We have a little sense and we ought to love one another. Sitting Bull here says that whenever you found us out, wherever his country was, why, you wanted to have it. It is Sitting Bull's country, this is. These people sitting all around me, what they committed I had nothing to do with it. I was not in it. The soldiers find out where we live, and they never think of anything good, it is always something bad. (Again shaking hands with the British officers.)

The Indians having risen, being apparently about to leave the room, the interpreter was then directed to ask the following questions :

Shall I say to the President that you refuse the offers that he has made to you? Are we to understand from what you have said that you refuse those offers?

SITTING BULL. I could tell you more, but that is all I have to tell you. If we told you more—why, you would not pay any attention to it. That is all I have to say. This part of the country does not belong to your people. You belong on the other side; this side belongs to us.

The CROW. (Shaking hands and embracing Colonel McLeod, and shaking hands with the other British officers.) This is the way I will live in this part of the country. That is the way I like them, (making a gesture of embrace.) When we came back from the other side you wanted to do something—to lie. You want us to go back to the other side; that is the reason why you stay here. What do you mean by coming over here and talking that way to us? All this country around here, I know, belongs to these people, and that is the reason why I came over here when I was driven out of the other country. I am afraid of God Almighty; that is the reason why I don't want to do anything bad. When I came over here I came to live with these people. My children, myself, and my women, they all live together. Those people that don't hide anything, they are all the people I like. I suppose you wanted to hear something; that is the reason you came over here. The people standing around here want to hear it also; that is the reason they stand around here. Sixty-four years ago we shook hands with the soldiers, and ever since that I have had hardships. I made peace with them, and ever since that I have been running from one place to another to keep out of their way. I was over across the line and staid over there, and I thought you people would take good care of me. You did not do so, and these people over here gave me good care. I have waited here three days, and I have got plenty to eat and everybody respects me. I came from the other side of the line, and I expect to stay here. Going back, you can take it easy. Go to where you were born, and stay there.

I came over to this country, and my great mother knows all about it. She knows I came back over here, and she don't wish anything of me. We think, and all the women in the camp thinks, we are going to have the country full of people. When I shook hands before, there were lots of people here then. Now I have come back in this part of the country again to have plenty more people, to live in peace and raise children.

The Indians then inquired whether the commission had anything more to say; and which the commission answered that they had nothing more, and the conference here closed.

After the conference closed, the Canadian authorities had an interview with the Indians, and, in reply to a request from the commission, Lieut.-Col. J. F. McLeod, commissioner of the Northwest Territory, addressed the commission the following letter as to the result:

NORTHWEST MOUNTED POLICE,
Fort Walsh, October 18, 1877.

GENTLEMEN: In answer to your note, I beg leave to inform you that after the interview of the commissioners with the Indians, I had a "talk" with the latter. I endeavored to impress upon them the importance of the answer they had just made; that although some of the speakers to the commissioners had claimed to be British Indians we denied the claim; and that the Queen's Government looked upon them all as American Indians who had taken refuge in our country from their enemies. I pointed out to them their only hope was the buffalo; that it would not be many years before that source of supply would cease, and that they could expect nothing whatever from the Queen's Government, except protection so long as they behaved themselves. I warned them that their decision affected not only themselves, but their children, and that they should think well over it before it was too late. I told them that they must not cross the line with a hostile intent; that if they did, they would not only have the Americans for their enemies, but also the police and the British Government, and urged upon them to carry my words to their camps; to tell all their young men what I had said, and warn them of the consequences of disobedience, pointing out to them that a few indiscreet young warriors might involve them all in most serious trouble.

They unanimously adhered to the answer they had given the commissioners, and promised to obey what I had told them.

I do not think there need be the least anxiety about any of these Indians crossing the line, at any rate for some time to come.

In haste. Most respectfully, yours,

JAMES F. McLEOD,
Lieut. Co¹. Commanding Northwest Mounted Police.

The commission left Fort Walsh on its return homeward on the morning of the 18th October, under escort of a detachment of the Canadian mounted police, arriving at the boundary on the afternoon of the 19th October, and was there joined by its escort of United States troops. Continuing its journey the commission reached Fort Benton on the morning of the 23d, and there embarked in Mackinaw boats. It descended the Missouri to Fort Buford, Dakota, arriving there on the 3d November. Leaving Fort Buford on the 4th November by ambulances, arriving at Bismarck on the 7th, and taking the Northern Pacific Railroad, it arrived at Saint Paul on the 8th, where it adjourned to meet in Washington on the 28th of November to submit its report.

In compliance with that clause of the foregoing instructions which directs the commission "to ascertain what danger there may be of hostile invasions on the part of Sitting Bull and the bands under his command upon the territory of the United States," the commission has the honor to report that they are convinced that Sitting Bull and the Indians with him will not seek to return to this country at present. It is believed that they are restrained from returning, partly by their recollection of the constant and harassing pursuit to which they were subjected during the last winter and spring by the troops under General Miles, a pursuit which ended only with their flight to foreign soil, partly by the assurances given them by the Canadian authorities that should they return with hostile intent they will become "the enemies of both governments," and in part by their belief that for some reason, which they cannot fathom, the Government of the United States very earnestly desires that they shall return. This belief has been confirmed and strengthened by the visit of the commission and the very favorable offers made to them. In their intense hostility to our government they are determined to contravene its wishes to the best of their ability. The most probable ultimate result is that these Indians, like those Sioux who, after the Minnesota massacres of 1862, sought and found an asylum in the British possessions, will in time become so accustomed and attached to their new country that they will regard it as their permanent home. At the same time it cannot be concealed that the presence of this large body of Indians, bitterly hostile to us, in close proximity to the frontier, is a standing menace to the peace of our Indian territories.

The tribes which occupy the region between the Upper Missouri and the 49th parallel have been for some time past restless, disturbed, and given to complaint. Among these tribes are the Yanktons, themselves Sioux, and the Assinniboines, kindred of the Sioux.

Though these tribes have been nominally at peace, there is no doubt that, during the last year and a half, many individuals from them have helped to swell those bands which have been engaged in open war. It is impossible to prevent constant communication between these tribes and the band of Sitting Bull; and so long as the latter shall remain as near to our frontier as they now are, they cannot fail to exercise a most injurious influence over the former, giving evil counsel and advice, stimulating disaffection, and encouraging acts of hostility. Besides, this body of refugees is not a distinct section of the Sioux Nation; it is made up by contributions from nearly every agency and every tribe; it is largely composed of young men whose families still remain at the various Sioux agencies.

Were it a distinct band that had separated itself from and broken off its associations with the rest of its people it would soon be forgotten, and would cease to exert any influence over those from whom it had separated; but the intimate relationship, the ties of blood, existing between the refugees and the agency Indians forbid us to hope for such a result. To the lawless and ill-disposed, to those who commit offenses against the property and persons of the whites, the refugee camp will be a secure asylum; not only an asylum on foreign soil, but an asylum amid their own kindred.

We have already an illustration of this danger in the fact that more than one hundred of the Nez Percés defeated at Bear's Paw Mountain are now in Sitting Bull's camp.

It is not the province of the commission to propose any measures in respect to this matter to be taken by the government, but they may be permitted to suggest that the evils which they apprehend may be in some degree avoided by a compliance on the part of the authorities of the Dominion of Canada with that rule of international law which requires that armed military or insurgent bodies which are driven by force across the frontier of a neutral state shall be "interned," shall be removed so far into the interior of the neutral state that they can no longer threaten, in any manner, the peace and safety of the state from which they have come.

In conclusion, the members of the commission desire to express their grateful sense of the courtesy with which they were received by Lieutenant-Colonel McLeod, Major Walsh, and the officers of police under their command.

ALFRED H. TERRY,
A. G. LAWRENCE,
Commissioners.

H. C. CORBIN, Secretary.

Eagle Wing Fan

Crazy Horse

MESSAGE

FROM THE

PRESIDENT OF THE UNITED STATES,

TRANSMITTING,

In compliance with a Senate resolution of July 7, 1876, information in relation to the hostile demonstrations of the Sioux Indians, and the disaster to the forces under General Custer.

JULY 13, 1876.—Read, ordered to lie on the table, and be printed.

To the Senate of the United States:

I have the honor to transmit herewith a report from General W. T. Sherman, together with the most recent reports received from Brig. Gen. A. H. Terry, as a response to the resolution of the Senate of the 7th instant, a copy of which is attached to this message.

U. S. GRANT.

EXECUTIVE MANSION, *July 8, 1876.*

IN THE SENATE OF THE UNITED STATES,
July 7, 1876.

Resolved, That the President be requested to inform the Senate, if not incompatible with the public interests, whether the Sioux Indians made any hostile demonstrations prior to the invasion of their treaty-reservation by the gold-hunters; whether the present military operations are conducted for the purpose of protecting said Indians in their rights under the treaty of eighteen hundred and sixty-eight or of punishing them for resisting the violation of that treaty; and whether the recent reports of an alleged disaster to our forces under General Custer in that region are true.

Attest:

GEO. C. GORHAM,
Secretary,
By W. J. McDONALD,
Chief Clerk.

WAR DEPARTMENT,
Washington, July 8, 1876.

To the PRESIDENT:

To enable you to answer the inclosed resolution of the Senate of July 7, I have the honor to submit the following brief statement of facts as exhibited by the records of this Department:

The Sioux or Dakota Nation of Indians, embracing various tribes, as the Yanktons, Yanctonnais, Brulés, Ogallallas, Minneconjous, Sans Arcs, Two Kettles, &c., have long been known as the most brave and warlike savages of this continent. They have for centuries been pushed westward by the advancing tide of civilization, till in 1868 an arrangement or treaty was made with them by a special commission named by Congress, whereby for certain payments and stipulations they agreed to surrender their claim to all that vast region which lies west of the Missouri River and north of the Platte, to live at peace with their neighbors, and to restrict themselves to a territory bounded east by the Missouri River, south by Nebraska, west by the 104th meridian, and north by the Forty-sixth parallel, a territory as large as the State of Missouri. The terms of this treaty have been liberally performed on the part of the United States, and have also been complied with by the great mass of the Sioux Indians. Some of these Indians, however, have never recognized the binding force of this treaty, but have always treated it with contempt, have continued to rove at pleasure, attacking scattered settlements in Nebraska, Wyoming, Montana, and Dakota, stealing horses and cattle, and murdering peaceful inhabitants and travelers.

On the 9th of November, 1875, United States Indian Inspector E. C. Watkins made an elaborate report to the Commissioner of Indian Affairs, in which he uses this language:

I have the honor to address you in relation to the attitude and condition of certain wild and hostile bands of Sioux Indians in Dakota and Montana that came under my observation during my recent tour through their country, and what I think should be the policy of the Government toward them. I refer to Sitting Bull's band and other bands of the Sioux Nation under chiefs or "head-men" of less note, but no less untamable and hostile. These Indians occupy the center, so to speak, and roam over Western Dakota and Eastern Montana, including the rich valleys of the Yellowstone and Powder Rivers, and make war on the Arickarees, Mandans, Gros Ventres, Assinaboines, Blackfeet, Piegans, Crows, and other friendly tribes on the circumference.

From their central position they strike to the East, North, and West, steal horses, and plunder from all the surrounding tribes, as well as frontier settlers and luckless white hunters or emigrants who are not in sufficient force to resist them.

After describing at great length their character and supposed numbers, given at a few hundred, he says:

The true policy, in my judgment, is to send troops against them in the winter, the sooner the better, and whip them into subjection. They richly merit punishment for their incessant warfare, and their numerous murders of white settlers and their families, or white men wherever found unarmed.

The force estimated as necessary to whip them was one thousand men.

This communication was submitted by the Commissioner of Indian Affairs, Hon. Edward P. Smith, to the honorable Secretary of the Interior, Z. Chandler, who in turn submitted it to the then Secretary of War, General Belknap, for his "consideration and action."

In a subsequent communication of the Secretary of the Interior, of December 3, 1875, to the Secretary of War, occurs this language:

I have the honor to inform you that I have this day directed the Commissioner of Indian Affairs to notify said Indians (Sitting Bull and others outside their reservation) that they must remove to the reservation before the 31st day of January, 1876; that if they neglect or refuse so to remove, that they will be reported to the War Department as hostile Indians, and that a military force will be sent to compel them to obey the orders of the Indian Office.

On the 1st day of February the Secretary of the Interior further notified the Secretary of War:

The time given him (Sitting Bull) in which to return to an agency having expired, and the advices received at the Indian Office being to the effect that Sitting Bull still refuses to comply with the directions of the Commissioner, the said Indians are hereby turned over to the War Department for such action on the part of the Army as you may deem proper under the circumstances.

162

During all the stages of this correspondence, the General of the Army and his subordinate commanders were duly notified, and were making preparations for striking a blow at these hostile savages, an enterprise of almost insurmountable difficulty in a country where, in winter, the thermometer often falls to forty degrees below zero, and where it is impossible to procure food for man or beast. An expedition was fitted out under the personal command of Brig. Gen. George Crook, an officer of great merit and experience, which, in March last, marched from Forts Fetterman and Laramie to the Powder River and Yellowstone Valleys, struck and destroyed the village of Crazy Horse, one of the hostile bands referred to by Indian Inspector Watkins, but the weather was found so bitter cold, and other difficulties so great arose, that General Crook returned to Fort Laramie in a measure unsuccessful so far as the main purpose was concerned. These Indians occupy parts of the Departments of Dakota and Platte, commanded by Generals Terry and Crook, respectively, but the whole is immediately commanded by Lieutenant-General Sheridan, who has given the matter his special attention. Preparations were then made on a larger scale, and three columns were put in motion as early in May as possible, from Fort Abe Lincoln, on the Missouri River, under General Terry; from Fort Ellis, in Montana, under General Gibbon; and from Fort Fetterman, under General Crook. These columns were as strong as could be maintained in that inhospitable region, or could be spared from other pressing necessities, and their operations are not yet concluded, nor is a more detailed report deemed necessary to explain the subject-matter of this inquiry.

The present military operations are not against the Sioux Nation at all, but against certain hostile parts of it which defy the Government, and are undertaken at the special request of that bureau of the Government charged with their supervision, and wholly to make the civilization of the remainder possible. No part of these operations are on or near the Sioux reservation. The accidental discovery of gold on the western border of the Sioux reservation, and the intrusion of our people thereon, have not caused this war, and have only complicated it by the uncertainty of numbers to be encountered. The young warriors love war, and frequently escape their agents to go on the hunt, or war-path, their only idea of the object of life. The object of these military expeditions was in the interest of the peaceful parts of the Sioux Nation, supposed to embrace at least nine-tenths of the whole, and not one of these peaceful or treaty Indians have been molested by the military authorities.

The recent reports touching the disaster which befell a part of the Seventh Regular Cavalry, led by General Custer in person, are believed to be true. For some reason as yet unexplained, General Custer, who commanded the Seventh Cavalry, and had been detached by his commander, General Terry, at the mouth of Rosebud, to make a wide detour up the Rosebud, a tributary to the Yellowstone, across to the Little Horn and down to the mouth of Big Horn, the place agreed on for meeting, attacked *en route* a large Indian village, with only a part of his force, having himself detached the rest, with a view to intercept the expected retreat of the savages, and experienced an utter annihilation of his immediate command. The force of Generals Terry and Gibbon reached the field of battle the next day, rescued fifty-two wounded men and buried two hundred and sixty-one dead men, including Lieut. Col. Geo. A. Custer, Captains Custer, Keogh, Yates; Lieutenants Cook, Smith, McIntosh, Calhoun, Hodgson, Rully, Porter, Sturgis, all of the

163

Seventh Cavalry; and Lieutenant Crittenden of the Twentieth Infantry, Lieutenant Harrington, Assistant Surgeon Lord, and Acting Assistant Surgeon De Wolff, are missing.

The wounded were carried back to the mouth of the Big Horn, in the Yellowstone River, which is navigable, and where there were two steamboats, one of which was sent down the river to Fort Abe Lincoln with the wounded, and to communicate these sad facts.

General Terry is therefore at the mouth of the Big Horn, refitting, and will promptly receive re-enforcement and supplies, and will resume his operations immediately.

Meantime General Crook had also advanced from Fort Fetterman, and on the 17th of June, eight days before General Custer's attack, had encountered this same force of warriors on the head of the Rosebud, with whom he fought several hours, driving the Indians from the field, losing nine men in killed; one officer and twenty men wounded. General Crook reports his camp as on Tongue River, Wyoming. Re-enforcement and supplies are also en route to him, and every possible means have been adopted to accomplish a concert of action between these two forces, which are necessarily separated, and are only able to communicate by immense distances around by their rear.

The task committed to the military authorities is one of unusual difficulty, has been anticipated for years, and must be met and accomplished. It can no longer be delayed, and everything will be done by the Department to insure success, which is necessary to give even an assurance of comparative safety to the important but scattered interests which have grown up in that remote and almost inaccessible portion of our national domain.

It is again earnestly recommended that the appropriation asked for repeatedly by General. Sheridan, of $200,000, be made, to build two posts on the Yellowstone, at or near the mouths of the Big Horn and Tongue Rivers.

Inclosed herewith please find copies of General Terry's report, just received by telegraph since the preparation of this letter.

Very respectfully, your obedient servant,

J. D. CAMERON,
Secretary of War.

[Telegram.]

PHILADELPHIA, *July* 8, 1876.

General W. T. SHERMAN, *Washington, D. C.:*

The following just received from Drum, and forwarded for your information:

CHICAGO, ILL., *July* 7, 1876—1.10 a. m.

General P. H. SHERIDAN, U. S. A.,
Continental Hotel:

The following is General Terry's report, received late to-night, dated June 27: It is my painful duty to report that day before yesterday, the 25th instant, a great disaster overtook General Custer and the troops under his command. At 12 o'clock of the 22d instant he started with his whole regiment and a strong detachment of scouts and guides from the mouth of the Rosebud; proceeding up that river about twenty miles he struck a very heavy Indian trail, which had previously been discovered, and, pursuing it, found that it led, as it was supposed that it would lead, to the Little Big Horn River. Here he found a village of almost unlimited extent, and at once attacked it with that portion of his command which was immediately at hand. Major Reno, with three companies, A, G, and M, of the regiment, was sent into the valley of the stream at the point where the trail struck it. General Custer, with five companies, C, E, F, I, and L, attempted to enter about three miles lower down. Reno forded the river, charged down its left bank, and fought on foot until finally completely overwhelmed by numbers he was compelled to mount and recross the river and seek a refuge on the high bluffs which overlook its right bank. Just as he recrossed, Captain Benteen, who, with three companies, D, H, and K, was some two (2) miles to the left of Reno when the action commenced, but who had been ordered by General Custer to return, came to the river, and rightly concluding that it was useless for his force to attempt to renew the fight in the valley, he joined Reno on the bluffs. Captain McDougall with his company (B) was at first some distance in the rear with a train of pack-mules. He also came up to Reno. Soon this united force was nearly surrounded by Indians, many of whom, armed with rifles, occupied positions which commanded the ground held by the cavalry, ground from which there was no escape. Rifle-pits were dug, and the fight was maintained, though with heavy loss, from about half past 2 o'clock of the 25th till 6 o'clock of the 26th, when the Indians withdrew from the valley, taking with them their village. Of the movements of General Custer and the five companies under his immediate command scarcely anything is known from those who witnessed them; for no officer or soldier who accompanied him has yet been found alive. His trail from the point where Reno crossed the stream, passes along and in the rear of the crest of the bluffs on the right bank for nearly or quite three miles; then it comes down to the bank of the river, but at once diverges from it, as if he had unsuccessfully attempted to cross; then turns upon itself, almost completing a circle, and closes. It is marked by the remains of his officers and men and the bodies of his horses, some of them strewn along the path, others heaped where halts appear to have been made. There is abundant evidence that a gallant resistance was offered by the troops, but they were beset on all sides by overpowering numbers. The officers known to be killed are General Custer; Captains Keogh, Yates, and Custer, and Lieutenants Cooke, Smith, McIntosh, Calhoun, Porter, Hodgson, Sturgis, and Reilly, of the cavalry. Lieutenant Crittenden, of the Twelfth Infantry, with Acting Assistant Surgeon D. E. Wolf, Lieutenant Harrington of the Cavalry, and Assistant Surgeon Lord are missing. Captain Benteen and Lieutenant Varnum, of the cavalry, are slightly wounded. Mr. B. Custer, a brother, and Mr. Reed, a nephew, of General Custar, were with him and were killed. No other officers than those whom I have named are among the killed, wounded, and missing.

It is impossible yet to obtain a reliable list of the enlisted men who were killed and wounded, but the number of killed, including officers, must reach two hundred and fifty. The number of wounded is fifty-one. The balance of report will be forwarded immediately.

R. C. DRUM,
Assistant Adjutant-General.

P. H. SHERIDAN,
Lieutenant-General.

Supplementary report from General Terry, received at War Department at 12 o'clock m.

PHILADELPHIA, *July* 8, 1876.

General W. T. SHERMAN, U. S. A.,
    War Department, Washington, D. C. :

CHICAGO, ILL., *July* 8.

General P. H. SHERIDAN,
    Continental Hotel, Philadelphia, Pa. :

General Terry's report continues as follows: At the mouth of the Rosebud I informed General Custer that I should take the supply-steamer Far West up the Yellowstone to ferry General Gibbon's column over the river; that I should personally accompany that column, and that it would, in all probability, reach the mouth of the Little Big Horn on the 26th instant. The steamer reached General Gibbon's troops, near the mouth of the Big Horn, early in the morning of the 24th, and at 4 o'clock in the afternoon all his men and animals were across the Yellowstone. At 5 o'clock the column, consisting of five companies of the Seventh Infantry, four companies of the Second Cavalry, and a battery of Gatling guns, marched out to and crossed Tullock's Creek. Starting soon after 5 o'clock in the morning of the 25th, the infantry made a march of twenty-two miles over the most difficult country which I have ever seen. In order that scouts might be sent into the valley of the Little Big Horn, the cavalry, with the battery, were then pushed on thirteen or fourteen miles farther, reaching camp at midnight. The scouts were sent out. At half past four, on the morning of the 26th, they discovered three Indians, who were at first supposed to be Sioux, but when overtaken they proved to be Crows who had been with General Custer. They brought the first intelligence of the battle. Their story was not credited. It was supposed that some fighting, perhaps severe fighting, has taken place, but it was not believed that disaster could have overtaken so large a force as twelve companies of cavalry. The infantry, which had broken camp very early, soon came up, and the whole column entered and moved up the valley of the Little Big Horn. During the afternoon efforts were made to send scouts through to what was supposed to be General Custer's position, and to obtain information of the condition of affairs; but those who were sent out were driven back by parties of Indians, who, in increasing numbers, were seen hovering in General Gibbon's front. At twenty minutes before 9 o'clock in the evening the infantry had marched between twenty-nine and thirty miles. The men were very weary, daylight was failing; the column was therefore halted for the night at a point about eleven miles in a straight line above the mouth of the stream. In the morning the march was resumed, and after marching nine miles Major Reno's intrenched position was reached. The withdrawal of the Indians from around Reno's command and from the valley was undoubtedly caused by the appearance of General Gibbon's troops. Major Reno and Captain Benteen, both of whom are officers of great experience, accustomed to see large masses of mounted men, estimate the number of Indians engaged at not less than 2,500; other officers think the number was greater than this. The village in the valley was about three miles in length and about a mile in width; besides the lodges proper, a great number of temporary brushwood shelter was found in it, indicating that many men besides its proper inhabitants had gathered together there. Major Reno is very confident that there were a number of white men fighting with the Indians. It is believed that the loss of the Indians was larger. I have as yet received no official reports in regard to the battle, but what is stated herein is gathered from the officers who were on the ground there, and from those who have been over it since.

ALFRED H. TERRY,
Brigadier-General.

R. C. DRUM,
Assistant Adjutant-General.

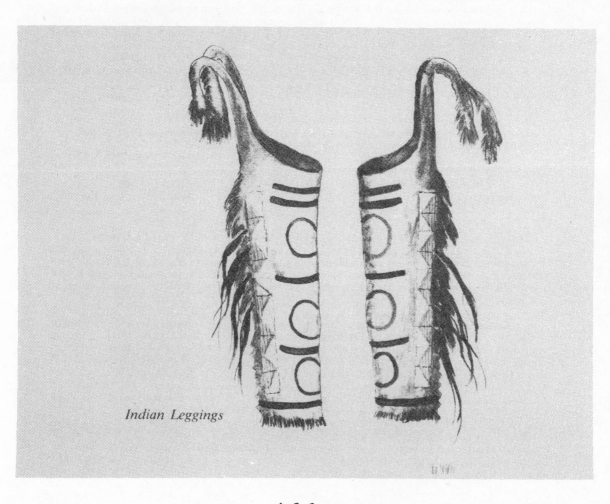

Indian Leggings

SENATE EXECUTIVE DOCUMENT NO. 33
45th CONGRESS, 2nd SESSION
PARTS 1 & 2

The Death of Lt. "Benny" Hodgson

MESSAGE

FROM THE

PRESIDENT OF THE UNITED STATES,

COMMUNICATING,

In answer to a Senate resolution of December 7, 1877, information in relation to the cost of the late war with the Sioux Indians.

FEBRUARY 21, 1878.—Read, ordered to lie on the table, and be printed.

To the Senate of the United States :

In answer to the resolution of the Senate, dated December 7, 1877, I transmit herewith reports from the General of the Army, the Quartermaster-General, the Commissary-General of Subsistence, and the Chief of Ordnance, showing " what has been the cost" (estimated) " of the late war with the Sioux Indians, and what the casualties of rank and file among the soldiers engaged in said Sioux war."

R. B. HAYES.

EXECUTIVE MANSION, *February 20, 1878.*

WAR DEPARTMENT,
Washington City, February 18, 1878.

SIR : I have the honor to return the resolution of the Senate, dated December 7, 1877, with reports from the General of the Army, the Quartermaster-General, the Commissary-General of Subsistence, and the Chief of Ordnance, showing " what has been the cost" (estimated) " of the late war with the Sioux Indians, and what the casualties of rank and file among the soldiers engaged in said Sioux war."

Very respectfully, your obedient servant,

GEO. W. McCRARY,
Secretary of War.

The PRESIDENT.

HEADQUARTERS OF THE ARMY,
Washington, December 14, 1877.

Respectfully returned to the Secretary of War, inclosing statement of casualties among the rank and file of the troops engaged in the late war with the Sioux, prepared by the Adjutant-General of the Army.

I am unable to answer that part of the resolution which relates to the cost of the war, but which no doubt can be obtained from the supply departments of the Army.

W. T. SHERMAN,
General.

Respectfully referred to the Quartermaster-General and Commissary-General for report as early as practicable.

By order of the Secretary of War.

H. T. CROSBY,
Chief Clerk.

WAR DEPARTMENT, *December* 14, 1877.

WAR DEPARTMENT,
QUARTERMASTER-GENERAL'S OFFICE,
Washington, D. C., February 18, 1878.

SIR: In reply to your instructions of the 14th December last, indorsed on the letter of the President of the United States, dated 7th December, 1877, transmitting the resolution of the United States Senate calling for information as to the cost of the war with the Sioux Indians, I have the honor to report, that I at length learn by telegraph from Colonel Holabird, chief quartermaster Division of the Missouri, that General Terry, commanding the Department of Dakota, estimates the cost of the Sioux war in that department at $992,808, of which $846,179 pertains to the Quartermaster's Department. That General Crook, commanding the Department of the Platte, estimates the cost of the same war in the Department of the Platte at $1,319,720, of which sum $1,048,182 pertains to the Quartermaster's Department. Total estimated cost of the Sioux war, therefore, is $2,312,531, of which $1,894,311 are charges against the appropriations of the Quartermaster's Department.

I am, very respectfully, your obedient servant,

M. C. MEIGS,
Quartermaster-General U. S. Army.

The Hon. SECRETARY OF WAR.

WAR DEPARTMENT,
OFFICE COMMISSARY-GENERAL OF SUBSISTENCE,
Washington, D. C., December 28, 1877.

SIR: In compliance with your indorsement dated December 14, 1877, referring to this office the Senate resolution passed December 7, 1877, I have the honor to submit herewith a report of the estimated cost to the Subsistence Department of the Sioux war of 1876–'77.

Very respectfully, your obedient servant,

R. MACFEELY,
Commissary-General Subsistence.

The Hon. SECRETARY OF WAR.

170

COST OF SIOUX WAR.

Statement showing the estimated cost to the Subsistence Department of the United States Army of the Sioux war of 1876–'77.

Value of subsistence stores lost	$17,486 12
Excess of cost of subsistence stores purchased in the Black Hills over cost of the same stores if supplied from depots	6,311 86
Total	23,797 98

R. MACFEELY,
Commissary-General Subsistence.

WAR DEPARTMENT,
Office Commissary-General Subsistence, December 28, 1877.

Statement of casualties among rank and file, United States Army, during the late war with Sioux Indians, commencing in February, 1876.

Organization.	Killed.			Wounded.		
	Commissioned officers.	Enlisted men.	Total.	Commissioned officers.	Enlisted men.	Total.
Medical department	1		1			
Second Cavalry		1	1		4	4
Third Cavalry		10	10	2	27	29
Fourth Cavalry	1	6	7		19	19
Fifth Cavalry		2	2		7	7
Seventh Cavalry	14	242	256		53	53
Fourth Infantry					3	3
Fifth Infantry		2	2		5	5
Sixth Infantry		1	1		1	1
Seventeenth Infantry					1	1
Twenty-second Infantry		1	1		2	2
Indian scouts		2	2		1	1
Totals	16	267	283	2	123	125

Aggregate killed and wounded, 408.

E. D. TOWNSEND,
Adjutant-General.

ADJUTANT-GENERAL'S OFFICE,
Washington, D. C., December 11, 1877.

QUARTERMASTER-GENERAL'S OFFICE,
December 14, 1877.

Noted and respectfully forwarded to the Commissary-General United States Army.

M. C. MEIGS,
Quartermaster-General U. S. A.

WAR DEPARTMENT,
OFFICE COMMISSARY-GENERAL SUBSISTENCE,
December 19, 1877.

Noted and respectfully returned to the Hon. Secretary of War.

R. MACFEELY,
Commissary-General Subsistence.

WAR DEPARTMENT, *December 20, 1877.*

Respectfully referred to the Chief of Ordnance for report as early as practicable.

By order of the Secretary of War.

H. T. CROSBY,
Chief Clerk.

COST OF SIOUX WAR.

ORDNANCE OFFICE, WAR DEPARTMENT,
Washington, January 14, 1878.

Respectfully returned to the Secretary of War.

The records of this office show that the value of the ordnance stores expended in action, lost on the battle-field, abandoned and destroyed for want of transportation, &c., in the campaign against hostile Sioux Indians, amounts to $70,466.23.

S. V. BENÉT,
Brigadier-General, Chief of Ordnance.

Ghost Shirt

MESSAGE

FROM THE

PRESIDENT OF THE UNITED STATES,

COMMUNICATING,

In answer to a Senate resolution of December 7, 1877, further information in relation to the cost of the Sioux war.

MARCH 26, 1878.—Read, ordered to lie on the table, and be printed.

To the Senate of the United States:

In further answer to the resolution of the Senate of December 7, 1877, as to the cost of the Sioux war, I transmit herewith copies of additional reports on the subject received from the Military Division of the Missouri.

R. B. HAYES.

EXECUTIVE MANSION, *March 25, 1878.*

WAR DEPARTMENT,
Washington City, March 22, 1878.

SIR: In connection with my letter of the 15th ultimo, submitting, in compliance with the resolution of the Senate dated December 7, 1877, reports as to the cost of the Sioux war, I have the honor to inclose copy of additional reports on the subject received from the Military Division of the Missouri.

Very respectfully, your obedient servant,

GEO. W. McCRARY,
Secretary of War.

The PRESIDENT.

[Telegram.]

ADJUTANT-GENERAL'S OFFICE,
Washington, December 18, 1877.

Lieut. Gen. P. H. SHERIDAN,
Commanding Division Missouri,
Chicago, Ill.:

The Secretary of War desires to have an approximate estimate of the cost of the late Sioux war, to enable him to answer a resolution of Congress.

E. D. TOWNSEND,
Adjutant-General.

HEADQUARTERS DEPARTMENT OF THE PLATTE,
Omaha, Nebr., January 18, 1878.

SIR: I have the honor to acknowledge the receipt of your telegram of December 19, 1877, and in reply to say that the approximate cost of the late Sioux war, so far as connected with the Department of the Platte, and as near as can be at this time estimated, amounts to $1,319,723.46.

Very respectfully, your obedient servant,

GEORGE CROOK,
Brigadier-General, Commanding.

To the ASSISTANT ADJUTANT-GENERAL, U. S. A.,
Headquarters Military Division of the Missouri, Chicago, Ill.

HEADQUARTERS DEPARTMENT OF DAKOTA,
Saint Paul, Minn., February 14, 1878.

SIR: In obedience to the telegraphic instructions of the Lieutenant-General, dated December 19, 1877, I have the honor to forward herewith an approximate estimate of the cost of the late Sioux war, so far as concerns the Department of Dakota, with the subreports upon which the approximate estimate is based.

I am, sir, very respectfully, your obedient servant,

ALFRED H. TERRY,
Brigadier-General, Commanding.

To the ASSISTANT ADJUTANT-GENERAL,
Headquarters Military Division of the Missouri, Chicago, Ill.

Approximate estimate of the cost of the late Sioux war to the Department of Dakota.

On what account.	Amount.
Quartermaster's department	$846,179 28
Subsistence department	35,728 50
Medical department	33,000 00
Ordnance department	75,000 00
Miscellaneous (telegrams)	2,900 00
Total	992,807 78

ALFRED H. TERRY,
Brigadier-General.

QUARTERMASTER'S OFFICE,
Saint Paul, Minn., December 26, 1877.

SIR: In compliance with your instructions of the 10th instant, I have the honor to submit herewith an approximate estimate of the cost of the late Sioux war in 1876–'77 to the Quartermaster's Department, as follows, viz:

Transportation of troops and supplies by steamer, including the hire of such vessels	$174,585 41
Transportation of troops and supplies by rail	260,000 62
Transportation of supplies by wagon, including hire of teams	195,599 17
Material for the repair of means of transportation	434 21
Hire of teamsters, packers, &c	47,561 97
Ferriage of troops and supplies	2,654 23
Hire of guides, scouts, special couriers, &c	16,252 74
Purchase of grain	70,367 50
Purchase of hay	100 00

Pay of extra-duty men	549	50
Purchase of buffalo overcoats	5,412	64
Purchase of mules	20,900	00
Purchase of horses	49,866	29
Purchase of camp-kettles	40	00
Purchase of tent-stoves	55	00
Pay of clerks	800	00
	$846,179	28

A considerable sum must have been paid in Chicago for transportation of troops and supplies by steamers, during the summer of 1876, of which no record has been made in the office of the department quartermaster.

No estimate is made of depreciation of property by wear and tear during the war, because no satisfactory calculation of the amount can now be made.

No account is taken of the loss of public animals, except as they were replaced by purchase, nor of other supplies forwarded to the troops, except as they were purchased in excess of the ordinary allowances or wants of the troops.

Very respectfully, your obedient servant,

BENJ. C. CARD,
Quartermaster, U. S. A.

The ADJUTANT-GENERAL,
Department of Dakota, Saint Paul, Minn.

HEADQUARTERS DEPARTMENT OF DAKOTA,
OFFICE CHIEF COMMISSARY OF SUBSISTENCE,
Saint Paul, Minn., December 28, 1877.

SIR: In reply to indorsement of December 20, 1877, from your office, on copy of telegram from Lieutenant-General Sheridan, of December 19th, instant, I have the honor to furnish the inclosed report. This contains all the information on the subject which I have been able to glean from my files, and it is, I suppose, incomplete. In order that the information required might be complete, all officers performing subsistence duty in this military department should be required to forward, with the papers enumerated in paragraph 2 of General Orders No. 12, headquarters Department of Dakota, February 12, 1870, a copy of each abstract of issues made in the month; and when the purchases, invoices, and transfers of stores are too numerous to be entered on the face of the returns of provisions, an abstract of each should accompany the return. At present the required information can be furnished complete only from the records of the office of the Commissary-General of Subsistence, United States Army, Washington.

Respectfully, your obedient servant,

M. R. MORGAN,
Major and Commissary Subsistence, Chief Commissary Subsistence.

The ADJUTANT-GENERAL,
Department of Dakota, Saint Paul, Minn.

COST OF THE SIOUX WAR.

Approximate estimate of the cost to the Subsistence Department in the Department of Dakota of the late Sioux war.

For subsistence stores issued to civilians employed with expeditions in the field, and to Indians, and for losses during the campaign $31,734 80

For hire of citizen herders, and for extra-duty pay to enlisted men in the subsistence department with troops in the field 3,993 70

35,728 50

M. R. MORGAN,
Major and Commissary Subsistence,
Chief Commissary Subsistence Department of Dakota.

OFFICE CHIEF COMMISSARY SUBSISTENCE, DEPARTMENT OF DAKOTA,
Saint Paul, Minn., December 28, 1877.

HEADQUARTERS DEPARTMENT OF DAKOTA,
MEDICAL DIRECTOR'S OFFICE,
Saint Paul, Minn., December 26, 1877.

SIR: I have the honor to report that I have made an approximate estimate of the expenses of the medical department during the Sioux war in 1876 and 1877, in excess of the requirements of the service in time of peace, viz:

For additional medical officers, hospital stewards, cooks, and nurses $25,000 00

For additional medical supplies for new posts and field service 8,000 00

33,000 00

As I do not disburse public funds, I have not the exact data for a more correct estimate, but believe the above amount will cover the expenses referred to.

Very respectfully, your obedient servant,

WM. J. SLOAN,
Surgeon, U. S. A., Medical Director.

To the ASSISTANT ADJUTANT-GENERAL,
Department of Dakota.

HEADQUARTERS DEPARTMENT OF DAKOTA,
OFFICE CHIEF ORDNANCE OFFICER,
Saint Paul, Minn., February 13, 1878.

SIR: In compliance with the instructions of the department commander, I have the honor to submit the following estimate of the cost of the Sioux war of 1876-'77.

The Ordnance Office, under a resolution of the United States Senate, has prepared a tabulated statement of losses, compiled from returns on file, chargeable to the Sioux war, from which it appears that about fifty thousand dollars should be credited to this department. I think that this estimate is too small, for it does not take into account losses that are not yet settled, the property being still borne on the returns. From a careful consideration of the amount of property furnished and that now on hand, I am of opinion that $75,000 will not more than cover the losses of the Ordnance Department, directly traceable to the Sioux campaign, in this command.

Very respectfully, your obedient servant,

O. E. MICHAELIS,
Captain of Ordnance, Chief Ordnance Officer.

To the ADJUTANT-GENERAL,
Department of Dakota.

COST OF THE SIOUX WAR.

[Memorandum.]

HEADQUARTERS DEPARTMENT OF DAKOTA,
Saint Paul, Minn., January 19, 1878.

Amount paid for telegrams received at and sent from the offices of the commanding general and adjutant-general, Department of Dakota, in relation to the Sioux war of 1876–'77 (approximate), $2,900.

GEO. D. RUGGLES,
Assistant Adjutant-General.

[Indorsements.]

HEADQUARTERS MILITARY DIVISION OF THE MISSOURI,
Chicago, February 26, 1878.

Respectfully forwarded to the Adjutant-General of the Army.
In the absence of the Lieutenant-General, commanding.

R. C. DRUM,
Assistant Adjutant-General.

HEADQUARTERS OF THE ARMY,
Washington, March 6, 1878.

Respectfully submitted to the Secretary of War. The inclosed reports, called for in accordance with Senate resolution of December 7, 1877, give the cost of the late Sioux war, as follows:

Department of the Platte.. $1,319,723 46
Department of Dakota.. 992,807 78

Total. Division of the Missouri, approximate..................... 2,312,531 24

W. T. SHERMAN,
General.

S. Ex. 35, pt. 2——2

177